The Unveiling
India

CS Sunny Pagare

Edited by Geetika K. Bakshi

INDIA • SINGAPORE • MALAYSIA

ISBN 979-8-89026-678-1

CONTENTS

Acknowledgements

This book has been a very special project, brought to fruition through the efforts of some very special people. I am deeply grateful to all those whose enthusiasm and energy transformed my vision for this book into reality, especially my wife, Adv. Madhavi Pagare, and my parents. Your commitment and sense of mission move me.

I am thankful to my publisher, Notion Press, for reposing faith in me and this work.

Having an idea and turning it into a book is as hard as it sounds. The experience is both internally challenging and rewarding. I especially want to thank Mr Swapnil Raje for making this happen and for insisting that this story deserved to be told interestingly.

I am also grateful to all the *Nari Shakti* who stepped in at the right time to assist me in this journey:

I owe an enormous debt of gratitude to Alka Sharma for assisting me in every part of this book journey.

I owe my sincere thanks to my friend and editor of this book, Geetika K. Bakshi, for diligently editing this work.

I express special thanks to Renuka Saptarshi, for drawing some beautiful sketches and designing the cover page for the book.

I'm eternally grateful to CS Aarti Mohadikar for reading my early drafts and assisting in my research work.

I'm also immensely grateful to Adv. Ruchi Mhatre, Mansi Morajkar and Shamli Shah, for drafting and proof reading the manuscript.

Most importantly, I am grateful to the Divine, without whose grace, not a single word could have been written.

– Sunny Pagare

Mumbai, August 2023

CHAPTER - I

INTRODUCTION

A famous US Author, Mark Twain, quoted in his book "Tom Sawyer's Adventures" (1835-1910)

"India is the crib of the human race, the birthplace of man's voice, history's mother, legend's grandmother, and grandmother of tradition. Our most precious and artistic materials in human history are preserved in India alone!"

On January 20, 2021, the Ministry of Culture officially declared January 23rd as the Day of Valor, officially known as *Parakram Diwas* or *Parakram Divas*, to commemorate Subhash Chandra Bose's birth anniversary to inspire the citizens of our country to act with determination against adversity, particularly the young in the face of Netaji. On this auspicious day, as the youth of this nation, we have decided to write this *Parakram* (courage/heroism) of our freedom fighters – in a book that illuminates the invisible events of our struggle for India's independence and attempts to rewrite history from a different perspective.

The history that was written by the British was a systematic and concerted attempt to use it as an instrument for demoralising indigenous people. The history we learned from grade 3 has been altered, falsified, and manipulated on a massive scale. Since our ancestors were educated under the British regime, they had enormously influenced psychology, and they sealed their lips and blindly obeyed Western philosophy to survive. The lessons of history they learned at British schools have had a negative impact on their minds and have resulted in low self-esteem and mistrust. The Indian history during the time of our predecessors, therefore, led to a serious inferiority complex.

The following is the history that developed a severe inferiority complex in the then Indians, our forefathers, as summed up by British authors. According to the British novelist, India barely stood out before the invasion of Alexander the Great. Following the conquest, the Greeks instructed the Indians in civilization. After the invasion by Alexander, the dynasties such as the Shakas, Huns, Kushanas, etc., constantly reminded the indigenous people that Muslim invaders were rather brave. Eventually, the British Isles ruled this troubled land with "peace and stability" through the introduction of a rule of law that Indians had never known before. This is how a good image of British rule was taken by narrating some history that shows how they did not rule us.

Conversely, the evidence demonstrates that seventeen invaders of India, including the British, invaded India, which has a never-ending impact on what we study and remember now.

First of all, King Darius of Persia, preceded by the great king Alexander of Greece, subjugated India. After them, King Demetrius, King Maues (Shakas) rulers of Afghanistan invaded India, the Pahlavi Dynasty Kings of Gondopherns, and King Kanishka of the Kushana Dynasty, as well as the Iranian and Kazakhstan Hun Dynasties, took over our land. These invaders stole and even drained our riches, both from India and her Indians. The Arabs were then followed by Afghanistan's cruel kings, Ghazani Mahmud and Ghori Muhammad. From Kazakhstan, Qutb al-Din Aibek (Slave dynasty) again dominated India, as well as Indian history over the years, and the Qutub Minar in Delhi remained a sign of his victories, as some historians claim.

The invasion then came from the Mongolian King Genghis Khan and the Uzbek king Babur with his dynasty of the Mughals, against whom the great warrior Chhatrapati Shivaji Maharaj battled and established a *Swarajya*. Aside from the Arabian, Iranian, and Mughal invasions of India, when the sea route to India was discovered, merchants from the east began invading India with the intent of trading, prima facie, and they later ruled India for more than 150 years. The Portuguese were the first to invade and the last to leave India. Then came the Dutch, the French, and finally, the British to conquer India. Over time, different dynasties turned to India to satisfy their appetite for conquest.

India suffered greatly from the resultant manipulation of history

Over the 1000 years of foreign rule by all of these invaders, millions of Indians were killed. One wonders why there's no memorial for the Hindu holocaust of the last 1000 years. Maybe centuries of mass killings have made them indifferent towards their own plight. This was the greatest genocide in history. There were not only genocides but also a drain of resources. Invaders from Islam stole Indian riches, while Christian invaders attempted to snatch the glorious past and amazing knowledge that Indians possessed and patent it for themselves. Because of this drain of both material and mental resources, India will never be a superpower as long as we allow "false" communist historians or disguised fascists to write India's history. The white man and communists have attempted to rewrite our heritage as per their ignorance towards the right things and wily hypocritic manipulations. Yet, we Indians are not so gullible that we will forget anything and accept the equivocation in concrete sources such as books. The position of the Indian National Congress and the 1942 Quit India movement are given much more prominence in our academic history textbooks. They place little value on the work of Netaji Subhash Chandra Bose and his Army and Navy Revolt of 1946. Paid historians have labelled this rebellion as a "Navy Mutiny," rather than an insurrection.

A Congress–Communist alliance took shape in Indian politics at the Centre almost from the time India became independent. This enabled Marxist historians to capture most of the influential academies, including universities. Their hold on history writing (and other social science subjects) grew stronger over time. As a result, they have written and managed to propagate a totally distorted historical account of every aspect and every period of Indian history. History textbooks still try to propagate a eulogy of Soviet communism. A decision to remove certain books written by well-known Marxist historians from circulation invited a chorus of "saffronisation." Isn't it strange that those who should have been charged with falsifying history were posing as victims? They have their disciples working in various fields who only read the same falsified history for years. Those fed on convictions of the Marxist kind have become an integral part of the mental setup of a large number of our educated masses.

The Indian Marxist historians continued to feed falsehoods to innocent Indian students for the sole purpose of meeting the current needs of communist politics in this country. What kind of historical writing was this? It remains a wilful falsification of history. It is nothing but communist propaganda.

The Undaunted Courage of a Lone Warrior

The then-Prime Minister, Jawaharlal Nehru, once commissioned a great historian to write the history of India's struggle for independence. He wrote a beautiful three-volume book in response to the Prime Minister's appeal, but J. Nehru rejected it, stating that it was not the one he was looking for. The thesis was discarded because the book did not discuss any of the work undertaken by Congress in the freedom movement. Mr Ramesh Chandra Majumdar, the great historian, was in charge. His work is so incredible that it should be used in textbooks as a reference point. With meagre resources, Majumdar worked alone and completed the majestic three-volume work in just seven years. It is still the most comprehensive, authoritative, and unchallenged work on India's freedom struggle. Indeed, Mr Majumdar's work has been discarded. Even Prof. Praful Chandra Gupta's work on Azad Hind Fauj has been sealed and preserved in the Defence Archive in Delhi, when, in fact, these works should be made public.

Revolts forced Britain's colonial masters to abandon India

Our liberation movement's trajectory is a tale of many armed movements and the creative minds that led them. These struggles continued to challenge British rule in India, one after the other. However, during and after World War – II (WWII), these struggles acquired great impetus and power. Following the Second World War, many new countries were created, and their freedom struggles served as an inspiration to our young fighters. The Indian National Army's revolutionary spirit had a major impact on the British-Indian armed forces. From March 1942 to 1946, there were nineteen uprisings in the Royal Indian Navy (RIN) alone; the most prominent among which was the rebellion of 1946, which rang the death knell of the mighty British Empire and paved the way for liberty.

Why Did the British Leave India? The Truth:

If we recall the excerpts from our history textbooks, they were more intent on convincing us that it was Gandhi's nonviolent revolution that forced the British to leave India. Some gullible Indians still believe in Bollywood's propagation of *"De di hume azadi bina khadag bina dhal."*

The initial revelation

Or if not the veracity, let us dig a bit to reveal the other side of the study. Two such discoveries demonstrate the contrary. Many quotes from a conversation between former British Prime Minister Clement Atlee and then-Governor of West Bengal Justice Phani Bhushan Chakraborty were revealed in General GD Bakshi's book "Bose: An Indian Samurai." According to the journal, Clement Attlee visited India in 1956 and stayed in Kolkata. He was the leader of the Labour Party and the British Prime Minister who signed the decision to grant India independence. When Attlee visited the country in 1956, P.B. Chakraborthy was the Chief Justice of the Calcutta High Court and the acting governor of West Bengal. "When I was acting Governor, Lord Attlee, who had granted us freedom by withdrawing British rule from India, spent two days in the Governor's palace at Calcutta during his tour of India," he wrote to the publisher of R.C. Majumdar's book "A History of Bengal." "I was having a prolonged conversation with him about the real motivations that had led the British to quit India." In the letter, he addressed Attlee's disclosure of the evidence, stating that the "Royal Indian Navy Mutiny, which began just after the dissolution of the INA, gave vent to India's attaining full

Independence and not to Satyagraha or nonviolent movements." This surprising discussion was first published in the Institute of Historical Review in 1982, by Ranjan Borra's piece on Subhash Chandra Bose, the Indian National Army, and the War of India's Liberation.

The second surprise

The year 1967 marked the 20th anniversary of our country's independence. The British High Commissioner, John Freeman, disclosed during a seminar on the occasion of the 20th anniversary that the Royal Indian Navy Revolt of 1946 increased the fear of another large-scale revolt along the lines of the Indian Revolt of 1857 among the 2.5 million Indian soldiers who had served in the Second World War. The British were absolutely petrified of a repeat of the 1857 Mutiny since they feared being slaughtered to the last man. As a result, the RIN figured prominently in the British decision to leave India.

Perhaps "forgotten mutiny" – Unravel the Unseen

Generally, what goes unnoticed is the history of continuous armed struggle that raged right from the uprising in the First War of Independence in 1857 to the Naval Revolt in 1946. Great warriors like Madan Lal Dhingra, Madam Cama, Lala Hardayal, Bhagat Singh, V.V.S. Aiyar, Shyamji Krishna Verma, Anantrao Kanhere, and several others were at the forefront of the armed struggle. The blood that was spilt was of these great warriors. The people that were killed or hanged were commoners like you and me. This freedom that we are enjoying now was the fruit of their sacrifices in flesh and blood. They lost their lives to give us this freedom, and we, in return, think standing for the National Anthem is a loss of our precious time!

The aim of writing this piece of unseen history is not to diminish Mohandas Gandhi's or Congress's significant contributions. We wanted to spark a discussion about the true significance of Netaji's Indian National Army position (INA). The involvement of the nonviolent movement dominates school textbooks. Meanwhile, the INA and other revolutionaries are dismissed in a few succinct pages. The time has finally come to analyse modern Indian history with an open mind, acknowledge opportunities and perspectives, and acknowledge the enormous contribution of these unseen heroes to India's independence. The time has come to uncover the facts in light of India's heritage and bring the work of the Royal Naval Ratings Mutiny ('colloquially known'), sometimes referred to as the "forgotten mutiny."

The 1857 Rebellion and the 1946 Navy Rebellion marked the beginning and culmination of the Quit India movement. British imperialism was still vulnerable to the Indian army's rebellion. The "First War of Independence", or the great Indian "Sepoy Mutiny" of 1857, as it was dubbed by the British, made a lasting impression on the psyche of British imperialism. During the Sepoy Mutiny, Hindus and Muslims showed unprecedented unity in India. When confronted with struggles, revolts, movements, uprisings, and revolutions, the imperialist and capitalist classes have always attempted and will continue to attempt to confuse, deflect, and undermine class struggle and international solidarity of the proletarian masses by using terminologies such as "mutiny," "coup," "Arab Spring," "green, orange, velvet revolution," and so on. They do this to discredit the event's or movement's progressive character and to conceal the underlying class contradictions and antagonisms. The British imperialists' reactions to the 1946 RIN (Royal Indian Navy) uprising were strikingly similar. This was a full-fledged revolt, not a mutiny insurgency backed by the Indian proletariat, especially Bombay's textile workers.

The goal of this book is to connect the dots between these two wars and shed some light on the international crises that were prevalent at the time of these interventions. The Chief Minister of Uttar Pradesh, while launching the centennial celebrations of the Chauri-Chaura incident in Gorakhpur on February 4, 2021, said that the government would organise programmes to honour freedom fighters who died during the course of the freedom struggle.

As we can see, the wind is shifting course, and the time has come to focus attention on the unseen and rewrite history that was never published!

CHAPTER - II

THE FIRST WAR OF INDEPENDENCE AND THE UNSUNG HEROES

In the introduction to this book, we saw how the British invaded India in the 16th century. Let's start from the beginning, the 18th century. While some people gave up hope under British rule, others began to believe that the British had turned a new leaf and were positively impacting the country. The British conveyed the message that Indians weren't quite ready or capable of gaining independence because they did not know how to govern themselves. This point of view gained popularity. Furthermore, the empire's apologists argued that improvements in colonial administration had begun to provide Indians with a "good government and a better life far more than mere animal existence!" On the contrary, we all know that the British continued to exploit behind this happy face. As the crescent of the British empire grew larger by the day, so did the severity of tyranny. Brave sons and daughters were born in this land to take vengeance and dwindle the crescent of the British Empire. As a result, the fall began!

Despite being a petite archipelago, Britain was able to establish one of the world's largest empires through colonialism. The epithet "the empire on which the sun never sets" describes the empire's size. The British East India Company raised the sun in India in 1599, thanks to a charter granted by Queen Elizabeth in 1600. It was formally registered as the British Joint Stock Company, and it was founded by John Watts and George White in order to trade with Asian nations in the South and South-East. This joint-stock company was once owned by British merchants and aristocrats.

When the British came, India was politically weak and economically prosperous. It was a simple matter for a group of English buccaneers, armed with the latest European artillery and morals, to defeat the bows and arrows, the elephants and the primitive musketry of the *rajahs*, and bring one Hindu province after another under the control of the British East India Company.

The Company's rule in India began in 1757 following the Battle of Plassey and ended in 1858 with the passage of The Better Government of India Act, 1858, which transferred power from the Company to the Crown through this Act and the Queen's Proclamation of 1858, resulting in the Crown assuming direct control of India in the form of the New British Raj. The name of the post of Governor-General of India was changed to Viceroy of India by the Act of 1858. The Viceroy was no longer appointed by the company but by the British government. The term "viceroy" refers to "the one who rules a country or province as the Sovereign's or King's representative and the one who is empowered to act in the Sovereign's or King's name." With its strong and efficient bureaucracy, this small island country, Britain, was able to gain control of many colonies. This potent bureaucracy in India was governed by the then-Governor-General of India, The Earl of Dalhousie (1848–1856), and Viscount Canning (1856–1858). The unexpected revolt of 1857 completely shook these compelling bureaucrats!

The Father of India's Revolution was born

A child was born into the Tilak family just one year before the First War of Independence in 1856, under the rule of tyranny and in an environment of defeatism and cynicism. Yes, indeed! Lokmanya Bal Gangadhar Tilak – a personality who needs no introduction! He was born in Chikhali, a village in Maharashtra's coastal district of Ratnagiri. Despite being born in the beautiful Konkan region, he was born and raised in a frustrated and sullen India, drawn into a whirlpool of despair and hopelessness in the aftermath of 1857.

What we really know beforehand is authentic or spurious

Although the revolt of 1857 is considered the first war of independence, more than 200 revolts against company rule occurred between 1770 and 1857. The origins of "Vande Mataram" can be traced back to the Bengal Sanyasi Andolan of 1770. More than 150 Hindu Sanyasis were gunned down by British troops during this andolan. Revolutionaries such as Mohan Giri, Devi Choudhrani, and Dheeraj Narayan, as well as farmers and saints, fought against British hegemony. It took nearly 30 years for the British to put an end to their dissent. It was during this andolan that the foundations of Indian nationalism were laid. Farmers and local tribes acted in this manner even before the First War of Independence in 1857.

The "First Revolt" and cruel intentions

Such a well-functioning administration and the British bureaucracy were overconfident, ignoring warnings of impending storms in the name of a REVOLT! The British referred to the Sepoy Mutiny as a corruption of the East India Company. A protest against the company demonstrated the company's rejection of British rule. For many years, the company attempted to demonstrate that it had legitimately governed Indians and provided them with equality before the law.

However, astute Indians with eyes wide open noticed that the concept of justice was nowhere applied in their cases. If a farmer filed complaints against an unjust zamindar, the prosecution was brought to trial in such a way that the roles of the plaintiff and the defendant were reversed, undermining the principles of equality. Failure to rectify grievances, however, was not the only cause of the 'Sepoy Mutiny,' because British vindictiveness and corruption, missionary activities, and the rapid introduction of European improvements all served to exasperate the fears of religious colonists. Naturally, this resulted in Anglophobia! The native Indians were not only enraged by the injustice, but the whites' racial superiority exacerbated the situation. By 1850, most Englishmen believed that their dominance over the entire world made them superior and that they would always be the dominant class.

The British were becoming increasingly dominant through a variety of tactics, one of which was the Doctrine of Lapse. Lord Dalhousie used this doctrine to annex the provinces of Satara, Jaipur, Sambalpur, Bhagat, Udaipur, Jhansi, and Nagpur. This dogma was a symbol of the British insensitivity to the Hindus' ancient right to adoption. By this time, the East India Company had intervened in kingship matters in several kingdoms. In fact, many consider this policy, known as the Doctrine of Lapse, to be the spark that ignited the First War of Independence in 1857. The British implemented a nefarious policy in which any princely kingdom where the ruler was declared "incompetent" or died without an heir would automatically lapse and be annexed by the British Empire. In a similar vein, he annexed the Kingdom of Oudh in 1856 under the guise of mismanagement. Kanpur was conquered by the Marathas in the 18th century. After forfeiting the Third Battle of Panipat to the Afghans and the Oudh King, Shuja-ud-Daulahin, in 1761, the city was taken over by the Oudh. The rulers of Oudh were unable to maintain complete possession, and it was eventually surrendered to the East India Company in 1801. Wajid Ali Shah's dethronement triggered a wave of resentment and anger all across the country. The kingdom of Oudh was fiscally exploited, and the Nawabs were reduced to complete reliance on the British. Dalhousie used the Nawab's negligence of state administration as a justification to merge the state with the British Empire. Peshwa Bajirao II, the Maratha ruler, was exiled to Bithoor following the Third Anglo-Maratha War. Because the Peshwas had no progeny, they adopted a young boy named Nana Dhondu Pant, the son of a Deccani Brahmin court official, and named him his rightful heir.

Another tactic used by the British was to suspend the pensions of provincial rulers such as Rani Jindan, the Queen of Maharaja Ranjit Singh. Further humiliating the ruling family, Lord Dalhousie annexed Punjab. Ranjit Singh's minor son, Dalip Singh, was overthrown and forced into exile in England. The Lahore Darbar's residences were auctioned off. The pensions of Nana Saheb and Lakshmi Bai of Jhansi were suspended in order to put a financial strain on them and compel them to surrender. The Nawab of Carnatic and Tanjore's titular sovereignty were also abolished.

A mutiny of resources

Along with the exploitation of India's natural resources, the British even implemented policies that facilitated the import of cotton goods from England, destroying local factories simultaneously. As a result of such policies, Indian markets were flooded with British goods, threatening the outright destruction of Indian manufacturers. Instead of taking bold steps to combat this, the East India Company got busy filling their pockets by buying cotton as a raw resource from Indians at a very cheap cost and then, selling them machine-made clothes from England at a rather hefty premium. Free trade and the failure to place protective duties on machine-made commodities utterly obliterated Indian manufacturing and thus, the economy.

The Ruination of East India

The East India Company's intervention was not limited to the manufacture or sale of goods but also resulted in the enactment of some laws that were viewed as an intrusion into the religious affairs of the natives. Thus, the British broke Hindu and Muslim taboos by incorporating tenets of Christianity into schools and colleges. Both General George Anson, the Commander-in-Chief of British forces in India, and Lord Charles Canning, Dalhousie's successor as Governor-General of India, promised to Queen Victoria that they would persuade Indians to opt for Christianity. Of course, Indians saw their attempts to enforce this promise as unwarranted interference in domestic affairs. Because of this context, Sir Syed Ahmed Khan wrote in 1857 that "All men, whether ignorant or well informed, high or low, felt a strong conviction that the British intended to force the Christian religion and foreign customs upon Hindus and Mussulmans alike."

Divide and Rule

Not only were these laws seen as an assault on Indian religious traditions, but also were the missionaries' activities. There was no need to interfere with religious traditions because it was a business or an MNC in today's words. Many historians claim that they were only involved in making money and not in spreading Christianity. Nevertheless, the facts paint a very different picture. In the 1850s, the directors of the East India Company in London instructed that cow and pig tallows (fats) be used instead of buffalo tallows. Despite British officers' repeated demands to use buffalo tallows rather than cow or pig tallows, the Directors insisted on using cow and pig tallows. Not just that, the bullet producers were instructed to combine pig and cow tallow so that both Hindu and Muslim soldiers got pig and cow tallow in their mouths! Why is this so?

This was achieved with the hope that once the Indian soldiers ingested the tallow, they would become corrupted and quickly disqualified by their respective societies from their respective religious sects, making a conversion to Christianity a much simpler task.

The original reason for the East India Company's desire to spread Christianity was to establish a 5 per cent-like population that felt alienated and threatened by the remaining 95 per cent, causing them to become more loyal to the company and allowing the company to easily control the remaining 95 per cent. As time passed, the reason for conversion shifted to the creation of a misconception that 'It was God's mandate to convert the entire world!'

The Charter Act of 1813 authorised Christian missionaries to penetrate the company's Indian Territory to spread their faith and western education. The Christian missionaries took every opportunity to reveal the atrocities that occurred in both the Hindu and Islamic religions. They condemned idolatry, mocked Hindu gods and goddesses, and attacked Hinduism and Islam's doctrine and principles. The teaching of Christian doctrines was made mandatory in missionary-run educational institutions. Thus, the British authorities' intervention in social norms and practices through constitutional amendments, as well as the government's support of Christian missionaries in their proselytising activities, instilled fear and hate in the minds of Indians.

The British did not stop there. When they introduced western education to India, they took the best of Indian education and attempted to take it to the west. A generous grant in 1830 to create the Sanskrit Chair at Oxford University was made by Colonel Joseph Boden, a British military officer with 25 years of service in India. He believed that "a more general and vital knowledge of [Sanskrit] would be a means of enabling my countrymen to proceed in the Conversion of the Natives of India to the Christian Religion, by disseminating a knowledge of the Sacred Scriptures (Bible) amongst them more effectually than just about every other means whatsoever." The Boden Chair of Sanskrit was founded at Oxford University in 1832 with this reserve to train missionaries in the Sanskrit language so that they could translate and disseminate the Bible into Sanskrit and preach to Hindus the 'truths of Christianity' encapsulated in Sanskrit terminology.

Both conversion and westernisation were used to demoralise the Indians. The abolition of allowances was one of the triggers that demoralised the sepoys. The British government used to abolish compensation and send the same troops to those provinces on lower pay. As a result of these measures, the Sepoys were humiliated. In 1844, four Bengal regiments declined to transfer to Sindh unless additional allowances were authorized. Mutinous spirit was also demonstrated by Sepoys in various provinces in the year 1849.

The passage of the General Service Enlistment Act sparked yet another wave of resentment among Indian soldiers. The Hindu soldiers were coerced into going on an expedition to Burma and Afghanistan, which went against their religious values. It was against their ancient customs to live among Muslims and take food and water from them. Furthermore, crossing the seas was forbidden by the religion since those who did so would forfeit their caste and be outcast by the superior members of society. Lord Canning's government passed the General Service Enlistment Act in 1856 in order to discourage Sepoys from denouncing their deployment abroad. By virtue of this act, all prospective recruits to the Bengal army were required to pledge allegiance that they would serve anywhere their services were required. These were the significant factors that paved the way for the First War of Independence – the Revolt of 1857!

The final call of Revolt did come with prior warnings

With so many rulers holding titles that already meant so little – already serving at the pleasure of the company and the growing interference of the company in religious matters, leading to an increase in atrocities – it became a source of immense unrest among the still rich and powerful rulers of these small kingdoms and their subjects, and it contributed to the growing unrest and gave birth to bickering.

Nana Saheb, who should have been Peshwa by now, was one of those who decided he wasn't going down without a fight. He chose to use force to reclaim his rightful title, as it seemed to be the only choice left, and began assembling an army. It is believed that hidden messages were sent out to Indian soldiers through chapatis/roti (round Indian bread) to remind them of their roots, evoke nationalistic feelings, and persuade them to enter the war. The company was completely unaware of the impending mutiny. Indeed, it is thought that one of the main reasons that the 1857 Uprising was so widespread was that the Indians were motivated by their myriad of quite real grievances, while the British had been lulled into what would turn out to be a false sense of their control over the land. Major-General Hugh Wheeler, then commanding officer of Kanpur, for instance, is said to have been so confident of his stance that he dispatched considerable forces to Lucknow when the revolt first erupted in May 1857. This proved to be a costly error, as trouble erupted in Kanpur not long after, on June 4, 1857. The company was totally caught off guard by Nana Saheb's assault. His army first raided the company treasury before targeting Wheeler's troops. The British East India Company's rule in India was supposed to end on the 100th anniversary of the Battle of Plassey.

Nana Saheb fought valiantly, leaving Wheeler with only 250 troops to protect over 1,000 British civilians. The business, outnumbered, was forced to seek refuge at All Souls' Church, along with their women and children. Nana Saheb's army imposed a blockade, preventing supplies from passing through, and the company was forced to surrender on June 24-25. Wheeler had already lost one of his sons in the rebellion. Nana Saheb later offered safe passage to those gathered in the church. It was agreed that the Englishmen and their families would travel to Allahabad by Ganga waterway on June 27. No one was to be harmed during this safe passage, according to Nana Saheb's directives. The Indian rebels became enraged when they saw the Englishmen in the warships and began shooting. Those who managed to escape the bullets were slaughtered with swords. Women and children were killed alongside the men. Later, this ghat was renamed as Massacre Ghat. When Nana Saheb was informed of the massacre, he arrived on the scene and managed to save some women and children. They were taken to Nana Saheb's private headquarters, a mansion recognised as Savada Kothi, and later relocated to cantonment quarters in Bibighar. Nana Saheb was officially crowned Peshwa the following month, in July 1857.

The company took the incident in Kanpur seriously. Major-General Henry Havelock, the British commander, ordered them to reassemble, forcing Nana Saheb's forces to withdraw. Havelock's attack enraged the Indians to the point that, in retaliation, the Indian rebels killed the English residents who remained at Bibighar and threw their bodies into a well. The incident was dubbed the Bibighar Massacre. Meanwhile, the company's attack on Nana Saheb persisted. They burned down Savada Kothi and the people who lived there, including Nana's daughter, Mainawati. The company then confiscated Nana Saheb's assets, which were estimated to be worth Rs 1 crore at the time. With this triumph, the British re-established their hegemony over Kanpur. Nana Saheb was forced to flee. His allies, including his nephew, Pandurang Nana Rao, and his general, Tatya Tope, were hanged. In reality, over 144 Indian soldiers were hanged on the Bibighar premises from a single, massive banyan tree.

Coercion and violence were used to assassinate revolutionaries arrested during these massacres. Colonel Neill forced the revolutionaries to lick the bloodied door of Bibighar and eat beef (if Hindu) or pork (if Muslim) before being hanged. Muslims were often sown into pig skins in order to humiliate the soldiers and give a message to those who may have considered mutiny. Following independence, the memorial garden was renamed Nana Rao Park. The giant banyan tree, where the 144 Indians were hanged, died in 2010, but a plaque commemorating what happened there has been erected. The Revolt of 1857 ignited the flames of Indian liberty. Yet, when one considers where the seeds were sown, one often thinks of Bengal, Allahabad, Delhi, and Punjab – rarely, if ever, Kanpur is taken into consideration, where so many suffered the consequences.

Before this uprising, the Indians' frustration was articulated through both violent mutinies and peaceful demonstrations. The Mutinies at Vellore (1806), Barrackpore (1824), Ferozpur (1842), mutiny of the 7th Bengal cavalry, mutiny of the 22nd N.I. in 1849, Revolt of the Santhals (1855-56), Kol uprising (1831-32), and other demonstrations by the citizens resulted in the revolt of 1857.

Women were no longer a sign of misery because they too led the revolution and played a heroic role. During the first war of independence, 50 women were executed by hanging. Even today, the trees on which they were hung are revered in Baghpat village. There are countless instances where women from Muzaffarnagar, Shamli, and Meerut fought and defeated British troops during the 1857 uprising, demonstrating their resilience. Not only were these women symbols of courage, but also of unity, as women from all castes and creeds, including Gujjars, Jats, Brahmins, Dalits, and Muslims, collaborated in the rebellion. Even after the men fled to Delhi following the rebellion, it was women like Avantibai who came aboard for the battle. They also specialised as informers and spies. There are reports from Madhya Pradesh that women used to dance in the British camp, passing on information to Indian soldiers in the British army through chits.

We had previously addressed the rebellion in Northern India, as many historians say that only North Indians participated in this revolt. In contrast, Shridhar Paradkar's book on the Indian War of Independence lists instances of rebellion against the British in the country's southern regions. Rangoji Bapu led a rebellion against the British in Satara in 1856. In 1857, soldiers from the Pune Armed Force, Mumbai Platoon, and the 27th Platoon of Kolhapur staged an armed insurrection. Bhima Naik invaded Sirpur in Khandesh, while Tatya Tope targeted Kargunda in 1858.

In 1857 and 1858, Bhagoji Naik battled British troops twice in Nashik, and Joglekar directed the battle in Trimbakeshwar. Andhra Pradesh was also affected by the rebellion. The British troops were attacked in February 1857 in Meedi in Parla village in the Kurnool district of Andhra under the command of Radhakrishna Dandsen. The 30th Platoon staged an armed revolt in Kadapa village and Jaggaiahpet, both in Andhra Pradesh. In July 1857, the Flag of Independence was hoisted in the Andhra Pradesh village of Machilipatnam.

In Karnataka, forces were united against the British in Jamkhandi and Bijapur, and in February 1857, the British troops were attacked by an army in Shorapur. While the rebellion in Maharashtra and Karnataka was spreading, Indian soldiers from the 29th Infantry in Belgaum rose up against the British. This rebellion swept through the southern states of Goa, Madras, and Kerala, with Dipaji Rane leading the revolt in Goa and the 18th platoon revolting in Madras alongside the Chingalpet uprising in 1858.

Place	Leader
Barrackpore	Mangal Pandey
Lucknow	Begum Hazrat Mahal, Birjis Qadir, Ahmadullah (advisor of the ex-Nawab of Awadh)
Kanpur	Nana Saheb, Rao Sahib (nephew of Nana), Tantia Tope, Azimullah Khan (advisor of Nana Saheb)
Jhansi	Rani Laxmibai
Bihar (Jagdishpur)	Kunwar Singh, Amar Singh
Gwalior/Kanpur	Tatya Tope
Assam	Kandapareshwar Singh, Manirama Datta
Orissa	Surendra Shahi, Ujjwal Shahi
Kullu	Raja Pratap Singh
Rajasthan	Jaidayal Singh and Hardayal Singh
Gorakhpur	Gajadhar Singh
Mathura	Sevi Singh, Kadam Singh

The well-planned 'Doctrine of Lapse'

The final wave of annexations occurred under Lord Dalhousie's reign as Governor-General. He came up with a policy known as the Doctrine of Lapse. According to the doctrine, if an Indian ruler died without a male heir, his realm would "lapse," or become part of the company territory.

According to this, no adopted son of the Indian king could be declared the heir to the throne. Only his foster father's personal belongings and properties would pass to the adoptive son. The adoptive son would not be eligible for any of his father's titles or pensions that he had previously received. This questioned the Indian king's long-held right to choose his or her own heir.

Due to the lack of a biological heir to the throne, several of the Indian princely states lost their lands to the British East India Company under the Doctrine of Lapse. After the policy's empowerment, a large number of Indian princes lived unhappy lives, which ultimately contributed to the Revolt of 1857.

Satara (1848), Sambalpur (1850), Udaipur (1852), Nagpur (1853), and Jhansi (1853) were all annexed using the same doctrine. Finally, in 1856, the company seized control of Awadh. This time, the British added a statement, claiming that they were obligated by duty to take over Awadh in order to liberate the citizens from the Nawab's "misgovernment"! Enraged by the humiliating manner in which the Nawab was deposed, the people of Awadh supported the 1857 popular revolt.

Rani Chennamma stood in defiance of the doctrine of lapse, a British annexation scheme, three decades before the 1857 mutiny. At the age of 15, she married Raja Mallasaraja of the Desai tribe. Chennamma's husband is said to have died in 1824, and their son died a couple of years later. The concept of lapse rears its head when a monarch dies without a direct heir to the kingdom. In plain terminology, the law stipulates that if a monarch dies without a male descendant, the kingdom's princely status is revoked, which ensures that the land is annexed into British India.

Following the deaths of her husband and son, Rani Chennamma adopted Shivalingappa and proclaimed him heir to the throne in 1824. The East India Company, on the other hand, did not find it acceptable. Rani Chennamma pleaded her case in a letter to Mount Stuart Elphinstone, Lieutenant-Governor of the Bombay Presidency, but the conviction was overturned, and war broke out.

The argument that deserves special consideration here is how many of the kings became impotent all of a sudden! This was due to the British nefarious games, which made the Kings addicted to alcohol. This was not any random occurrence, but rather a well-planned conspiracy that culminated in the doctrine of lapse!

The doctrine of lapse: 'not so fictitious facts'

The revolution served as a sign of unity and patriotism. It exemplified the Indians' resentment of the company's laws. The rebellion mirrored the collapse of the East India Company and its bureaucracy. As a consequence, the next chapter in Indian history, the Transfer of Power, transpired! The East India Company relinquished control of Indian administration to the crown, i.e., the Queen, through the Government of India Act of 1858. It marked the end of the era of conquest and expansion, and the Queen's proclamation stated that there was no need for "extension of territorial possessions" and vowed to uphold native princes' rights to honour and integrity as their own. The Act of 1858 abolished dualism in Indian affairs and made the crown solely responsible for managing Indian affairs. Following this, the Indian Councils Act of 1861, the Indian High Court Act of 1861, and the Indian Civil Service Act of 1861 were passed, bringing about fundamental changes in the administrative set, i.e., the executive, legislative, and judicial administrations of India. The British policy against Indian states shifted dramatically, and the states were now perceived as the empire's bulwark against potential threats. The Indian army was reorganised extensively, and the number of European troops in the army was boosted. All of the higher-ranking positions in the armed forces were intended only for Europeans. The strategy of incorporating Indian representatives into legislative and administrative matters was enacted. The Indian Councils Act of 1861 provided a cautious launch in this direction. The rebellion left a legacy of ethnic animosity. Because of the Sepoy mutiny, people of Indian descent as a whole were labelled untrustworthy and subjected to slurs, humiliation, and contemptuous treatment. The era of colonial expansion was succeeded by a more subtle era of economic exploitation. The policy of 'divide and rule' between Hindus and Muslims was initiated as a result of the revolt's depiction of unity. The British disposition toward social reforms altered from what it had been before 1857. They were now resisting reforms that could harm their empire, and as a result of this rebellion, the British became overly protective.

System of education - low-level and lethal policy

The education system was often structured in such a way that the information imparted was of poor quality, and the system was entirely unequal. The scheme devised by the British to enslave *Bharat* and its people was our new "education system," which transformed *Bharat* and *Bhartiya* into "India and Indians." The term "Indian" is a distorted version of the British term for indigenous tribes of the American continent.

The year 1857 was significant not only in terms of the armed revolt but also in terms of the reform that was taking place in the educational sector, which eventually grew by leaps and bounds. This year saw the establishment of three major universities: the University of Calcutta, the University of Madras, and the University of Bombay. It was a big deal at the time because we were under the British East India Company, which wanted to introduce growth for the sake of making its own job easier.

The Law Member in the Viceroy's Executive Council presented a blueprint to shape Indian education for enduring colonial rule in the British Parliament on February 2, 1835, popularly known as the Macaulay Minute, wherein he enshrined, "We must at present do our best to form a class who may be interpreters between us and the millions whom we govern, a class of persons Indian in blood and colour, but English in taste, in opinion, in morals and intellect."

The Macaulay scheme was followed by Charles Wood's Despatch, reinforcing compulsory English education in the government and aiding educational high schools and higher education.

Sir Charles Wood's Despatch on Education, published in 1854, is regarded as the Magna Carta of English Education in India. It stated that the government's educational policy aimed to teach Western education. It proposed the establishment of primary schools (vernacular languages) at the lowest level, high schools in Anglo vernacular, and district-level colleges (English medium). The education sector changed marginally after the Queen's Proclamation, but the corporation had never received significant attention in the areas of education prior to that. Even the meagre sum of One Lakh set aside for education could not be invested until 1833. The company only emphasised educating members of the aristocracy and middle classes, resulting in a substantial disparity between different classes of Indian citizens. Their educational system's sole purpose was to train clerks who would carry out the company's administrative work smoothly. It clearly demonstrates the company's selfishness. All subjects were taught in English, and the study of Indian languages was discouraged. All those who underwent English training considered themselves superior to others, and thus, a unique sect was born, who were Indians only by blood and colour but considered themselves English in their thinking and way of life. There were hardly any funds set aside for the education of Indian women because the British saw women's education as useless. On the other hand, they were worried about offending Indian people since conservative Indian opinion was against educating their women. The English government paid no attention to science and technological education. Only three medical colleges, one each in Calcutta, Bombay, and Madras, and one engineering college, one in Roorkee, were founded after 1857. Since admission to these colleges was only available to Europeans, Indians were almost disregarded.

This was the aftermath of the First War of Independence, but we still need to cast doubt on the facts unearthed after a couple of millennia that assisted in uncovering the truth. People in Ajnala exhumed the mortal remains of India's freedom fighters who were massacred in the First War of Independence. Historians retrieved the remains of 282 martyrs from a well inside the premises of Gurudwara Shaheed Ganj, 30 kilometres from Amritsar. They uncovered 90 skulls, 170 jaws, 5000 teeth, and hundreds of bones after three days of excavation. However, apart from that, they were able to find British-era coins and medals. These were the remnants of Indian soldiers from the 26th Bengal Native Infantry, deployed at Mian Mir cantonment near Lahore, who'd already revolted against the British and were marching towards Ajnala after hearing of the mutiny in Meerut and other places in 1857. By assassinating two British officers near Lahore, these troops, numbering about 500, challenged the British Empire. To react, Fredrick Cooper, the then-British deputy commissioner of Amritsar, ordered action against the troops. While many were killed in this action, 282 Indian soldiers were captured and brought to Ajnala, where many were killed and thrown into the well, while others were forced into it alive. A 10-foot layer of soil was put on them to disguise the reality that had been unveiled after all these years.

Bahadur Shah Zafar - a great betrayer of the Great Revolt of 1857, or the First War of Independence

Bahadur Shah Zafar supposedly led the First War of Independence from the front. The Sepoys bestowed the title "emperor of Hindustan" on him only because they were looking for and desperately hoping for leadership. Bahadur Shah Zafar reluctantly took the leadership but betrayed the sepoys.

Even as Bahadur Shah maintained the façade of leading the fight against the British, he opened a secret parallel track with them: he offered them full support to crush the sepoys.

Bahadur Shah sent out letters to various British military officers, for example, to the Lieutenant Governor of Agra, informing them of the location and other details of the sepoys in Delhi.

However, one of his most macabre acts of treachery occurred after a month, when the Great Revolt erupted. Even as the sepoys were engaged in intense fighting with the British in and around Delhi, a fight they fought in Bahadur Shah's name, he sent a message to General T. Reed, Commander-in-Chief, who headed the British unit besieging Delhi. In turn, T. Reed conveyed this message to John Lawrence, the Chief Commander of Punjab.

Cynical as it may sound, the terms of Bahadur Shah Zafar's betrayal were rather cheap. He offered to sell himself for a pittance, given his own tall claims about being an emperor and royal pensions. However, the British ruthlessly crushed the Great Revolt before Bahadur Shah could carry out his betrayal and had to abjectly surrender.

Quite naturally, members of the secular cult of Indian history writing regard him as a tragic hero and a freedom fighter. Writing a fat time dedicated to projecting this weakling and traitor as a "tragic figure of the eponymous monarch... and abidingly fond of the arts of peace," as William Dalrymple has done in The Last Mughal, must take a special talent in perversion.

Unsung heroes of India: An inquest

Mangal Pandey was an Indian soldier in the British army who is credited with being a key figure in the Sepoy Mutiny, India's First War of Independence in 1857. Mangal Pandey was the same person who inculcated national resentment by inciting Indians against the British. His 34th Bengal Native Infantry was made up of Brahmins. When a new Enfield rifle was introduced in India in the mid-1850s, his major conflict with the company began. The rifle's cartridges were rumoured to be greased with animal fat, particularly cow and pig fat. A soldier had to bite the bullets in order to activate them in the rifle. Cow fat is regarded as sacrilegious by Hindus, whereas pig fat is considered sacrilegious by Muslims. As an outcome, the use of the cartridges threatened their religious beliefs and frustrated the Indian soldiers. On March 29, 1857, Pandey and his fellow sepoys rose up in revolt against the British officers on March 29, 1857, and even attempted to shoot them. Mangal Pandey was arrested and condemned to death on April 18. However, fearing a Sepoy rebellion, British authorities hanged him 10 days earlier on April 8.

Mangal Pandey, Rani Laxmibai, Tantia Tope, Nana Saheb, and Bahadur Shah Zafar fought alongside tens of thousands of other valiant men and women. The Sepoy mutiny has been written by them. Much has been written about the aforementioned leaders. Apart from these, there are a few other unsung heroes who gave their lives in the 1857 uprising. Their account must be revealed, and that period of history must be retained.

Kunwar Singh, the legendary king of Jagdishpur, also known as Babu Kunwar Singh or Kuer Singh, was a prominent leader during the first war of independence in 1857. When the uprising reached Bihar, Kunwar Singh was called upon to lead a select band of armed soldiers against the troops under the command of the British East India Company. Kunwar Singh was 80 years old when he took up arms against the British. He fought a good fight, harried British soldiers for nearly a year and remained invincible until the end.

Kunwar Singh, who belonged to the royal Ujjainiya (Panwar) Rajput house of Jagdispur, currently a part of Bhojpur district, Bihar, India, took charge of the men who had revolted at Danapur, Bihar on July 25. Two days later, Singh, along with his men, occupied Arrah, the district headquarters. On August 3, Major Vincent Eyre rescued the town, defeated Singh's men, and burned Jagdishpur.

History has it that during the uprising, his army was forced to cross the Ganges. Brigadier Douglas' soldiers started shooting at their boat. Singh's left wrist was smashed by one of the gunshots. Singh thought that his hand had become unusable and that there was an additional risk of infection due to the bullet shot. He pulled out his sword and severed his left hand near the elbow, offering it to the Ganges.

The troops under the authority of the East India Company were comprehensively routed in their final fight, fought on April 23, 1858, near Jagdishpur. On the 22nd and 23rd of April, despite being injured, he battled heroically against the British army, driving them away with the support of his army, bringing down the Union Jack from Jagdishpur Fort, and hoisting his flag.

He returned to his palace on April 23, 1858, and died three days later on April 26, 1858, passing on the mantle to his successor and brother, Amar Singh II.

On April 23, 1966, the Republic of India issued a commemorative stamp to honour his contribution to India's freedom struggle. In 1992, the Bihar government founded the Veer Kunwar Singh University in Arrah.

Rango Bapuji Gupte was Chatrapati Pratapsingh of Satara's most trusted advisors. When the British dissolved Pratap Singh's princely state in 1839, Bapuji went to England as a diplomat to defend the state's case before the British parliament. He lived in London for 14 years, where he studied English. When Rango Bapuji returned to India, he took an oath to fight for India's independence at Rohideshwar. He met Nanasaheb Peshwa and assisted him in assembling an army for the 1857 revolt. Following the rebellion, the British took possession of his ancestral home, Kari, near Bhor. Rango Bapuji was the first Indian diplomat in Indian history to make the journey to England and present facts about Pratapsingh to the British parliament. He was amongst the masterminds behind the 1857 Revolt. Seetaram, the son of Rango Bapuji, led the Satara revolt in 1857 at the behest of Chatrapati Shahu Maharaj. The late Prabodhankar Thackeray, Bal Thackeray's father, penned the biography of this brilliant lobbyist.

Azizun Bai; one of the most intriguing tales is that of the Kanpur courtesan, Azizun Bai. Kanpur witnessed vicious fights between Nana Sahib's and Tatya Tope's forces versus the British. Azizun Bai's position in the Kanpur battles has been described by both colonial and Indian historians. Unlike many of the other women who had joined the rebellion, she had little to gain and had no personal animosity. She was simply greatly affected by Nana Sahib. Her legacy lives on among the citizens of Kanpur. She used to dress in male attire and ride with the soldiers on horseback, armed with a set of handguns. She was in the procession when the flag was raised in Kanpur to commemorate Nana Sahib's initial victory.

The cavalry was headquartered in Kanpur, and she was particularly close to one of them, Shamsuddin. The sepoys congregate at her residence. She also compiled a group of women who went around fearlessly cheering on the military men, attending to their wounds, and privately supplying arms and ammunition. She made one of the gun batteries her base of operations for this mission. She spent the entire conquest of Kanpur with the soldiers whom she considered her comrades, and she was still armed with handguns herself.

Bhima Nayak, Nemad's Robin Hood, played an important role in the rebellion. Because of his defiant acts, the British were terrified. He was instrumental in uniting the adivasis of Khandesh, consequently facilitating Ambapani's revolt. The available sketch of this generous Robin Hood has sparked a lot of debate. Tatya Tope and Bhima Nayak are said to have interacted when Tatya Tope toured Nemad. However, his death certificate recently surfaced, revealing that he died in Port Blair on December 29, 1876. This brave Robin Hood was difficult to detain, but he was intercepted due to deceit by one of his men.

In 1857, Baburao Shedmake led the Gond rebellion in Maharashtra's present-day districts of Chandrapur and Gadchiroli. When the Raja of Nagpur died without an heir, the area of Chanda district was brought under British rule in 1854, thanks to Lord Dalhousie's ruthless "Doctrine of Lapse."

In March 1854, the British took possession of Chanda, and R. S. Ellis of the Madras Civil Service became the first District Collector of Chanda. The Raj-Gond families owned several *zamindars* in the district. These also predated the Marathas' arrival in the 18th century. Naturally, these families resented the British, especially the annexation of their territory. One such zamindar was Molampalli, which comprised 24 villages in today's modern Chandrapur township. Baburao Shedmake, the Zamindar of Mollampalli, was a 25-year-old resident. He was born on March 12, 1833, in Kishtapur village, Aheri tehsil, Gadchiroli district, but hardly anything is documented about his family or formative years. In early March 1858, Shedmake gathered a force of 500 tribal youths and trained an exceptionally fearless militia. He was able to conquer the entire Rajgad Pargana of the Chanda district with this force.

When word of the uprising reached Chandrapur, the District Collector, Mr Chrichton, designated a unit of the British army to suppress it. On March 13, 1858, British forces confronted Shedmake's army near Nandgaon-Ghosari. They culminated in a decisive battle, with Shedmake emerging victorious. He completely routed the British army, causing substantial losses in troops and equipment. In Chandrapur, a small memorial exists at the site where Baburao Shedmake was executed. Though the Revolt of 1857 in Chandrapur and surrounding regions has been all but forgotten in the rest of India, tribal myths, legends, and songs among the locals keep it afloat.

CHAPTER - III

THE ERA OF RE-ESTABLISHMENT AND RECLAMATION OF WHAT WAS ALMOST LOST

Following the rebellious year of 1857 and the exhibition of the Queen's Proclamation, the British attempted to reclaim their rule. The old Mughal emperor, Bahadur Shah II, was put behind bars at Rangoon, and thus, Delhi was reclaimed. Lucknow was also captured by the then-British Commander-in-Chief, Colin Campbell, but the insurrection continued in some parts of Oudh in the form of guerrilla warfare.

There were some significant reasons why the revolt failed. During the rebellion, some local rulers, including the Scindia of Gwalior, the Nizam of Hyderabad, the Nawab of Bhopal, and the rulers of Patiala, strongly backed the British. The Indian Historical Catastrophe! Following that was the scarcity of the most significant factor; the problem faced by our brave Indian soldiers even today – the scarcity of modern equipment. Our heroes, like Abhimanyu, learned how to combat oppression in their mother's womb and had the *"josh"* in them from birth. Nevertheless, the weapon systems accessible to the insurgents were of inferior quality. We had efficient hands for combat, but those brave hands were not provided with efficient arms. And as a consequence, the rising revolution was oppressed, and the first war of independence collapsed! And we lost our independence for over the next 100 years.

The British officers had the best equipment at their disposal and a framework that facilitated them in pulverising the 1857 rebellion. They were able to put a stop to the revolution thanks to modern weapons, transportation, and communication. The table below summarizes the locations as well as the officers who reclaimed them during the revolution.

Sr. No	British Officers	Places recaptured by them
1.	General John Nicolson	On September 20, 1857, he seized Delhi and died soon after from a mortal wound sustained during the uprising.
2.	Major Hudson	In Delhi, he was successful in assassinating Bahadur Shah's sons and grandsons.
3.	Sir Hugh Wheeler	He fought valiantly against Nana Saheb's forces until June 26th, 1857. Later, on June 27th, the British forces surrendered with the condition of safe passage until Allahabad.
4.	General Nail	In June 1857, he captured Banaras and Allahabad, and at Kanpur, he killed Indians in vengeance for the killing of Englishmen by Nana Sahib's troops. He was killed in the battle at Lucknow.
5.	Sir Colin Campbell	He played a role in the final recovery of Kanpur on December 6, 1857, and the final reoccupation of Lucknow on March 21, 1858. On May 5, 1858, he also recaptured Bareilly.
6.	Henry Lawrence	On July 2, 1857, he was the chief commissioner of Awadh when he was assassinated during the seizure of British residency in Lucknow.
7.	Major General Havelock	On July 17, 1857, he defeated Nana Sahib's force and died in Lucknow in December 1857.

The island's 70-year shame has finally been erased

Hundreds of sepoys were bayoneted or shot at in a rage of British vengeance. In the 1857 Revolt, British soldiers assassinated many freedom fighters in Allahabad, Kanpur, and Lucknow. Having followed their crushing of India's first independence movement, the British named several islands, settlements, and cities after British army officers.

1. As a tribute to the former president on his second death anniversary in July 2017, the Odisha government renamed

Wheeler Island (titled "after Sir Hugh Massy Wheeler") in Bhadrak district, as APJ Abdul Kalam Island.

2. In the Andaman, Havelock Island was named after Major General Sir Henry Havelock, while Neill Island was named after British Brigadier General James Neill, and Ross Island went by the name of marine surveyor Daniel Ross. In December 2018, Havelock Island, Neill Island, and Ross Island in the Andaman were officially renamed Swaraj Deep, Shaheed Deep, and Netaji Subhash Chandra Bose Island, respectively, to commemorate the 75th anniversary of Netaji Subhas Chandra Bose raising the Indian national flag during the liberation struggle.

After-effects of the failed revolt

Following the rebellion, it became much more necessary for the British government to mend relations with the Indians, and they began to make efforts. One of them was the Government of India Act of 1858. The Indian Civil Services were established under Section XXXII (32) of the act. On paper, this is one of the best decisions of the British Parliament! And if an Indian decided to pass the ICS test, they had to travel to England! Yes, those are the carrots shown to the Indians in order to placate them. On November 1, 1858, Queen Victoria issued her Proclamation announcing that from thenceforth, India would be ruled in the name of the British Monarch by a Secretary of State, effectively destroying the company's rule. The Government of India Act of 1858 was passed in order to end the company's rule and shift control to the British crown as a consequence of the rebellion. Following the enactment of this act, the British Governor-General of India was appointed to the position of viceroy, making him the monarch's representative.

The Queen's Proclamation was labelled "Magna Carta of the People of India" since it identified the principles of justice and religious tolerance as the Queen's guiding policy. The document also granted amnesty to all Indians, except for those who had explicitly participated in the assassination of British officers during the rebellion. Queen Victoria reassured the Indian princes in her proclamation that their territories would not be annexed unilaterally and that they would have the privilege to adopt in order to continue their lineage. Lord Canning declared to the Princes, Chiefs, and People of India this Proclamation, which outlined a new British policy of permanent support for native princes and non-intervention in religious matters.

Allahabad (Ilahabad), now officially known as Prayagraj, has been an important city from time to time

An eye is always kept on Allahabad and the politics that goes on there because it is the city that has brought India so many Prime Ministers and where the seeds of the Emergency were sown. It is not only significant now, but Allahabad was also significant during the revolt and its aftermath. It was a preferred region, not only by the Mughals, but also by the British East India Company and, later, the Crown! This historic city was proclaimed the capital of British India for one day on November 1, 1858, when Lord Canning read Queen Victoria's Proclamation, taking direct control of British India from the East India Company. As a measure, it witnessed the transition of power in 1858!

The city of Allahabad witnessed an uprising when the sixth native infantry posted within the fort killed several Englishmen.

The Governor-General of India during the mutiny chose Allahabad as his permanent residence after the rebellion. Then Lord Minto, the then Governor-General of India, transformed the field where Lord Canning read the queen's declaration into a splendid park. In 1908, a marble pillar, famous as the "Proclamation pillar," was raised and the busts of Queen Victoria and Edward VII were mounted on it. However, apart from this park, there is a cemetery that holds the graves of British commandants and soldiers who died during the 1857 rebellion. Today, the Archaeological Survey of India has designated this cemetery as a protected monument.

Allahabad was named the capital of the North Western Provinces in 1858, ushering in a new era for the city as it was transformed from a decaying Mughal town into a genteel British Raj city. Under the supervision of Commissioner Cuthbert Bensley Thornhill, a new White Town was designed on a grid-iron pattern. Cannington was the title given to this new settlement, which would have been the largest before the British transformed New Delhi in the early twentieth century. Many historians believe that Sir Edwin Lutyens' architectural layout of Allahabad became the model for New Delhi.

Civil Service in India

The Indian Civil Service (ICS), also known officially as the Imperial Civil Service, was the elite higher civil service of the British Empire in British India under British rule. They were created by the British Parliament under Section XXXII (32) of the Government of India Act 1858. During the company's governance, civil servants were nominated by the company's Directors and then sent to Haileybury College in London for advanced training, after which they were sent back to India with the required amount of training. Based on a study submitted by Lord Macaulay, the idea of a merit-based modern civil service was introduced in 1854. Entry into civil services was made on the basis of competitive examinations as an outcome of the Select Committee's recommendations, and a Civil Service Commission was established in London in 1854 for the same purpose, with examinations beginning in 1855. These exams were only held in London, and the syllabus had a strong emphasis on European Classics. The maximum age for taking the exam was 23, and the minimum age was 18! As an effect, it has become challenging for Indian candidates to even consider taking this exam. It was an impossibility for the Indians before until every Indian had the means to travel to London for that exam and the books to prepare for that exam. Despite this, Shri Satyendranath Tagore, brother of Shri Rabindranath Tagore, became the first Indian to qualify for this test. Three years later, four more Indians achieved success as a result of his example. As the number of Indian civil servants rose, India petitioned for the examination to be held in India too. However, since this was merely a formality for the British, they refused the applications, fearing that there would be too many successful Indian civil servants in the services. This demand was not agreed upon until after the First World War and the Montagu Chelmsford reforms. From 1922 onwards, the Indian Civil Service Examination was held in India, with the first exam held in Allahabad and then, in Delhi under the auspices of the Federal Public Service Commission. The Indian Civil Service (ICS) was the administrative arm of the British Raj in India and was strongly associated with colonial rule, and it was many British accounts of the ICS officers' rule provided the depiction of them as Dictators.

Unsurprisingly, the ICS was a focal point of nationalist sentiment prior to independence; perhaps more surprisingly, the newly independent Indian state chose to keep the ICS framework and staff largely intact after 1947.

Bipin Chandra Pal, "Father of Revolutionary Thoughts"

Bipin Chandra Pal was born in Sylhet, now in Bangladesh, on November 7, 1858. Bipin Chandra Pal, renowned as the "Father of Revolutionary Thoughts" in India, was a man with a plan to rekindle the flame of nationalism in his people's hearts and drive the evils of colonial rule from their sacred motherland. Bipin Chandra Pal was also a well-known name as a teacher, social reformer, speaker, writer and journalist.

Since childhood, his thoughts were clearly visible and he never shied away from speaking his mind. As candid as he remained in his public life, he was equally forthright and revolutionary in his private life. After the death of his first wife, he married a widow which was a big step in those times.

As soon as he joined the Congress, Bipin Chandra Pal quickly established himself as a big leader. Soon, he became friends with Lala Lajpat Rai and Bal Gangadhar Tilak. Together, the three adopted the fiercest forms of protest against revolutionary change and soon became famous in the country as 'Lal Bal Pal.'

Poorna Swaraj, the Swadeshi movement, boycott and national education became major parts of the country's independence movement, to which the name of Aurobindo Ghosh was also added along over time.

Ram Janmasthan Nihang Sikhs

During this rebellion and its aftermath in our history, a major event occurred, the ramifications of which were felt by Indians before the Ram Mandir Judgment was issued by the Hon'ble Supreme Court of India. An FIR dated November 30, 1858, stated that 25 Nhihang Sikhs entered the Babri Masjid structure. The superintendent of the Babri Masjid lodged this complaint with the Thanedar of Awadh. According to the FIR, the Nihangs were performing Hawan and other religious rituals inside the Masjid. It is further said that they scribbled "Ram! Ram!" in charcoal on the Masjid's walls. According to the article, Hindus had access to Lord Ram's birthplace, the Janmasthan, which is located outside the Masjid but within the same complex. They had been visiting the birthplace for a long time, but they had recently begun visiting the Masjid and worshipping there as well. For several weeks, Thanedar had to evict them from the masjid. This FIR is an excellent piece of evidence demonstrating that the Muslim group did not have sole control of the system. This document contributed to the demise of the argument that Hindus were denied entry to the Masjid. Due to ongoing local disturbances, the British government agreed to fence the birthplace to isolate it from the rest of the land parcel in 1859.

An Anecdote of Unfamous Heroes:

Maniram Dutta Barua (1806-1858), popularly known as Maniram Dewan, led the first major fight for independence in Assam during the revolt. He came from a powerful Assamese family, and his ancestors held prominent status in the Ahom kingdom. In his formative days, he was a dedicated British government officer, serving as a *tehsildar* and a *sheristadar*. Maniram Dewan was the one who told British officials about the Assam tea cultivated by local tribes, which culminated in the British establishing a tea plantation in Assam. As time passed, his allegiance shifted to the eponymous Ahom King, Purandar Singha, who appointed him as Prime Minister of his kingdom, and Maniram Dewan became a fierce critic of British rule. He was opposed to the oppressive tax scheme, exploitation of the local economy, and the introduction of opium production, among other things. He was also resistant to the decision to nominate Marwaris and Bengalis to the post of Mauzadars in Assam, alleging that the locals were overlooked during the process. He then petitioned the Calcutta Sardar Court for the return of administration to the Ahom King. However, the appeal was denied by the court. Following this rejection, he began constructing his network in Calcutta in order to overthrow the British government. The revolt of 1857 served as a catalyst for him, and he saw it as an opportunity to reestablish Ahom rule in Assam. He intended to initiate a revolt against the British with the assistance of King Kandarpeswar Singha and other local leaders. They planned the revolt in August 1857, which Maniram Dewan conducted from Calcutta and determined that Kandarpeswar Singha would liberate Jorhat on Durga puja, and then other towns such as Sivsagar and Dibrugarh would be liberated. Unfortunately, this strategy was discovered before it could be carried out as several letters concerning the rebellion were intercepted by British officials. Maniram Dewan was detained in Calcutta and transferred to Jorhat in Assam. These letters were intercepted by Special

Commissioner Captain Charles Holroyd, who also served as a judge in the trial in which Maniram Dewan was identified as the plot's mastermind. Maniram Dewan and his associate Piyali Barua were publicly hanged on February 26, 1858. He was a businessman as well as a government official and a freedom fighter. Following the discovery of tea in Assam with his assistance, the British appointed him as a Dewan of the Assam Tea Company in 1839. After about a year, he resigned from his position and founded his own tea plantation, becoming the first Indian to grow tea commercially in Assam by establishing two tea gardens. Apart from tea, he also dabbled in gold procurement, salt processing, iron smelting, goods manufacturing, boat and brick making, ivory work, ceramics, agricultural products, and so on. Following his death, the British government auctioned off Maniram Dewan's tea estates in Senglung and Cinnamara, which were purchased for a pittance by the British tea company's George Williamson. However, this proved to be a terrible investment for the company since these loyal Maniram Dewan labourers declined to work with the British owners. Later, the Cinnamara tea estate was purchased by the Jorehaut Tea Company, which is now owned by Assam Tea Corporation. The Senglung Tea estate, on the other hand, was abandoned and lost in time before even being rediscovered in 2014.

CHAPTER - IV

ENGLISH DURING THE 1860S

1. The Theory of Species Origin was published

Some events occurred in the 1860s that were rare for Europeans to accept. In November 1859, Charles Darwin's theory of the origin of species was published. His theory creates the impression that humans evolved from monkeys. Conversely, religious fundamentalists claimed that humans are a special creation of God Almighty, and as a result, their theory was contested by fundamentalist Europeans. They found it difficult to embrace and saw it as heresy. To demonstrate their opposition, these fundamentalists resisted the spread of this doctrine in schools and colleges in the United States and Europe. They were of the view that evolution is merely a theory without any supporting evidence, and thus it should not be taught as a part of the curriculum at schools. They maintained that the theory of evolution is demonstrably incorrect since there are no historical records that show apes evolving into humans.

Although fundamentalists were vehemently opposed to the theory, it was effective in transforming the theological landscape. It undermined the foundational belief of "creator-based" religion, leading to the emergence of the fundamentalist backlash recognized as Creationism and Intelligent Design to this day!

Darwin's theory was founded on observations made in the Galapagos, Patagonia, and Australia, but not on the Indian subcontinent. Darwin never visited India. Considering its vast biological diversity and the access he could have gained through the growing British presence in India, the exact reason he didn't come to India was that the British never welcomed him, since they thought Darwin didn't need to come to India! On the other hand, it could come as a surprise that the British wanted to send the Beagle on a voyage of scientific discovery to South America and the Pacific because these were the areas where they lacked expertise. On the contrary, many Indians, such as bureaucrats, army officers, planters, and private citizens, gathered a large amount of knowledge about Britain's vast new possessions. Darwin was given all of this knowledge on a silver platter. He may not have visited India, but the Origin of Species and its sequel, The Descent of Man, are jam-packed with information from India that he gathered from the far-flung network of correspondents he established during the long following years of the Beagle voyage when he struggled to understand evolution by natural selection and its implications and gathered the massive amount of evidence he knew would be needed.

Mr Felix Padel Charles Darwin, Charles Darwin's great-great grandson, has worked closely with the Adivasis in eastern India. He is a self-employed anthropologist with degrees from Oxford and Delhi University. Darwin is enthralled by tribal peoples' indigenous cultures.

"The British did not build, but rather de-developed India," said Mr Felix Padel Darwin at a national seminar on "Social Ecology and Environmental Movements in India" at Lucknow University. The British conquered India because it had been developed for a long time and the British were militarily developed. In terms of multi-cultural ethos and manufacturing skills, India was much more integrated than Britain. Following British rule, the standard of manufacturing in many areas, such as cloth, deteriorated dramatically and entered a "de-developing" phase.

2. An unusual death: Thomas Babington Macaulay

While the mystery of the origin of human life captivated the world, a death caused by a heart attack shocked the world. It is not uncommon for someone to die of a heart attack nowadays, but it was unusual in 1859. It was Thomas Babington Macaulay who advocated the westernisation of India and the Indians. His aim was to overthrow Indian culture by instituting a British education system in India and distracting Indians from their heritage. He also desired to steer young Indian minds away from the direction of nationalism and into other fictitious pleasures, so that they would not remain in a proper state and thus become robots in the possession of foreign forces. Much of this culminated in the plunder of Indian wealth and the Indians becoming slaves. Thomas Babington Macaulay was the evil genius behind such an education scheme and the demise of Indian society. This British education system robbed Indians of their identity by instilling so-called English culture not only in their ideas but also in their morality and taste. They attempted to contaminate the Indian blood and colour through these efforts. These measures taken by the British show that they wanted the Indians to transition from Indian culture to western civilisation.

Macaulay and his racist British mafia in all their arrogance decided that "a single shelf of good European literature was worth the whole of native literature of India," and that "all the historical information which has been collected from all the books…in the Sanskrit language is less valuable than what may be found in the most paltry abridgements used at preparatory schools in England." What is more amazing is the fact that Macaulay passes this judgement *after* admitting that "I have no knowledge of either Sanskrit or Arabic." Certainly. But he had full knowledge of the workings of imperialism of which he was a willing slave and substantial beneficiary.

While doing all of this evil work, he intended to write a history of England from 1688 to 1820, or until George III's death. But, on December 28, 1859, he died of a heart attack, leaving behind his major work, "The History of England from the Accession of James II." On January 9, 1860, he was buried in Westminster Abbey, near a statue of Joseph Addison, in Poets' Corner. Because he had no heir, his lineage ended with his death.

A colonial mentality continues to govern the Indian education system. Despite the passage of more than six decades after independence, we have failed to establish a vibrant, high-quality, free, and widespread primary education system.

It is time to abandon Macaulay's vision of India and build a nation of people who are Indian in blood and colour, as well as in tastes, beliefs, morals, ethics, and intellect.

The Lady Guardian: Rani Suryamani (1859)

When the rest of India was pacified by the Act of 1858, it was in 1859 that the British government solidified its roots in Odisha, and the people of Puri were forced to face a great calamity. Their king, Gajapati Birakishore Dev, died, leaving Srimandira in the hands of his queen, Rani Suryamani Patamadhehi, and his adopted son, Dibuasingha Dev. The Princess of Suvarnapur (now Sonepur) was Rani Suryamani. Despite her skill as an archer, she was unprepared to manage this massive living temple in the absence of her husband. Since their adopted son was just four years old, he was unable to become superintendent of the temple. In such a tough position, she made the courageous decision to become the custodian of the Jagannath temple and the Puri Raj estates. Her administration was flawless after 32 years as a custodian. Rani Suryamani carried out the tasks assigned to her to the best of her ability, and as a result, she was able to put an end to the sevayats' uprising.

1860-End of the Second Opium War

Many Indian, American, and Spanish families were busy making money from poppy seeds in the mid-nineteenth century, which contributed to the Opium wars, much to everyone's surprise. Opium was the cause of a large amount of money produced all over the world. Karl Marx investigated the moral and economic effects of opium on the global industry. Opium was manufactured in India under the monopoly of the East India Company and smuggled into China by entrepreneurs. Of course, this smuggling was not easy; it came at the expense of two armed conflicts in China in the mid-nineteenth century between powers from Western countries and the Qing dynasty, which ruled China from 1644 to 1911. The first opium war was fought between the Chinese and the British in 1839, and it lasted until 1842. And the second Opium War, also known as the Arrow War or the Anglo-French War in China, began in 1856 between Britain and France against China and ended in 1860.

British agents smuggled tons of opium into China in exchange for tea, legally and illegally, taking silver in return. Millions were turned into addicts in China and India even as laws were passed against opium in Britain. Journalist-playwright Thomas Manuel asserts in his packed-with-facts book Opium Inc: How a Global Drug Trade Funded the British Empire that the British Raj in the 19th century was a narco-state – a country sustained by trade in an illegal drug.[1]

At its peak, opium was the third-highest source of income for the British in India – after land and salt. Bombay money was used to fund these opium wars! Bombay, the country's financial and business hub, was built on these tiny poppy seeds, which produced enormous income. Mr Claude Markovits, a great historian, once said that "Bombay was first the Medellin and then the Manchester of India". Medellin was the headquarters of Pablo Escobar, the 20th century's king smuggler. This was the size of Bombay's opium trade market, which was sustained by opium trading companies like Jardine Matheson, whose closest partner was Sir Jamsethji Jeejeeboy, the man who founded half of Bombay! He was the first Indian to be knighted and was the king of opium in Bombay!

Queen Victoria appointed Jeejeeboy as the first Baronet of Bombay in 1857.

While the poor Indians were squeezed to ensure bumper poppy harvest and production and sale of opium, many Indians made 'super profits' from the trade. Besides Calcutta, opium was shipped out of Bombay too, with the British collecting their fees and Indian merchants making a killing.

---

1   https://thewire.in/books/book-review-opium-inc-british-raj-narco-state

The Banana Stem: Shields to the Garo Warriors (1872)

Meghalaya's first Garo freedom fighter was born in Samanda village near Williamnagar in the East Garo Hills region. He was a Garo warrior who ambushed a troop of British soldiers in the state. A contingent of British soldiers from Tura went to the East Garo Hills to conquer the area in 1872. The Garo tribe, who refused to hand over possession of their homeland to the western invaders, met resistance from the British forces. To fight back, the soldiers established a camp near Chiso Bibra in the village of Matcha Rongkrek. Togan Nengminja planned an assault on the camp to prevent the British from invading the area. As a result, he and other Garo warriors raided the camp at night, preying on the sleeping soldiers. Though the attackers initially succeeded, the noise of the assault woke the other soldiers up, and they immediately launched a retaliatory attack. Garo warriors armed with conventional guns were unable to stand up to the British rifle. The Garo warriors suffered heavy losses, and Pa Togan Nengminja was shot and killed on the spot. To cover themselves from bullets, Pa Togan Nengminja and his warriors used shields made of plantain banana stems. He reasoned that once the bullets reached the shield, they would cool down and lose momentum. Needless to say, it did not succeed, but it does point to the warriors' preparation before the assault. Although they were incapable of defeating the rifle, the banana shield is an indication of the Garo tribe's intelligence and preparation.

A decade that witnessed the birth of legends and events that are still shaping history!

October 6, 1860: The Emergence of Immortal Penal Law Codification!

Yes, indeed! You heard that right; the IPC, or the Immortal Penal Code, was drafted in 1860 and is still totally legitimate after 160 years! The Indian Penal Code was implemented under colonial rule in an effort to put a common criminal code in India to correct the flaws in *Mohammadi* law that existed at the time. Some aspects of the code were adapted from the Napoleonic Code and the Louisiana Civil Code of 1825, notwithstanding its origins in English law. In 1827, an effort was made to introduce a penal code under the direction of then-Governor Mr Elphinstone, which was termed the Elphinstone Code. However, the attempt was a failure. In 1833, the Charter Act was passed, which made provisions for the enactment of laws in India. Thus, the process of law-making in India was commenced. The First Law Commission of India was established in India as a result of this Act. This paved the way for the development of the legendary "Indian Penal Code of 1860." The Law Commission of India was headed by Lord Thomas Babington Macaulay, the brains behind the IPC. He wrote the entire code, which he introduced to Parliament in 1856. Barnes Peacock proposed several amendments to the Code before it was presented in Parliament and before its presentation in the Legislative Assembly. After a delay caused by the 1857 rebellion, the Indian Penal Code was eventually passed on October 6, 1860. Regardless of the fact that the code went into effect on January 1, 1862, it did not apply to the princely states, since they had their own legal systems.

A Cambridge law graduate, Macaulay, was active in codifying the mishmash of laws that applied in various parts of the world into a draught code. He was never a serious player, but he dabbled in writing and politics. He was so obsessed with politics that, after being elected to the House of Commons twice, he saw his political and financial future as bleak. He came to India as a member of the Governor-Council. A general's annual salary of ten thousand pounds was offered to the 34-year-old Macaulay for chairing India's first law commission.

The Most Controversial Offense - Sedition Is Revealed

When Macaulay drafted the Indian Penal Code, India was still ruled by the company. To ensure that no one dared speak out against the company's rules, Macaulay included provisions in the IPC that addressed this issue. He stipulated that someone who, by speaking or writing, attempts to incite feelings of dissatisfaction with the government in the East India Company's territories would face life imprisonment or banishment for three years. Since it was loosely based on old English law, this provision did not use the word sedition directly. The draft of the code was completed in 1837, but the 1857 Revolt served as a catalyst in the process of implementing the draft. The legislation was enacted in 1860, a year after Macaulay's death. However, the sedition clause was left out of the code. This oversight was corrected ten years later with the addition of Section 124-A to the Indian Penal Code.

Surat Income Tax Agitation, 1860

In 1860, the introduction of the Income-tax Act in India by James Wilson led to widespread resentment among the population. On November 29th, a small disturbance took place in Surat in this connection that came to be known as the Income-tax Riot.

The residents of Burhanpuri Bhagal, one of the central quarters of the city, gathered in large numbers and declared that they would not fill in the income-tax forms and that they would close down their shops until the tax was repealed. The crowd, which numbered around three thousand people, was ordered to disperse, but it refused to do so. It was only the lathi-charge of the mounted police that compelled the dispersal of the gathering. During the confrontation, some thirty people were arrested. Out of those arrested, twenty-four were convicted and sentenced to six months of imprisonment with hard labour.

This riot demonstrates the growing bitterness of Indians against the oppressive policies of the colonial government. It also serves as a reminder of the power of collective action and the importance of standing up against injustice.

1861 – Archaeological Survey begins in India

Mr Alexander Cunningham established the Archaeological Survey of India and served as its first Director-General. He was a retired army engineer who was appointed as Archaeological Surveyor not because he had any special knowledge, but because in September 1842, when he was still a Lt.A.D.C to the Governor General, Lord Auckland, he proposed a scheme for falsifying Indian archaeology in a letter to Col. Sykes as an 'undertaking of vast importance to the Indian Government politically and to the British public religiously so that the establishment of the Christian religion in India could eventually succeed.' Cunningham attributes Muslim authorship to a large number of Hindu townships and buildings in order to achieve this aim.

Since the British founded this archaeological department, we began our study of history with Stone Age man and the mesmerising culture of Harappa and Mohenjo-Daro! There was no archaeological department in India before the establishment of British rule. Misleading records were available during the long Muslim rule that preceded the British in India due to Muslim practises of capturing and misappropriating Hindu temples and palaces in order to convert them into mosques and tombs. As a result, when the British arrived in India, all of the historic buildings were in the hands of Muslims.

Following this, the British not only falsified Indian history for political purposes, but they also consulted the Muslims who occupied the buildings and documented their bluff. The Muslims were well aware that if they spat up the true past, they would lose control of those massive structures and monuments. Based on this deception, an archaeological department was established in India.

Indomitable Madam Bhikaji Cama born on September 24, 1861

Since the vast majority of Parsees in India were British stooges, they did not participate in the freedom struggle. Nevertheless, there are still exceptions. Madam Bhikaji Cama, born on September 24, 1861, in an affluent Parsi household, was a radical firebrand freedom fighter and tireless propagandist for Indian independence. She has lived in France since she was banished from India and Britain. Her father, Sorabji Framji Patel, was a well-known merchant who was active in industry, education, and philanthropy in the city of Bombay. But she was drawn to the Indian nationalist movement instead of the wealthy and business world. She had a talent for languages and quickly became adept at arguing for her country's cause in various circles. Later, in 1885, she married Rustomji Cama, a well-known lawyer. There were several incidents of disagreement between the couple as she became more interested in socio-political issues. She relocated to London due to marital problems and poor health.

On March 12, 1862, James Bruce, 8th Earl of Elgin, was appointed Viceroy of India

In 1862, James Bruce, the 8th Earl of Elgin, was the first viceroy who had been directly appointed by the crown and was subject to the Secretary of State for India. He was also the first viceroy to use Peterhoff, Shimla, as his official residence.

Elgin Road is named after James Bruce, the only Viceroy buried in India (buried in the churchyard of St. John in the Wilderness at Dharamshala). Three of James' cousins who died in Kolkata before the construction of the Scottish Cemetery are buried in South Park Cemetery.

Netaji Subhash Bose spent his formative years in Calcutta on Elgin Road. This house was the hub of his political operations, and it was from here that Netaji escaped house arrest. As a result, this is the house most closely associated with Netaji; thus, it is now a museum known as "Netaji Bhawan."

High Courts in India - History

A legal system based on recorded judicial precedents, now known as the common law system, arrived in India with the British East India Company in 1726, thanks to a charter granted by King George I. This charter resulted in the creation of Mayor's Courts in Madras, Bombay, and Calcutta (now Chennai, Mumbai, and Kolkata, respectively). Following its success in the Battle of Plassey, administrative functions began to take on the task of judicial functions. By 1772, the company had replaced the Mughal legal system by extending its courts beyond these three major cities.

Following the First War of Independence in 1857, the Empire experienced the next major shift when authority abruptly transitioned from the company to the Crown. The legal system, too, had undergone a transformation. The Supreme Courts took the place of the Mayor Courts, and these courts were later transformed into the first High Courts through letters patent approved by the Indian High Courts Act passed by the British Parliament in 1862. The need for separate judicial bodies for various states was the impetus for the passage of this act. As a result, the British government agreed to replace the then-existing Supreme Court and Sardar Adalat with the High Court.

Calcutta was India's first city to have its own High Court. The "High Court of Judicature at Fort William," now recognised as the High Court of Calcutta, was constituted by the Letters Patent dated May 14th, 1862, which was issued under the Indian High Courts Act of 1861, which vested in the Queen the power to issue charters and letters patent to erect and establish the High Courts of Calcutta, Madras, and Bombay. Later, on August 14th and 15th, the cities of Bombay and Madras saw the establishment of high courts. The Letters Patent established the High Courts' authority and powers. The duties of superintendence of the lower courts and enrolment of lawyers were now delegated to the respective High Courts in the cities. In 1862, Sir Barnes Peacock was appointed as the first Chief Justice of the Calcutta High Court, and in 1863, Justice Shri Sumboo Nath Pandit became the first Indian to be appointed as a judge of the Calcutta High Court.

A legal system was developed. The personal and religious laws of the monarchs were supplanted with codified laws. Even European citizens were placed within the jurisdiction, but only European judges could hear criminal cases. The legal system became more intricate and expensive. Wealthy people had the power to influence the system. There was much opportunity for trickery, fraud, and deception. Long-running legal proceedings meant that justice was delayed. The courts grew overworked as litigation rose. European judges frequently lacked knowledge of Indian traditions and customs.

Kiang Nongbah was publicly hanged by the Britishers in Jowai town on December 30 1862

Kiang Nongbah or U Kiang Nangbah was a Pnar (a matrilineal sub-tribal group of the Khasi people) freedom fighter who was publicly hanged by the Britishers in Jowai town on 30 December 1862.

Towards the close of 1860, income tax was also levied in addition to the house-tax. There was an apprehension in the air that tax would also be levied on betel and betel nut. Imposition of these taxes created turmoil amongst the *Jaintias* and they rose again in a fierce rebellion in 1862. The leader and guiding spirit in this rebellion was a young man, U Kiang Nongbah. In the first rebellion, he kept his identity secret and thus, avoided arrest. He was extremely shrewd and a great organiser. He contacted all the Dolois and Sirdars without causing any suspicion. He managed to hoodwink the British Intelligence Service. They had no trace of his movements and activities. Yet, ultimately, he was defeated because of the superior might of the British. In the unequal fight that ensured, hundreds of Jaintias were killed and U Kiang Nongbah was betrayed, captured and hanged publicly to strike terror into the hearts of the Jaintias on December 30, 1862.

"Brothers and sisters, please look carefully at my face when I die on the gallows. If my face turns towards the east, my country will be free from the foreign yoke within 100 years; if it turns towards the west, my country will remain in bondage for good."

These were the last words U Kiang Nangbah said to the British at the gallows.

A postage stamp was issued by the Government of India to commemorate him in 2001. A government college (Kiang Nangbah Government College) was also opened at Jowai, Meghalaya, in 1967 in his honour. 'Kiang Nangbah Monument' is located on the banks of the Myntdu River in Jaintia Hills District, Meghalaya. This beautiful hollow tower-like structure of typical Jaintia design was erected by the Jaintia tribe.

1863 – Birth of Yodha Sanyasi

Swami Vivekanand delivered speeches that were generally regarded as the founding documents of Hinduism. Narendranath Dutta, born into a Kayastha family on the auspicious day of Makar Sankranti in Shimla Pally, Calcutta, was born on the 12th of January, 1863. Who could have predicted that a boy from an ordinary family, whose father was an esteemed lawyer practising in the High Court of Calcutta, would one day grow up to be one of the greatest sages in world history? On his birth anniversary, the whole nation celebrates "National Youth Day." He essentially was and still remains an Indian youth icon who inspired millions through his call that embeds the nectar of Hindu scriptures and philosophy in itself.

The National Youth Festival is held every year to provide exposure to our talented youth at the national level, along with galvanising them towards nation-building.

Behind the mighty intellect of Swami Vivekananda was an extremely accomplished Yogic master well-established in the highest state of self-realization. Many such mysterious, inexplicable, and interesting events surrounded Swami Vivekananda.

Swami Vivekananda was a great intellectual and scholarly monk who put Hinduism on the world map. He also had a profound impact in the United States – a legacy that roughly lasted till about the 1950s. Celebrities who were inspired by him included J.D. Salinger, Nikola Tesla, and others.

John Laird Mair Lawrence, 1st Baron Lawrence, became Viceroy of India on January 12, 1864

While on a home visit in 1863, John was sent back to India as Viceroy upon the sudden and unexpected demise of Lord Elgin. His tenure as Viceroy lasted from 1864 to 1869.

His proclaimed goals were to consolidate British strength. The greatest disappointment of Lawrence's tenure, however, was the Orissa famine of 1866, which killed an estimated one million Indians. Part of the criticism centred on his decision to relocate the government apparatus to the cooler hills of Shimla, which were geographically distant from the seat of power in Calcutta. In response, Lawrence offered his resignation, which was declined by Viscount Cranborne.

1865 – The birth of the man who coined the phrase "Simon Go Back!"

Lala Lajpat Rai, a social reformer and freedom fighter, was born on January 28, 1865, in Dhudike, which is now part of Punjab's Moga district. His father was a scholar of two languages, Persian and Urdu, and his mother was a religious lady who helped instil strong moral values in the children. He received his primary education at the Government Higher Secondary School in Rewari (then in Punjab), which is now in Haryana. In 1880, he enrolled at Lahore's Government College to study law. He enjoyed reading and was profoundly moved by the values of patriotism and nationalism articulated by Giuseppe Mazzini, the Italian revolutionary leader.

The Hindu Mela is a political and cultural festival that started in 1867 in Calcutta

In 1867, a national festival proudly titled "Hindu Mela" was born in Bengal with twin objectives. The first was to invoke the spirit of patriotism and the second was to rouse Hindu society to its forgotten greatness. The Hindu Mela was suffused with devotional and patriotic songs, but it was not explicitly anti-British. But with the memories of the 1857 War of Independence still fresh in their mind, the British colonial Government kept an eye on this Mela.

Generally speaking, an outgrowth of the Hindu Mela was the staging of the first political play, *Bharatmata* in 1873 – a development that alarmed the British immediately. The brilliant success of Bharatamata spurred others to adopt this medium for nationalistic purposes. The Bengali stage was being transformed in unforeseen ways. In less than a year, Bharatamata was followed by *Purubikram*, authored by Jyotirindranath Tagore, the elder brother of the more famous Rabindranath. He topped this feat in 1875 with another play, *Sarojini*.

Hindi-Urdu controversy

After the revolution of 1857, the power came into the hands of the British Parliament and the expansion of education was greatly accelerated. In this context, the Hindus of Bihar and United Provinces (modern Uttar Pradesh) requested the Government that instead of using Persian and Arabic script as the language of official work, Devanagari script and Hindi should be given the status of second official language. The reason behind this was that Hindi was a regional language and Devanagari script could be written and read by the general public. As soon as the government considered this suggestion as more pragmatic and wanted to accept it in 1867, Sir Syed Ahmad Khan started opposing it and launched a campaign to make Urdu the second official language.

His reason behind this was that Urdu was the common language of Muslims. He was engaged in the promotion and propagation of the

Urdu language through his writings since the end of Mughal rule and the schools and colleges established by him taught in Urdu medium. But his view was narrow and limited to Muslims only. On the other hand, non-Muslims like Hindus and Christians objected to Urdu being the second official language. There were two main arguments against his Urdu: first, it was not the language of the common people and second, its script is foreign, and the general public did not know how to read and write. For Sir Syed Ahmad Khan, the insistence of Hindus to make Hindi the second official language was in some way a symbol of the decline of the influence of centuries-old Islamic culture in India. He argued that Urdu Muslims and Hindus alike have political and cultural heritage. But, due to bitter memories of past Muslim rule, the Hindus were not at all willing to carry on a legacy in which both script and vocabulary are beyond the comprehension of the general public.

The success of the Hindi movement was natural as it was close to the masses in terms of script and spoken language. Yet, Sir Syed Ahmed Khan took it as Hindu dominance and started promoting Urdu as a symbol of Muslim heritage and as the language of the Muslim intellectual and political class. Using the Urdu language, he started pushing for issues centred on Muslims exclusively. His approach further accelerated the mass polarization as educated and intellectual Muslim elites adopted Urdu as their spoken language. Later on, Urdu became the heart of the Two Nation Theory.

Lakshminarasu Chetty died In 1868 in financial poverty and patriotic richness

Gazulu Chetty was born in 1806 to a wealthy indigo merchant, Sidhulu Chetty, in Madras. On completion of his initial education, Chetty entered the family trade and succeeded as a businessman. He entered politics and devoted money to social and philanthropic causes. During the mid-19th century, Christian missionaries indulged in open proselytization in public institutions in the Madras Presidency. Their proselytization activities were allegedly favoured by officials of the British government, who preferred native Christians to Hindus in higher appointments in order to entice Hindu Indians to embrace Christianity. The religious stance of the Madras government was frequently condemned by the Hindu population. Chetty supported their cause and launched agitations against conversions. On 02 October 1844, Chetty founded the Crescent, the first Indian-owned newspaper in the Madras Presidency for the "amelioration of the condition of Hindus." But right from the beginning, the newspaper faced strict government opposition. An advertisement sent to the Madras government for insertion into the government publication Fort St George Gazette was rejected. Further, the government resolved to enact a law wherein a Hindu convert to Christianity would not lose his ancestral right to own property. This was severely condemned by the Hindu community of Madras who, under the leadership of Chetty, presented a memorial to the Governor on 09 April 1845. The government eventually withdrew its plans after prolonged discussions with the agitators. Around this time, the Madras government tried to introduce the Bible as a standard textbook for the students of Madras University. Students were often questioned on points connected to Christian theology and were denied government posts if their knowledge of Christian texts was found wanting. Hindus of the Madras Presidency protested against these measures. Chetty presided over a protest meeting at the Pachaiyappa College on 07 October 1846 in which it was resolved to send a memorandum to the Court of Directors of the British East India Company. Their efforts were successful and the move to introduce Christian theology into the curriculum was disbanded. In 1853, the government once again tried to introduce the Bible into the educational curriculum, but its efforts were thwarted by George and John Bruce Norton and Chetty.

He passed away in 1868. Love for the *Rashtra* and *Dharma* animated all his life. He gave his everything for the welfare and dignified future of Hindus. He understood how the colonial system was tearing away at the cultural matrix of the Hindus by destroying temple lands and temple revenues, how it was also destroying the peasants by changing the land ownerships in villages, and creating insufferable human misery.

His was an important insight – a *Hindutva* insight indeed, long before even Savarkar expounded *Hindutva*.

Richard Southwell Bourke became 4th Viceroy of India

On January 12, 1869, Richard Southwell Bourke, 6th Earl of Mayo was appointed as the fourth Viceroy of India. He was commonly referred to as "Lord Mayo" in his hometown. He consolidated India's borders and reorganised the country's finances. During his term, the first census was conducted in 1872.

On February 8, 1872, the Viceroy of India, Lord Mayo, was assassinated at Hopetown, Port Blair, Andaman Islands, by a convict, Sher Ali Khan, a Pathan from India's North West Frontier Province (NWFP). It was an odd irony that, when the British Empire was lauded as an immense and never-ending reign, the same sun was indirectly responsible for the death of its Viceroy.

Sher Ali served in the British army and was responsible for the deaths of Indian freedom fighters during the 1857 uprising. He was imprisoned in Andaman because he murdered one of his own family, Hyder. The altercation was about property.

Sher Ali, after the assassination of Lord Mayo, declared in his trial that the reason for the killing was *Jihad* (doing the deed 'by order of God'). Lord Mayo was India's sole Viceroy to be assassinated while in power.

Mohandas Gandhi or "Bapu" was born on October 2, 1869

Mohandas Gandhi was born on October 2, 1869, in a trading family in Porbandar, a small town in Gujarat. The day is now celebrated as Gandhi Jayanti.

Gandhi studied law at the Inner Temple in London. After unsuccessfully attempting to practise in India, he moved to South Africa in 1893 and returned to India in 1915.

He was the pioneer of some of the phenomena like Non-violence, Civil Disobedience, *Satyagrah,* etc. These were the ways he used to fight against the British.

The Wahabi movement was crushed in 1870

Our story begins with the death of the super-bigot, Syed Ahmad Barelvi, widely credited as the founder of the Wahabi "movement" in India. He was the grand-disciple of the ultra-fanatic, Shah Waliullah, and followed his footsteps loyally. He marshalled support by writing fanaticism-dipped letters to the Prince Kamran of Herat, Amir Nasrullah of Bukhara and the Nizam of Hyderabad. Of them, the Nizam's brother became his most devoted disciple and sent him men and money.

Syed Ahmad also set up various Khalifas throughout India – a vast network of fanatics headed by members of the Islamic clergy and other prominent men from the community. After Maharaja Ranjit Singh died in 1839, Ahmad's Khalifas captured large parts of the region to the east of the Sindhu River. This was the beginning of the Wahabi "movement." The British quickly woke up to this threat, quelled the Wahabis in 1847 and wrested back the region.

When the Wahabis noticed the speed, ferocity, and sweep of the First War of Indian Independence against the British, they stuck to their founding charter; they stood completely aloof from it because it was eminently *haram* to cooperate with the infidel Hindus. They also went a step further by issuing a formal Proclamation "inviting all Mahomedans in India to arm and fight for their religion." Next, they published a Fatwa "declaring that it was the duty of all Mahomedans to make religious war and that otherwise, their families would be destroyed and ruined."

It was time to cut the root itself. As we noted earlier, the spectacular and repeated successes of the Wahabis were because the Khalifa network of Muslims in mainland India supplied them with money, men, and material. This source had to be burnt for good. Accordingly, the British launched a massive manhunt of prominent Wahabi leaders across India and arrested most of its masterminds. The trials at Ambala, Patna, Malda, and Rajmahal yielded a great harvest. These Wahabi leaders were transported for life.

With that, the Wahabi movement was completely crushed in 1870.

However, in the highly secularized history of the 1857 war of independence, the selfsame Wahabis are painted as having waged the First War of Independence. From the start, the Wahabis regarded their revolt as a struggle for Muslim independence. It was an all-out Jihad for the restoration of pure Islamic rule in India. The underlying impulse of the Wahabi "movement" was Islamic, not Indian; its ultimate goal was to establish Dar-ul-Islam throughout India.

Guess who was the latter-day inheritor of the bigoted Wahabi impulse germinated by Shah Waliullah and put into practice by Barelvi? His name is Sir Syed Ahmed Khan, the patron saint of the secularists.

Sir Jadunath Sarkar, one of the greatest Indian historians, was born on December 10, 1870

Jadunath Sarkar was born in Karachmaria village in Natore, now in Bangladesh, to Rajkumar Sarkar, the local Zamindar on 10 December 1870. In 1891, he graduated in English from Presidency College, Calcutta. In 1892, he topped the Master of Arts examination in English at Calcutta University and in 1897, he received the Premchand-Roychand Scholarship.

Jadunath Sarkar was *nulli secundus* in the realm of pioneering and fundamental scholarship in history. Jadunath Sarkar's works are notable not merely for their level of detail but also for their singular quality of being authoritative. But the more astonishing fact is that he didn't write "single" (i.e., independent) volumes but he authored multiple volumes on the same subject. He was thus also a pioneer in the preservation of records and documents and the building up of archives.

Jadunath Sarkar towered over the entire discipline of history and historical research for over two decades, marshalling facts from primary sources, producing definitive histories and demolishing shoddy and mediocre scholarship by his contemporaries. He also made a lot of enemies who, unable to rebut his arguments, embarked on a vicious plot to bring him down personally.

He wrote the blunt truth about Muslim rule in India. But more infuriatingly, he also wrote about the courageous, valorous magnificence of Chhatrapati Shivaji Maharaj.

Jadunath Sarkar had done an extensive empirical study of the Mughal Empire in the context of Indian history by clearly delineating various aspects like administration, agriculture and so on. However, the Left tried to belittle this evidence-based approach to Indian history. In a recent biography of Jadunath Sarkar, the scholar is astonished to note that Irfan Habib in his book, "Agrarian System of Mughal India" does not refer to Jadunath Sarkar even once. In a sense, non-Left historians have been systematically wiped out of the pages of history, so that the Left does not have to deal with uncomfortable facts which do not suit their narrative.

Jadunath Sarkar was unceremoniously removed from the very institution he had helped set up and build – the Indian Historical Records Commission. By the 1970s, Jadunath Sarkar's body of work was almost entirely banished from academia.

But a worse fate followed the death of Jadunath. In 1973, Indira Gandhi's education minister, the Islamic bigot, Nurul Hasan coaxed her to set up something called "The Centre for Studies in Social Sciences" in the very home of Acharya Jadunath Sarkar. All the objects in his house had been removed.

The Cow Slaughter in 1870: Malicious utterance

The East India Company conquered Punjab in the mid-nineteenth century. Following this conquest, a sect known as the "Namdhari Sikhs" arose, with their spiritual home in Bhani Sahib in the princely state of Malerkotla, which is now part of the Sangrur district. The Namdhari Sikhs are widely regarded as among the region's first challengers to colonial rule. They became known as the 'Kukas,' and their movement was defined by the concepts of non-cooperation, civil disobedience, and special reforms for women. They were also well-known for promoting vegetarianism. They were also involved in the cow protection movement that arose in British India. An ox slaughter at Malerkotla in January

1872 sparked a full-fledged skirmish between a party of Namdhari Sikhs, Malerkotla officials, and British administrators. Even after Satguru Ram Singh, the Namdharis' chief, advised restraint, violence continued. This led to the notorious public execution without trial of over 60 people, including children, who were bound to cannons and blown away. Also today, a monument stands in Malerkotla to remind us of this heinous execution and the dirty politics that was carried out for cows!

The British used their infamous divide-and-rule strategy not only in 1905 but its seeds were sown much earlier by giving Muslims open permission to slaughter cows in the Punjab region. This was a deliberate tactic to provoke their Hindu and Sikh neighbours. In 1871, the desecration of the Golden Temple and other Gurudwaras resulted in the sacrifice of Namdhari Sikhs. In Amritsar, Ludhiana, and Raikot, they were executed without trial.

These occurrences were fuel to the already raging fires of discontent, making people realise that freedom will be hard-won! This 'Kuka movement' was viewed as a cornerstone that would end British rule.

Though some Mughal rulers, such as Akbar, recognised the importance of cow protection to appease the majority Hindu sentiment, it was with the Sikhs that cow protection began as a political response to the persecution of Indians.

According to Guru Gobind Singh's Oogardanti Baani, which is included in the Dasam Granth:

"Give me this command that I may grab Turks and destroy them. The great evil of cow-killing may I stop in this world. The throne of the Mughals may I destroy.

Fulfil this desire of mine. May the suffering of cows stop. May the victory of the true Guru resound throughout the world."

The prominent Sikh ruler Maharaja Ranjit Singh used to sentence cow slaughterers to death. It should be noted that the death penalty was prohibited under Sikh law. It was previously permitted only in cases of cow slaughter, whereas, even an attempt to assassinate the King had no death penalty. It is, therefore, not surprising that the first Gaurakshini Sabha was founded in Punjab in 1882. Cow slaughter was prohibited not only by Sikh rulers but also by Maratha rulers.

Robert Clive, an alleged opium user himself, was the one who began it all! The individual who stabbed himself with a pen knife after being unable to bear the agony of the disease caused by opium addiction. He was the one who palpably assured Indian Muslims that eating beef was a religious requirement. He made cow slaughter a vote-bank problem and decided to sever India's agricultural backbone by targeting the sacred cows. In pursuit of carrying out this mission, he opened the first cow slaughterhouse in India in the year 1760 in Kolkata. The Slaughter House was so large that it could slaughter over 30,000 cows a day[2]. So, anybody can get an idea about how many cows were slaughtered in a year! And this activity continued for a century, leaving very few cattle for agricultural needs, and thus, succeeded in breaking the backbone of the Indian economy! The main source of survival for major Indians was and even today is Agriculture. Since there were fewer cows, there was less cow dung available, which meant less urea and phosphate to keep the soil fertile. To address this problem, Britain began importing artificial manure and gaining profit from such imports. What a mercantile mind they possessed!

In 1893, Viceroy Lansdowne wrote, "While she [Queen of England] agrees on the relevance of perfect justice, she believes that Muslims require more security than Hindus, and they are by far the more loyal. Although Muhammad's cow-killing is used as a justification for the agitation, it is actually aimed at us, who slaughter many more cows for our army, & c., than the Muhammadans."

In his book, "The Creation of the Indian National Congress: 1892-1909," Dr P C Ghosh quotes the then Viceroy, Lord Lansdowne, as saying, "The cow protection movement transformed the Indian National

---

2   https://www.dailypioneer.com/2017/sunday-edition/shed-your-colonial-mindset-over-cows.html

Congress from a foolish debating society into a real political force, backed by the most dangerous elements in native society."

Protecting Cows became a sign of Hindu self-respect, as cow slaughter was used to denigrate Hindus. The movement soon spread across North India, which had seen the worst of the Hindu persecution. Between 1880 and 1893, hundreds of gaushalas (cow shelters/homes) were built, as well as several public meetings and awareness campaigns were held. Cows did, in reality, pose a serious challenge to the British Raj.

Unrest among the Santhals in June 1871

The Dumka district in Jharkhand witnessed widespread unrest and mobilization among the Santhals in 1871.

After crushing the massive Santhal uprising of 1855-1856, the British government instituted a thorough enquiry into their conditions in an effort to pacify them and ensure that such a rebellion would not occur again. However, the peace established did not prove to be long-lasting, as the colonial regime slowly began rolling back the protections offered to the tribe under the Santhal Parganas Act of 1855. The Santhal agriculturalists of Dumka in particular were agitated at the prospect of being forced into poverty by the nexus of excessive revenue demands by the colonial regime, and the extortionate rates of interest charged by the moneylenders, who were the only source of loans in the absence of a cheap credit system. There were even instances of the peasants being thrown out of the lands that they themselves had reclaimed from the forests due to failure to pay the revenue on time. In such conditions, the Santhals organized processions to the Office of the Assistant Commissioner at Dumka in 1871 demanding immediate resolution for their grievances. The Assistant Commissioner responded by imposing fines on some of the Santhal men for disturbing the public peace. To this instigation, the agitators responded by threatening another *hool* (rebellion) if their grievances were not resolved soon.

This threat of the Santhals threw the administration into a state of panic. In just a few months, the 'Santhal Pargana Settlement Regulation

1872' was introduced, under which arrangements were made to restore lands to those peasants who had been evicted previously, maximum limits were introduced on the interest rates on loans that could be charged from the Santhals, and a number of other steps were taken to improve their conditions.

The 1st Earl of Northbrook, Thomas George Baring, was appointed Viceroy of India

On May 3, 1872, Thomas George Baring, 1st Earl of Northbrook (famously known as Lord Northbrook), was appointed as the Viceroy of India. His greatest achievements came as an ambitious reformer focusing on the improvement of the standard of governance in the British Raj.

On August 27, 1894, Lord Northbrook announced Assam as a separate province under a Chief Commissioner. To give a Royal welcome, the Assam administration built the Gateway of Assam, popularly known as "The Northbrook Gate," standing on the Itakhuli hill near the Sukreswar temple of today's Panbazar. It is the only completely surviving monument of the colonial era. The place where the Northbrook gate is located is also of utmost significance as the historic Battle of Saraighat was won at this very place on a Friday in March 1671.

Sri Aurobindo, the famous sage of Pondicherry was born in Calcutta on August 15, 1872

Sri Aurobindo was born as the son of Dr K. D. Ghose and Swarnalata Devi. Dr Ghose on the 15th of August in the year 1872 in Kolkata, India. He was named Aurobindo Akroyd Ghose. His parents wanted his upbringing to be in the European style. So, they got him enrolled in the Loreto Convent School at Darjeeling.

When he was seven years old, he was sent to England for the completion of his education. He did his schooling from St. Paul's School in London and graduation from King's College, Cambridge. Side by side, he learnt several foreign languages like Greek, French, Italian, German, Latin, and Spanish.

He passed the Indian Civil Service Examination with great credit in 1890. Failing, however, to stand the required test in horsemanship, he was not allowed to enter the Covenantal Service of the Indian Government. But, returning to India, he became the Vice-principal of the State college in Baroda. He was held in great respect by the Maharaja of Baroda.

Aurobindo's scholarship soon attracted the notice of all. He was loved by the educated classes in Baroda State. He was exceedingly popular with the general public. Sri K.M. Munshi was one of his students. Munshi admired and loved Aurobindo. To the younger generation, Aurobindo became a veritable god and by them, he was called "Aru Da", meaning "elder brother Aurobindo". Aurobindo married Mrinalini Devi.

It was in 1893 that Aurobindo came back to India. He drew a salary of Rs. 750/- in the Baroda Educational Service. From 1893 to 1906 he drank deep from the fountains of Sanskrit and Bengali literature, philosophy and political science. He then resigned from his job and joined the Bengal National College on a salary of Rs. 150/-. He plunged headlong into the revolutionary movement. He was a great figure in the nationalist movements of the time.

Aurobindo, along with his brother Barindra Ghose, founded the secret revolutionary organisation called the Anushilan Samiti which was inspired by the nationalist ideas of Bankim Chandra. The Anushilan Samiti believed in militant nationalism and political violence in order to end British rule in India. To this end, it was involved in a number of assassination attempts, bombings and dacoities, besides publishing nationalist literature through its journals that were considered incendiary by the British and promptly banned.

As time passed by, Sri Aurobindo began losing interest in politics and started concentrating on spirituality. He came across a yogi named Vishnu Bhaskar Lele, who showed him the path of the Hindu practice of yoga.

Hona Bhagoji Kenglia and the Koli resistance of 1873-74

Honya Bhagoji Kengle was a freedom fighter from the Jamburi region in the Poona (now Pune) district of Maharashtra. He was a member of the Koli tribe and led them during the uprising of 1873-74. The Kolis were heavily oppressed by money lenders and British officials.

In the 19th century, the Koli tribe suffered from a severe famine that spread across Deccan. The money lenders demanded harsh and unreasonable penalties from the famine-stricken population, with support from British law courts. This angered the tribes, and in 1873, Kengle raised a group of Kolis and rebelled against the money lenders by conducting attacks and robberies. The rebellion spread throughout the western parts of Pune, Ahmadnagar, Nasik, and the eastern sub-divisions of Thana. To suppress the revolt, a special police force was sent to the hills, and a reward of 1000 rupees and 200 to 600 rupees was announced for Honya and his followers, respectively. Although he was able to escape and evade the authorities until 1876, he was eventually caught by Major H. Daniel.

British authorities labelled Honya as 'the Coeur de Lion' or a 'Lion Heart' for the bravery he showed during the rebellion. His resistance also inspired the Deccan riots of Maharashtra in 1875.

Insurgencies of North East India

The advent of the British rendered the Ahom Kingdom extinct by 1838. From 1839 to 1873, the region was administered by the British as part of the Bengal Province. The plan to use NE India as a cushion from Myanmar/China was mooted under the Coupland Plan by earmarking the region as Crown Colony. The British could not exercise direct colonial control over several parts of the region. Thus, Christian Missionaries were deployed to penetrate deep into the remote areas. As history shows, the Christian Missionaries were hugely successful to the extent that almost 97 per cent of Nagaland is fully Christianised: that is, successive generations of tribals have been completely cut off from their original roots.

Parts of the NE region were classified as 'Excluded Area' or 'Partially Excluded Area' and brought under the ambit of the 'Inner Line Regulation' thus serving ulterior British interests of preventing access to the so-called outsiders.

This isolation and separation denied the national mainstream to the tribals and inhibited their exposure to modern developments in various spheres. The people in the plains considered the hill tribes uncivilized while the hill tribes considered them outsiders and looked upon them with distrust thus laying the foundation for hostility in the region.

The Bhagirath Manjhi Movement of 1874

The tribal population of the country was greatly affected by the oppressive colonial forest laws and settlement operations meant for surveys and censuses by British anthropologists, cartographers, etc. This led to a string of movements which were affected by one cause or the other. Bhagirath Manjhi, a resident of the Taradih village of the Godda district of Jharkhand was the leader of one such movement.

Bhagirath Manjhi was a part of the Santhal uprising of 1855. By the 1870s, there was a growing discontentment among the Santhals due to the settlement operations conducted by the colonial administration. Manjhi channelised the grievance into a resistance against payment of taxes and the formation of a political organisation. In 1974, severe famine and scarcity were underway. Manjhi organised the masses by making political statements where he stated the right of the Santhals over the land and no alien rule had demanded taxes from them. A shrine set up at Godda was demolished by Deputy Commissioner Boxwell and Manjhi was sentenced to imprisonment. Extra troops were also stationed in the area in order to quell uprisings if they arose. Bhagirath was released in 1877 but continued working and spreading the sentiments in a clandestine way.

The movement led by Bhagirath Manjhi was an important step towards strengthening the resolve of the Santhals against the British. The anxiety of the administration over the potential fear of an uprising revealed that the British could not have functioned without native support despite it being the custodian of administrative power.

The Iron Man of India was born on October 31, 1875

The Iron Man of India, Sardar Vallabhbhai Patel, was born on October 31, 1875, in Nadiad, in the Kheda district of Gujarat. He was a prominent member of Congress, a successful barrister, and a leader in India's fight for independence. He made an immense contribution to widening the support for the non-cooperation movement in Gujarat.

He was a senior leader of the Indian National Congress who played a leading role in the country's struggle for independence. He was a successful lawyer. He subsequently organized peasants from Kheda, Borsad, and Bardoli in Gujarat in non-violent civil disobedience against the British Raj. Under the chairmanship of Sardar Patel, the "Fundamental Rights and Economic Policy" resolution was passed by the Congress in 1931.

Sardar Patel worked tirelessly to cajole, threaten, persuade, and out-manoeuvre hundreds of princely states into acceding to the Indian Union. The one state where he was overruled by Jawaharlal Nehru was Kashmir when in December 1948 the state was taken out of the charge of Sardar Patel and placed "under the charge of Goplalswami Ayyangar."

The 31st of October is celebrated as the Rashtriya Ekta Diwas (National Unity Day) in India to commemorate the birth anniversary of Sardar Vallabhbhai Patel. The decision to honour the Iron Man of India on his birth anniversary was taken after Prime Minister Narendra Modi assumed office in 2014.

Prime Minister Narendra Modi inaugurated the Statue of Unity, the world's tallest statue, with a height of 182 metres (597 feet) on October 31 2018, on the Narmada River in Gujarat. It depicts Indian statesman and independence activist Sardar Vallabhbhai Patel, who was the first deputy prime minister and home minister of independent India.

1876-1880; Edward Lytton, Viceroy whose reign was marred by controversies

Between 1876 and 1880, Edward Robert Lytton Bulwer-Lytton, 1st Earl of Lytton, served as Viceroy of India. Queen Victoria was proclaimed Empress of India during his reign, and he served as British Ambassador to France from 1887 to 1891. During his reign as Viceroy, Queen Victoria became Empress of India, but he also faced numerous challenges. His ruthlessness in both domestic and international affairs made his presidency controversial. The way he addressed the Great Famine of 1876-1878, as well as the second Anglo-Afghan War, paved the way for many critiques. His thoughts on Social Darwinism were said to have influenced his policies. His son, Victor Bulwer-Lytton, 2nd Earl of Lytton, was born in India and later served as Governor of Bengal and as acting Viceroy for a brief period. The senior earl was also the father-in-law of Sir Edwin Lutyens, the architect who designed New Delhi.

The Two-Nation Theory

The Two-Nation Theory was first promulgated by Syed Ahmad Khan, the founder of the Aligarh Muslim University.

Syed Ahmad Khan said in 1876, "I am convinced now that Hindus and Muslims could never become one nation as their religion and way of life was quite distinct from each other."

Seven years later, he voiced similar sentiments. He said, "Friends, in India, there live two prominent nations which are distinguished by the names of Hindus and Mussalmans…To be a Hindu or a Muslim is a matter of internal faith which has nothing to do with mutual relationships and external conditions…Hence, leave God's share to God and concern yourself with the share that is yours…India is the home of both of us…By living so long in India, the blood of both have [sic] changed."

Twelve years later, he stated, "Now, suppose that the English community and the army were to leave India, taking with them all their cannons and their splendid weapons and all else, who then would be the rulers of India? …Is it possible that under these circumstances two nations—the Mohammedans and the Hindus—could sit on the same throne and remain equal in power? Most certainly not. It is necessary that one of them should conquer the other. To hope that both could remain equal is to desire the impossible and the inconceivable. But until one nation has conquered the other and made it obedient, peace cannot reign in the land."

The idea that Islam encapsulates a separate nation is even more ancient than that. Karl Marx, the Father of Communism, stated in 1854, "The Koran and the Mussulman legislation emanating from it reduce the geography and ethnography of the various people to the simple and convenient distinction of two nations and two countries; those of the Faithful and the Infidels. The Infidel is "Harby," i.e., the enemy. Islamism proscribes the nation of the Infidels, constituting a state of permanent hostility between the Mussulman and the unbeliever."

The Dramatic Performances Act

The now-forgotten Dramatic Performances Control Act of 1876 was passed by Viceroy Lytton under the Prime Ministership of Benjamin Disraeli to specifically crush opposition to colonial British rule in India. A furious "Lord" Northbrook passed an emergency ordinance on February 29, 1876, "empowering the Government of Bengal to prohibit certain dramatic performances which were scandalous, defamatory, seditious, obscene or otherwise prejudicial to the public interest." The Act was indeed repressive legislation aimed at destroying the forces of Indian nationalism.

During the repressive British rule in India, demonstrators used any available weapon to demonstrate their opposition to British rule. One of those strategies was drama. The British government paid heed and enacted the Dramatic Performances Act to curb such demonstrations through dramas. The Calcutta National Theatrical Society staged the production of Dinabandhu Mitra's play '*Nil Darpan*' in 1872, which revealed the persecution of Bengali farmers at the hands of British indigo planters. It received favourable reviews in the regional language press, but it enraged the British government, which demanded that the play's performances be halted.

Upendranath Das's two dramas, '*Sarat Sarojini*' and '*Surendra Binodini*', exemplified Indian resentment of British racial discrimination. When these plays were staged at the Great National Theatre, they caused quite a sensation among those who witnessed them. Several such plays questioning and subverting British rule were performed over the next few years, leading to the creation of a law known as the Dramatic Performances Act, of 1876 (DPA).

Post-independence also, several plays, including Nil Darpan, *Anandmath*, and Marathi playwright Vijay Tendulkar's classic text *Sakharam Binder*, were forbidden from being performed in India.

CHAPTER - V

QUEEN VICTORIA IS ANOINTED EMPRESS OF INDIA

While Wilhelm I was elevated to the title of "Emperor of Germany" in 1873, Queen Victoria was interrogating her secretary about her acceptance as an official title on the other end. The Queen's anointment as Empress of India was made easier by a change in Prime Minister in 1874. Because then-British Prime Minister Benjamin Disraeli was a staunch conservative, he declared Queen Victoria Empress of India in 1877. Although the transfer of power from the Company to the Crown occurred in 1858, this proclamation of title was a move to further integrate the monarchy with the empire and bond India more closely to Britain.

The Royal Titles Bill was introduced in the British Parliament in 1876 in order to make this revelation. It was met with hostility from liberals, who believed that the title would be associated with absolute power. Since Prince Albert's death, Queen Victoria opened Parliament in person for the first time to announce the change in the Royal title.

On January 1, 1877, the celebrations in Delhi, known as the Delhi Durbar, began in response to the imperial proclamations. The celebrations were conducted by Viceroy Lord Lytton at the time. More than 400 Indian princes, chiefs, bureaucrats, and their retinues had amassed in Delhi by the end of 1876 to prepare for the major occasion. While Queen Victoria was quietly celebrating the new year with her family at Windsor Castle on January 1, 1877, a huge celebration was taking place more than 4,000 miles away in Delhi, India, to honour the Queen's new imperial role as Empress of India.

Unfortunately, the Emperor and Empress were unable to visit India before the country declared independence in 1947. George abdicated his Emperor title to become King of India, and Elizabeth became Queen of India. India became a republic at the same time as the Commonwealth was established, and they lost their titles as well. In 1961, their daughter, Queen Elizabeth II, paid her first visit to India.

Although Queen Victoria famously never visited India, it is not difficult to access evidence of the "Empress of India" in the country that served as a major piece of her imperial jigsaw. Her name lives on in the Victoria Public Hall in Chennai, the Victoria Road in Bengaluru (Bangalore), and the Victoria Terminus, Mumbai's main railway station (later in 1996, it was renamed as Chhatrapati Shivaji Terminus and Chhatrapati Shivaji Maharaj Terminus in July 2017). But she is most apparent in Kolkata (Calcutta), in the pale marble and architectural nobility of the Victoria Memorial.

The Great Famine of 1876-1878 - the defeat of humanity!

At the point when Lytton was caught up with commending the announcement of Queen Victoria turning into the Empress of India, the subjects of this Empress were struggling with the consequences of a severe dry season that caused crop disappointment in the Deccan Plateau. This famine affected south and north-eastern India, as well as the British-managed administrations of Madras, Bombay, and the regal provinces of Mysore and Hyderabad. In the middle of the pageantry of the Delhi Durbar, India was experiencing one of the most egregious starvations in its history. The Great Madras famine, which lasted from 1876 to 1878, reached its apex in 1877, consuming around 6,000,000 Indians. The primary cause of the drought was an extremely dry season in India's breadbasket, the Deccan Plateau, which caused a severe food shortage and massive famine across the subcontinent.

Although famine was affecting a large number of Indians, Viceroy Lytton praised the flight of record tonnes of wheat out of India. He prioritised industrialist benefits over starving insurance there, making his residence questionable by ignoring the current string of catastrophic gatherings.

The Vernacular Press Act, 1878 - An initiative by Lytton

The colonial Government passed another equally mercenary legislation – the Vernacular Press Act, of 1878. Its provisions were similarly brutal and broke the spine of several Indian language publications and their owners and journalists.

In 1878, Lord Lytton enacted the Vernacular Press Act, often known as the Gagging Act, which authorised the government to seize publications that printed subversive information. This act was enacted to quell the voices raised by vernacular newspapers. This demonstration was the outflow of dissatisfaction with regard to the British system in oriental dialects.

The foundation that made Lytton pass this Act was a blast in the Indian language Press in the country. The age of Hindi journalism began in 1826 with the publication of '*Uddanta Martanda*' from Kolkata and gradually spread with *Bangdoot, Banaras Akhbaar, Gyandeepak, Malwa Akhbaar, Gwalior Gazette, Payam-e-Azadi, Samachar Sudha Varshan, Lokhit, Marwaad Gazette, Jodhpur Government Gazette*, and others. All of these periodicals were created with the covert goal of raising awareness of British policies and, as a result, catalysing the independence struggle. Many newspapers debuted in 1860, namely The Times of India (1861), The Pioneer (1861), The Statesman (1875), and The Hindu (1878).

With so many newspapers on the market, British citizens were concerned that this medium of information dissemination would endanger their reign. So, to limit the freedom of the burgeoning glory, Lord Lytton passed the Vernacular Press Act to check the opportunity of a flourishing Indian press and express their wrath by publishing nationalist articles advocating Swaraj, publicly criticising British rule, and pushing for people to take action. They jeopardised not only their businesses but also their lives by exposing themselves to the fury of the British Raj. Lord Lytton established laws through this act in 1878, requiring newspaper editors to sign a bond promising not to print material that was probably going to cause sensations and would incite displeasure with the British government. As a result, a wave of resentment toward the British spread quickly. However, these oppressive measures were not sufficient to stop the Indian Press. They kept on scrutinizing the British Government. As a result, Lord Rippon rescinded the Act in 1882.

The Vernacular Press Act was eventually repealed in 1882 but made a sinister comeback in the form of the notorious censorship regime of Sanjay Gandhi.

The Second Anglo-Afghan War

The second Anglo-Afghan conflict, which lasted from 1878 to 1880, was fought between the British Raj and the Emirate of Afghanistan. During the battle, Afghanistan was governed by Sher Ali Khan of the Barakzai line. This was a piece of an incredible game between the British and the Russians. This long conflict of 3 years was divided into two sections. The first started with the British attack on Afghanistan. It was a fast triumph for the British and this triumph constrained Amir-Sher Ali Khan to escape. Ali's successor, Mohammad Yaqub Khan, promptly tried for some degree of reconciliation because of which the Treaty of Gandamak was endorsed on May 26, 1879. Following the pact, the British sent an envoy and a mission to Kabul led by Sir Louis Cavagnari. However, on September 3rd, this mission was massacred, and the conflict was renewed by Ayub Khan, resulting in Yaqub's abdication. This was the second phase of the war, which concluded in September 1880 with the British decisively defeating Ayub Khan outside Kandahar. Following this loss, the British installed a new Amir, Abdur Rahman Khan. At that point, he sanctioned and affirmed the Gandamak pact once more.

Periyar E.V. Ramasamy born – Father of the Dravidian Movement

E V Ramasamy, popularly known as EVR, is hailed as 'Periyar' by his followers. He was born on September 17, 1879, in Erode. He was a demagogue who used the social evils which were then prevalent, or perceived, as a capital for his propaganda. He was neither a rationalist nor a humanist. He was anti-Hindu and pro-British. By equating him to Bhimrao Ramji Ambedkar, many are doing a great disservice to the memory of Ambedkar, who was a great nation-builder and a patriot.

EVR advocated racial hatred against Brahmins. He was explicit in his agenda. The magazine he edited, published articles praising the ascendancy of Adolf Hitler and warned Brahmins in Tamil Nadu that they should learn from the plight of Jews in Nazi Germany and opt for course correction. Even after the fall of the Nazi regime, the approach of EVR, particularly when he addressed his cadre, was the same.

While EVR is hailed as a great liberator of women, there is barely any evidence of him participating in the most crucial women's rights movement of his time – the struggle for the Sarda Act. It is a well-known fact that EVR and his movement were mainly pro-British and they also supported the Muslim League in its pro-Pakistan demand.

The ideology of the Dravidian movement can be traced back to the works of Bishop Robert Caldwell, an evangelist and a linguist who aggressively popularized the idea of an Aryan invasion of India. In Caldwell's analysis, the Aryans sent their agents, the sly Brahmins who, through their faith, now known as Hinduism, enslaved the Dravidian people who were given the title of 'Shudra.' The main aim of Caldwell in projecting the Aryan-Dravidian divide was to make way for mass conversions because many in South India were led to believe that Hinduism is a racist cult dominated by the Aryan Brahmins.

This belief was turned into a combative political ideology by Periyar. He saw all of South India as a separate nation from the rest of what he called the 'Aryanstan.' To the bulk of his Tamil and other South Indian admirers, he presented Hinduism as a racist, Aryan-Brahminical cult as per Caldwell's diktat. By the 1940s, as India approached independence from Britain, he feared that North India would take the place of Britain to dominate South India.

Periyar responded by calling for a separate nation, comprising Tamil, Telugu, Malayalam and Kannada-speaking regions—roughly corresponding to the then Madras Presidency but failed to get British approval. Fortunately, his mangled views were only accepted in present-day Tamil Nadu, while other South Indian regions – Telangana, Andhra Pradesh, Kerala, and Karnataka rejected them without batting an eyelid.

Periyar bemoaned the independence of India from British rule as he believed that the South would now become "Sanskritised" leading to a subjugation of the Tamils by the Aryans. And so, the concept of Dravida Nadu was reduced down, and restricted to Tamil Nadu. This then led to a proposal for a union of the Tamil people of not only South India but including those of Sri Lanka as well. This proposal for a "sovereign Tamil" raised concerns among the Sinhalese politicians in Sri Lanka.

Rampa Rebellion In 1879

Chedalandakondla Bheema Reddy organized an armed group of Rampa Reddies in Andhra Pradesh. Rampa Reddies attacked a Forest Ranger post in defiance of the oppressive forest laws. Along with Karam Tamman Dora, Ambel Reddy and other leaders, he attacked British forces at several places. Guerrilla wars were fought in regions between the Golconda hills of Visakhapatnam and Bhadrachalam taluk. Many including Chedalandakondla Bheema Reddy died on the battlefield and many were hanged.

Resistance of Poligars of Kurnool in 1800

The Poligars, holders of *pollam* or estate (zamindars, feudal chiefs) of the Rayalseema area fought against the British in 1800. Their main functions were to collect taxes, maintain law and order and maintain troops for the king. There were 80 Poligars in the locality. They refused to accept the authority of the British and pay cess to the Company. Thomas Munroe, the Principal Collector of the region ordered the Poligars to lay down arms and follow the order of the Company. A nationalist Poilgar Narasimha Reddy attacked the Company treasury at Koilakuntla and marched towards Cumbam. After a grim battle with Captain Holt, Narasimha Reddy escaped to Nizam territory. He was apprehended after six weeks and was hanged in full view of the people at Koilakuntla. After 18 months, Munore finally managed to bring the revolting Poligars under control.

The 'Chapekar Brothers'

The Chapekar Brothers

The three Chapekar brothers were born in Chinchwad.

Damodar Hari Chapekar (Born: 1869)

Balkrishna Hari Chapekar (Born: 1873)

Vasudeo Hari Chapekar (Born: 1880)

Damodar Hari Chapekar's family originally hailed from Velaneshwar in Konkan, Maharashtra, but his forefathers migrated to Chinchwad in Pune, where Damodarpant was born on June 25, 1869. Damodarpant and his brothers Balkrishna and Vasudev have wanted to contribute to the Free India movement since they were children. Damodarpant used to do many 'Surya-namaskars' every day to prepare himself for revolutionary actions; he also practised running while covering a distance of 11 miles in an hour.

Damodar's father, Hari, had mastered Sanskrit and was preparing to become a Kirtankar – a person who made a career by singing Kirtans while travelling to different places. Taking up the profession of a Kirtankar, on the other hand, was frowned upon in the highly conservative Chitpavan Brahmin group to which the Chapekars belonged.

Arya Mahila Samaj

Pandita Ramabai founded the Arya Mahila Samaj on November 30, 1882.

So, who is Pandita Ramabai, and what contribution has she made to Indian society?

Ramabai, who was born in a Brahmin household in 1858, was given the title of 'Pandita' by the Calcutta senate at the age of 20 for her proficiency in Sanskrit. Widowed at the age of 22, she founded the Arya Mahila Samaj to promote women's welfare. The next year, she moved to England for further studies and publicly converted to Christianity under the Anglican Church of England during her stay. After a few years in England, she went to America to raise funds for the establishment of a residential school for upper-caste Hindu widows.

During her fundraising drive, she wrote the book 'The High Caste Hindu Women' to raise awareness of the condition of Hindu women.

She disclosed her missionary intent after portraying this ugly picture of Indian society. "I believe that those who regard the preaching of the gospel of our Lord Jesus Christ to the heathen as so important that they will spend millions of rubles and hundreds of valuable lives in its accomplishment will consider it of the utmost importance to prepare the way for the spread of the gospel by throwing open the locked doors of the Indian Zenanas (homes)," she says.

Shanti Sadan, a religious-neutral residential school for high-caste widows, was founded in Mumbai in 1889. However, since her covert proselytising efforts became public, the school was dogged by controversies. With tales of rampant conversions circulating, the astonished guardians pulled their daughters from the school. Ramabai redoubled her proselytising efforts, unfazed. She eventually transferred her school to Kedgaon (near Pune) and renamed it Mukti Sadan to emphasize the missionary nature of her organisation.

To support her conversion activities, funds poured in from all around Europe and America. Her mission's financial clout was such that she supplied financial help to missions in Korea and China regularly. Ramabai, a former Brahmin woman, was regarded by the Anglican Church as an outstanding resource for proselytising among the higher caste. They described her as "one of India's daughters whom we felt God was preparing to bring a ray of light back to that benighted land."

Now, the point is, why does Indian academia refer to her zealous missionary efforts as social reforms, and in such hagiographic terms? Are the NCERT and the humanities department of the opinion that abdicated women from Hinduism is a sort of social reform? Is the word "social reform" just valid when the "reform" is aimed at Hindu society?

Chapekar Club

Poona (now Pune) became the epicentre of various problems as the Chapekars flourished, including the Age of Consent Bill, the Sharadashram of Pandita Ramabai, a Christian convert, and the Hindu-Muslim riots. The Kesari and other local periodicals were advocating the cause of orthodoxy, and in this climate, the Chapekars came to suspect that the reformers and Muslims were attempting to disgrace the Hindu religion at the behest of the British administration. They felt compelled to act in defence of their beliefs.

Damodar founded the 'Chapekar Club,' where he gathered like-minded youth and inspired them to rebel against the British administration.

They established the "Chapekar Club" for physical and military training, as well as the "Society for the Removal of Obstacles to the Hindu Religion." They attacked prominent social reformers in the dark, smeared tar on the Queen's monument near Bombay's Esplanade, and set fire to the examination pandal. They became active participants in the Ganapati melas when they lustily sang songs glorifying Chhatrapati Shivaji Maharaj for "his daring actions and exhorting the audience to stake their lives on the battlefield in a national war to pour blood on the earth of the enemy who destroyed Hinduism."

Frederick, George Samuel Robinson, 1ˢᵗ Marquess of Ripon, had been appointed viceroy of India

On Gladstone's return to power in April 1880, Lord Ripon succeeded Lord Lytton as Viceroy of India. He ended the *Second Afghan War* by recognising Abdor Rahman Khan as the emir of Afghanistan and removing the Indo-British expeditionary forces from the nation in 1881, reversing some of his predecessor's decisions. He liberalised India's internal administration, reduced the salt tax, enlarged the powers of locally-elected administrations, and attempted to stabilise land taxes (but failed). He repealed the Vernacular Press Act of 1878, giving local-language media the same freedoms as English-language media. In 1881, he enacted legislation to ameliorate labour conditions slightly. His Ilbert Bill (1883) was only enacted after he removed his contentious section granting Indian judges the same rights as European judges in handling cases involving European defendants. In 1884, he resigned.

Kesari - Marathi Newspaper

On January 4, 1881, Kesari began as a simple Marathi tabloid and evolved into a biweekly, triweekly, daily, and finally an e-paper, while continuing to serve its loyal readership in Marathi.

In reality, it had a two-day older English twin, '*Mahratta,*' a magazine that also marked its 140ᵗʰ birthday recently after reaching various depths and peaks, and both predate the establishment of the Indian National Congress in 1885.

Tilak, then 25, Gopal G. Agarkar, its first Editor, Mahadev B. Namjoshi, Vaman S. Apte, and Ganesh K. Garde founded "Kesari" (meaning Lion in Sanskrit) as a tabloid with a group of like-minded young friends. Today, it is the only vernacular language newspaper that has been published without interruption by a trust for the past 140 years.

The 'Kesari' has existed for over a century, pursuing the goal of *'Swaraj'* in the pre-Independence time, and then *'Su-raj'* in the post-Independence time. Throughout, it has had an impact on the people of Maharashtra in various ways, affecting all aspects of the country's social-academic-political-economic life.

During the freedom movement, Lokmanya Tilak utilised it as a weapon to arouse the masses, promoting Swadeshi alongside Swaraj, and uniting the common folk through huge celebrations of festivals such as Ganeshotsav in the state.

In addition to Marathi, "Kesari" was temporarily published in Hindi and Gujarati, as well as "Mahratta" in English, to cater to the broadest sense of readership, from commoners to the classes, and defied the might of the British authorities despite imprisonment for its owners or editors.

Book by Bishop Robert Caldwell published in 1881 - 'A Political and General History of the District of Tinnevely'

Bishop Robert Caldwell (7 May 1814 – 28 August 1891) was a missionary for the London Missionary Society. He arrived in India at age 24 and studied the local language to spread the word of the Bible in a vernacular language, studies that led him to author a text on the comparative grammar of the South Indian languages.

While serving as Bishop of Tirunelveli (alongside Edward Sargent), Caldwell researched the history of Tirunelveli. He studied palm leaf manuscripts and Sangam literature in his search, and made several excavations, finding the foundations of ancient buildings, sepulchral urns and coins with the fish emblem of the Pandyan Kingdom. This work resulted in his book A Political and General History of the District of Tinnevely (1881), published by the Government of the Madras Presidency.

Gloating about his successes in Bengal, Thomas Babbington Macaulay wrote thus to his father in 1836:

"Our English schools are flourishing wonderfully... The effect of this education on the Hindoos is prodigious. No Hindoo, who has received an English education, ever remains sincerely attached to his religion... It is my firm belief that, if our plans of education are followed up, there will not be a single idolater among the respectable classes in Bengal thirty years hence."

Twenty years later, Bishop Robert Caldwell would publish his A Comparative Grammar of Dravidian or South-Indian family of Languages in which he holds that

The [Tamil] language is probably the earliest cultivated on the Dravidian idioms, the most copious and that which contains the largest portion and the richest variety of indubitably ancient forms

It wouldn't be an exaggeration to claim that this among other glowing epithets about the language in his book on Tamil Grammar formed the bedrock of Tamil linguistic separatism, and gave the much-needed manure for the racist theories of Dravidian separatism to fully flower and eventually capture political power.

In the realm of Dravidian ideology, Robert Caldwell was a demigod who has numerous busts and statues dedicated to him across Tamil Nadu. A postage stamp too, was issued in his honour by the Indian Government in 2010.

He further traces the beginnings of Tamil literature to not earlier than the 10th Century CE. Now, this posed an enormous problem for the Dravidian champions of those days because, among other factors, this ideology chiefly rests on the antiquity of the Tamil language.

The fact that 80 per cent of Tamil Nadu's population[3] is under the reservation umbrella is the direct outcome of the Dravidian ideology. This umbrella will only expand as long as this ideology gets an uninterrupted run.

---

3   https://www.dharmadispatch.in/history/how-the-dravidianists-ravaged-the-tamil-heritage-and-gifted-tamil-nadu-to-the-global-church

Indeed, the biggest beneficiary of Dravidian discourse has been the Church. Over the years, it has shrewdly used the Aryan versus Dravidian, the Tamil versus non-Tamil, and the Brahmin versus the non-Brahmin fault lines to steadily gain converts and foot soldiers. According to the 2011 Census, Christians form 46.85 per cent of Kanyakumari, the highest in the state. Vast tracts of coastal Tamil Nadu are now Christian.

1882 - Vande Mataram - the first song to represent nationalism - was published in the novel Anandamath, by Bankim Chandra Chatterjee

Vande Mataram (I revere thee mother) is a patriotic hymn inspired by the pages of this masterpiece, sung by the novel's idealistic and nationalist saints striving for the liberation of their motherland. The Vande Mataram hymn was written in 1875 which was at least seven years before "*AnandaMath*" was published. The hymn, and especially the chorus of Vande Mataram, became extremely popular among the Bengali youth of Chattopadhyay's era (Hindu and Muslim alike) and quickly became a pan-India symbol of resistance to foreign authority.

It rose to national prominence as a result of events in Bengal's Barisal region. It is a little-known fact that Muslims' opposition to the chorus of Vande Mataram (which continues to this day) was not instant and was the consequence of a number of causes.

If truth is to be told, the song came very close to becoming India's national anthem because of its importance in mobilising and uniting Indians throughout the freedom struggle. However, Tagore's 'inoffensive' Jana Gana Mana was adopted as the national anthem of the newly formed Republic of India despite Chattopadhyay's far more popular canto.

The Ilbert Bill

The Ilbert Bill was a bill introduced in 1883 by Viceroy Ripon for British India that sought an adjustment to existing laws in the nation at the time to allow Indian courts and magistrates to trial British offenders in criminal cases at the District level, which was previously prohibited. It was named after Courtenay Ilbert, the Council of India's newly hired legal counsel, who recommended it as a compromise between two previously proposed measures. However, the bill's presentation sparked fierce opposition in Britain and among British settlers in India, escalating racial tensions before it was enacted in 1884 in a severely reduced form. The acrimonious issue heightened tensions between the British and Indians and served as a precursor to the creation of the Indian National Congress the following year.

The bill's most vociferous opponents were British tea and indigo plantation owners in Bengal, led by Griffith Evans, who were concerned that Indian judges, unlike British justices, would not forgive their maltreatment of Indian workers.

As a result of public opposition to the Ilbert Bill by a majority of English women, Viceroy Ripon (who had presented the Bill) enacted an amendment requiring a jury of 50% Europeans if an Indian judge was to face a European on the dock. Finally, a compromise solution was reached: jurisdiction to try Europeans would be granted to both European and Indian District Magistrates and Sessions Judges. In all situations, however, a defendant would have the right to a jury trial, with at least half of the members being European. The law was then passed as the Criminal Procedure Code Amendment Act 1884 on January 25, 1884, and went into effect on May 1, 1884.

The Father of the Indian Armed Rebellion Died

On February 17, 1883, Vasudev Balwant Phadke, one of India's first revolutionaries in the freedom struggle, died. His insurrection may have influenced the story of Bankim Chandra Chattopadhyay's novel Anandamath in a roundabout way (1882). Phadke was born on November 4, 1845, in the Shirdhon hamlet of Panvel Taluka in Maharashtra's Raigad district.

Phadke was recognised as the "Father of the Indian Armed Rebellion" since he served as an inspiration to certain other freedom fighters. AnandaMath, a patriotic tale by Bankim Chandra Chattopadhyay, incorporated several contemporary acts of patriotism undertaken by Phadke throughout his freedom struggle. Because the British government opposed it, Bankim was forced to print up to five editions of the book to scale back these stories.

Here are other intriguing realities about the father of Indian armed resistance, who died at the age of 38. He loved acquiring skills like wrestling as a child. He eventually relocated to Pune and worked as a clerk in the military accounts department for 15 years. Phadke was moved by the sufferings of the farmer community during the British Raj. Swaraj, he believed, was the sole solution to their problems. He was the first Indian to tour for political propaganda.

In 1875, he formed the Ramoshi revolutionary organisation with the aid of the Kolis, Bhils, and Dhangars communities in Maharashtra to defeat the British. Phadke and his companions Vishnu Gadre, Gopal Sathe, Ganesh Deodhar, and Gopal Hari Karve declared their 200-strong militia outside Loni, which was eight miles north of Pune, on the night of February 20, 1879. It was most likely India's first revolutionary troop.

Phadke and his soldiers raided rich English businesspeople to raise finances for their armed battle and to provide for famine-stricken farmers. In May 1879, Phadke delivered his famous statement condemning the government's exploitative economic practises and warning them. Copies of the proclamation were sent to the Governor, collectors, and other government officials, causing a stir across the country. Phadke rose to prominence after capturing the entire control of Pune for a few days by catching British soldiers off guard during one of his surprise raids. In 1860, three social reformers and revolutionaries, Phadke, Laxman Narhar Indapurkar, and Waman Prabhakar Bhave, established the Poona Native Institution, later known as the Maharashtra Education Society.

When the British increased their stranglehold on him, he was forced to flee Maharashtra. He visited the Shree Shaila Mallikarjuna temple, a Jyotirlinga in the district of Kurnool, Andhra Pradesh. Phadke was apprehended in 1879 and taken to a jail in Aden, Yemen since the British were concerned about the Indian public's reaction to his detention. In February 1883, he escaped from jail by yanking the prison door off its hinges, but he was quickly apprehended again. He went on a hunger strike till he died on February 17th. He was 38 years old.

During the Freedom fight, some radicals planned an armed revolt. The Revolutionary Nationalists were their moniker. Vasudev Balavant Phadke was among the first revolutionaries to organise a shadowy cabal.

The Damodar and Balakrishna Chapekar brothers were close associates of this shadowy group. They were both arrested and executed by hanging.

The Birth of Vinayak Damodar Savarkar

Vinayak Damodar Savarkar, given the prefix 'veer' (brave), was born on Monday, May 28, 1883, in the village of Bhagpur near Nashik in a Chitpavan Brahmin family. Vinayak was one of four children born to Damodarpant Savarkar and Radhabai, the others being Ganesh (Babarao), Mainabai, and Narayan.

He lost his mother at a young age. Savarkar was a quiet boy, spending his early childhood reading, meditating and exploring various villages. However, as he grew up, he realized that he had one more mother – Bharat Mata.

The idea of freeing India shaped Savarakar's whole life. Numerous freedom fighters have risen against tyrants of different ages in Bharat. King Porus fought Alexander, Emperor Chandragupta Maurya fought Greek invaders; Emperor Lalitaditya Muktipada fought against the Shahi Turks (invaders from Central Asia), Raja Mihira Bhoj fought the Arab invaders, and Chhatrapati Shivaji Maharaj fought the Mughals and many more.

These stories inspired Veer Savarkar very much in his childhood, and he made a vow to himself that he would invest every precious breath of his life into serving his *Matra Bhoomi* (Motherland) – Bharat. He firmly decided to save his second mother – Bharat – and was willing to sacrifice every ounce of his life. Savarkar always had a choice to settle for a peaceful life after his education, take up a clerk's job, wear fanciful suits and eat royal cuisines. But some men can never sell their conscience nor trade their soul, and Savarkar was one of them.

Veer Savarkar was born between Karl Marx's death and Mussolini's birth. Karl Marx, the Prophet of the Proletariat, died in a London corner seventy-five days before Savarkar's birth, and Benito Mussolini was born sixty-two days later, shaping the future of Italy.

According to legend, Savarkar was allegedly questioned, "Have you read Marx?" "Ask Marx - did he read Savarkar?" Savarkar had reacted in his style.

Now, given that Savarkar was born in the same year as Marx's death, when and where would the poor Marx have read Savarkar?

Yet, Savarkar's statement may imply that Marx's anthropological thought is radical and profound; however, Savarkar's thinking and work are equally radical and profound. Only Savarkar's ideas have a 'frame of reference' of 'nationalism.'

Savarkar was born into the illustrious caste of Chitpavan Brahmins, which produced Nanasaheb of 1857 fame, Vasudeo Balwant Phadke, Lokmanya Tilak, and others, all of whom fought to wrest the crown of Independence from the British.

He had always enjoyed reading since he was a child. He was frequently spotted at libraries, where he read newspapers such as Kesari, Kal, and others. As a child, he read Short History of the World. He studied Indian history beginning with the Vedas. He was well-versed in both Sanskrit and English literature. Among the works he read were biographies of Mazzini, Garibaldi, Napoleon, Lenin, and Trotsky, among others.

He read the Bible and the Quran. He also read the works of thinkers such as Spencer, Mill, Darwin, Huxley, and Emerson, among others. He knew half of Rabindranath Tagore's works by heart.

Veer Abhimanyu is the tragic hero of the sacred writing. Every Indian grows up hearing his or her ancestor's story of bravery and sacrifice on the battlefield. We are told that elders bestow various blessings on Abhimanyu before he enters the dharma kshetra Kurukshetra; some wish him victory, while others wish him a long life.

But his maternal uncle, Bhagwan Krishna, could not be a prophet. All he has to say to the valiant warrior is "*Yashasvi bhava.*" After all, even evil men can win battles from time to time. Many adharmis may live for a long time. Only the righteous achieve permanent *yash*, with time as their witness and an incredibly grateful nation to propagate their *gaathas*, generation after generation.

Veer Savarkar is the tragic hero of India's independence struggle, who had it much worse than Abhimanyu. He didn't have the luxury of laying down his life in single combat. He had to fight a lot of people for a long period of time. His fight lasted for several decades. Perhaps this is why he is so loathed.

The Earl of Dufferin was proclaimed Viceroy of India

On December 13, 1884, the Earl of Dufferin was proclaimed Viceroy of India.

Shimla's century-old Viceregal Lodge, which was established during Lord Dufferin's viceroyalty, served as the Viceroy of India's official residence. Among those who lived in this edifice were the Earl of Dufferin, the Marquis of Lansdowne, the Earl of Elgin, and Lord Curzon.

From 1884 until 1888, Lord Dufferin was Governor General of India and Viceroy. He had held several major political and diplomatic positions. During his tenure, the Third Burmese War resulted in the annexation of the entire country of Burma, and the Burmese monarch was exiled to India. In the year 1885, A.O. Hume established the Indian National Congress (INC). The Panjdeh Incident occurred in Afghanistan in 1885, which was a significant political event. Russian forces took the Afghan area south of the Amu Darya, near the town of Panjdeh, which is now in Turkmenistan. This resulted in an awful diplomatic crisis between Russia and Great Britain.

Murshidabad district in West Bengal witnessed a disastrous famine in 1885

The famine saw a high number of mortalities in various parts of the district. While Khargram lost 31 people to starvation, 24 men of Kandi committed suicide at the railway track, unable to bear the pangs of hunger. But the way that the colonial government approached the famine was inadequate to meet the needs of the victims.

The lives lost during the Murshidabad Famine of 1885 were tragic instances of British irresponsibility and misgovernance in the Indian subcontinent.

Indian National Congress – Bombay

After receiving approval from Viceroy Dufferin, Allan Octavian Hume established the "Indian National Union" in May 1885. It was affiliated with the government and acted as a forum for the expression of Indian public opinion. With 72 delegates in attendance, the Indian National Congress was founded on December 28, 1885, at Gokuldas Tejpal Sanskrit College in Bombay (Now Mumbai). The inaugural session, chaired by Womesh Chandra Bonnerjee, approved a resolution expressing discontent with the current governance system and demanding council reforms. In response, Lord Dufferin formed a commission to restructure the councils, which culminated in the Indian Councils Act 1892. In India, this act established the principle of representation.

Dadabhai Naoroji, K.T. Telang, Pherozeshah Mehta, D.E. Wacha, B.M. Malabari, and N.C Chandavarkar from Bombay were among the gathering eminent leaders in the hall of the Gokuldas Tejpal Sanskrit College, Bombay; M.G. Ranade and G.G. Agarkar from Poona; Dewan Raghunath Rao, P. Rangiah Naidu, P. Ananda Charlu and S. Subramania Iyer from Madras (now Chennai); Womesh Chunder Bonnerjee and Narendra Nath Sen from Calcutta (now Kolkata); Lala Baijnath from Agra; and Allan Octavian Hume from Simala.

The Congress party was created by A.O. Hume, a former ICS officer, to prevent a planned national rebellion against British rule. When he learned of the subterranean stirrings of this revolution, Hume was scared out of his wits. By 1878-79, he had received intelligence from various parts of India that "*Swamis*, monks, *sanyasis*, and religious devotees held in the highest veneration by the people, who had widespread support among the masses of the lowest strata of the population, were determined to do something, and that something meant violence." This intelligence was put into seven volumes, which included news bulletins from British agents. Here's a summary of what was intended.

In other words, a re-enactment of the events of 1857. Only this time, lessons had been learnt, and strategizing had been more deliberate and well-planned. In less than a quarter-century. If the second revolution had risen, the trajectory of Indian history would have been irreversibly altered.

A.O. Hume's vision is admirable. He spoke in the honeyed tongue of satan, directly borrowing from the worst of Biblical traditions. It was one of the first manifestations of the barbarous White Man's Burden. He turned himself overnight into a friend and well-wisher of Indians after retiring as a servant of the colonial British Indian Government. And he chose his audience with care.

On March 1, 1883, he wrote an Open Letter to the Calcutta University graduates. It was a "request" to form an organisation dedicated to the "mental, moral, social, and political regeneration of the people of India." The letter was impassioned and emotional, and it elicited the intended response. The Indian National Union was established. The intended audience was a deracinated class of Bengali Hindus whose minds had been fully blow-dried by English schooling at that point.

On the side, A.O. Hume addressed to the viceroy of India, Duffrein, and the following is a quotation from his letter:

> A safety-valve for the escape of great and growing forces, generated by our own action, was urgently needed, and no more efficacious safety-valve than our Congress movement could possibly be devised.

The other effect of Hume's devious scheme was that it effectively, but only temporarily, halted the surge of tremendous philosophical, spiritual, intellectual, social, political, and nationalist forces that had been shaping up over the previous half-century to eventually become the Modern Bharatavarsha's Renaissance. The indefatigable Surendra Nath Banerjee, who was recognised, admired, and feared even in England, was one of the greatest thinkers of the movement. When W.T. Stead, a British writer and editor, met him, he created a pun on his name, "Surrender-not Banerjee."

And guess who A.O. Hume's new INC's first president was? Not Surendra Nath Banerjee, but W.C. Bonnerjee, a seminal Macaulayite fabrication who was so embarrassed by his real name—Umesh Chandra Banerjee—that he garbled it as Womesh Chunder Bonnerjee.

R.C. Majumdar characterises him as follows:

"...the election of W.C. Bonnerjee as President...provides a good indication of the political opinions of the Congress' founders. Mr Bonnerjee led the life of an Englishman, avoiding, if not mocking, all manifestations of political agitation."

W.C. Bonnerjee later defended Surendranath Banerjee in court in a contempt case, but our evaluation should be based on spiritual beliefs. The appropriate thing for Bonnerjee to do was to decline the presidency and instead offer it to Surendra Nath Banerjee. Bonnerjee, predictably, decided that India was not the right country for him and moved to England, where he ran for office on a Liberal Party ticket and failed in 1892.

Now the question might arise in your mind why was Surendra Nath Banerjee excluded from the INC's formation? Because he was an extremist, according to Hume. So, who exactly were these 'peacemakers?'

The second session in 1886 also heralded what can be called the Surendra Nath – Tilak era, the second phase of the pre-independence history of the Congress. This was truly the most glorious period of the Congress

Third Anglo-Burmese War

During Lord Dufferin's reign, the Third Burmese War resulted in the annexation of all of Burma, and the Burmese King was banished to India.

Upper Burma was annexed in 1886. Lower Burma was annexed by Lord Dalhousie, but upper Burma remained independent, with King Thebau developing a strong relationship with the French. The British were annoyed by the Burmese ruler's rising French influence and lack of cooperation with the British, notably concerning the Bombay Burma Trading Company's access to China via Burmese territory. Lord Dufferin's warning was ignored by the monarch of Upper Burma. Upper Burma was invaded by the British, and the King submitted within two weeks.

He was imprisoned and transported to Madras. The regions of Burma were annexed to British India on January 1, 1886, while Lower Burma was annexed as a province of British India on September 25, 1886, with Sir Charles Bernard as the first chief commissioner. The British were heavily chastised for their aggressive behaviour. Many commentators referred to it as "unjust" and a manifestation of imperialism. Thibaw was a self-governing monarch who was allowed to establish diplomatic relations with any country. There was significant opposition in "Myanmar is a country in Southeast Asia. Burma was favoured as a Crown Colony by Indian leaders. Like Ceylon, for example, rather than an Indian province.

After the Revolt of 1857, the British took the last Mughal King, Bahadur Shah Zafar, as a prisoner to Rangoon, where he died. But did you know that the last king of Burma, King Thibaw, spent his final, similarly bleak years as a political prisoner in Ratnagiri, Maharashtra?

The third Anglo-Burmese war of 1885 was brief and decisive. While the first two Anglo-Burmese wars resulted in British rule of coastal Burma, the third conflict effectively terminated Burmese independence. Mandalay's capital was easily conquered, and the monarchy was seized by the British Empire.

Then, there was the issue of what to do with the King and Queen, who was still immensely popular. It was customary practise at the time to exile rulers to faraway nations. Sri Lanka's last king had been exiled to Vellore, whereas Bahadur Shah Zafar had been exiled to Rangoon, where he died in 1862. The British chose Ratnagiri, a distant and remote town on India's Konkan coast, to transfer Thibaw as far away from Burma as possible.

In April 1886, King Thibaw, Queen Supalayat, and their four daughters came to Ratnagiri. For the exiled king and his family, a huge home with 30 rooms was built. The magnificent Thibaw's Palace, as it was known, still survives today. Life in the palace was challenging. The King and his family were under virtual house arrest in the palace, enduring severe financial hardship. There were rumours that the King was forced to sell his valuable Burmese rubies, some of which are still reported to be in the possession of Ratnagiri's Sahukar (money lender) families.

King Thibaw died alone and in melancholy in 1916, at the age of 58. His anguish over the loss of his country, along with the hardships of his exile, led to his death at a young age. He was laid to rest in a tiny grave at the Christian cemetery in Ratnagiri. His wife, Queen Supayalat, and other family members returned to Burma after he died in 1919. However, his daughter, who had married a local royal retainer, elected to remain. The palace was soon turned into British offices and eventually, operated as a government polytechnic college.

For a long time, the military dictatorship of Burma (now Myanmar) refused to recognise its former ruler. President Thein Sein of Myanmar visited Ratnagiri to pay his respects at King Thibaw's grave only in 2012 after democratic governance in Burma was restored.

The Bombay Burmah Trading Corporation, which sparked the third Anglo-Burma war in 1885, is still in operation and is part of the Wadia group, which is led by Nusli Wadia.

Rajanna Anantayya and his role in the Gudem Agitation

The tribal communities in India were demonized and penalized during British rule as the latter considered tribes to be uncivilized and viewed them with suspicion. In Gudem, the tribal hill people strongly opposed interference from outsiders, as it posed a threat to their customary way of life. With the growing clout of traders, moneylenders, and forest officials, the tribals found in Rajanna Anantayya of Anakapalli district of Andhra Pradesh, a leader that led their agitation in 1886.

There were efforts by the native elite to deceive hill people into unfair contracts and trap them in debt bondage. When legal remedy was sought, the courts were apathetic to the needs of the tribal communities. In addition, taxes were levied on their two primary sources of income: the production of locally brewed alcohol and woodcutting. As a result, there was growing resentment, which turned into a full-fledged agitation in 1886 under the leadership of Rajanna Anantayya.

The last Nizam of the Princely State of Hyderabad Mir Osman Ali Khan is Born

Mir Osman Ali Khan born on 6 April 1886, was the last Nizam (ruler) of the Princely State of Hyderabad, the largest princely state in British India. He ascended the throne on 29 August 1911, at the age of 25 and ruled the Kingdom of Hyderabad between 1911 and 1948, until India annexed it. He was styled as His Exalted Highness (H.E.H) the Nizam of Hyderabad and was widely considered one of the world's wealthiest persons of all time.

Mir Osman Ali's delusion was primarily based on the fact that he had completely terrorized his majority Hindu subjects into submission. The spirit of Hindus under his regime had truly fallen into the pits. This reality also fuelled Nizam's fantasy of becoming the head of the entire Muslim world. However, when the Western powers permanently crushed the Ottoman Empire, the Nizam was heartbroken.

The Nizam, who ruled over almost 16 million people, 85 per cent of whom were Hindus, used every trick in the book to retain his independence as the British prepared to leave India.

The Nizam pleaded with the British to help him remain an independent state. He tried to buy the port state of Goa from the Portuguese to retain maritime access. He approached the United Nations to build support for his cause. He loaned money to Pakistan and built a large army in defiance, of his Standstill Agreement – an agreement which was to ensure the status quo as India and the Hyderabad state held talks – signed with India. He allegedly stole weapons from Pakistan.

Having exhausted all possible ways to reason with the Nizam, Sardar Patel had in 1948 ordered the military operation termed "Operation Polo," which resulted in the defeat of the Nizam and subsequent annexation of Hyderabad to the Union of India on 18 September 1948.

CHAPTER - VI

MAY 25, 1886 – THE FATHER OF THE INDIAN NATIONAL ARMY WAS BORN

Rash Behari Bose was born on May 25, 1886, in the West Bengal district of Purba Bardhaman, in the village of Subaldaha.

As early as February 1915, he launched the Ghadar Conspiracy, which intended to spark an insurrection in India. Ghadarites who had been tried and trusted were despatched to several cantonments to infiltrate the British army. With the war raging in Europe, most of the soldiers had left India, and the remaining could be handily won over, according to RB Bose. The revolt failed, and most of the revolutionaries were imprisoned. Rash Behari, on the other hand, eluded British intelligence and made his way to Japan.

Rash Behari Bose also visited Thailand and established a network foundation for nationalistic Indians. Bose founded the Indian Independence League (IIL) in Bangkok, with affiliates in Malaya. Rash Behari Bose founded the Indian National Army (INA) after Singapore surrendered to the Japanese. Rash Behari handed over this organisation to Netaji Bose.

KM Munshi, An Architect of Modern India born on December 30, 1887

Kanaiyalal Maneklal Munshi was born on December 30, 1887 in Bharuch, Gujarat. He excelled in academics and enrolled at Baroda College for higher education. Here, one of his teachers was the revolutionary leader, Sri Aurobindo Ghosh, who influenced Munshi to join the freedom struggle.

In Bombay, Munshi joined Annie Besant's Home Rule League and met many leading freedom fighters of the time such as Surendranath Banerjee and Gandhi. He participated in the Civil Disobedience Movement and was imprisoned twice.

In 1907, after topping his BA and LLB exams, Munshi arrived in Bombay to practice law, and after three years, registered as a lawyer at the Bombay High Court. His law degree would later help him take part in framing the Indian Constitution when he was appointed a member of the Drafting Committee under Dr BR Ambedkar.

Due to his penchant for education and literature, Munshi took a sabbatical from his legal career in 1920 and established the Gujarati Sahitya Sansad to promote Gujarati literature. He also wanted to focus on his own writing, for which he had already earned fame. His Patan trilogy, a work of historical fiction, written in Gujarati and based on the Chalukya rule in Gujarat, was very well-received. Interestingly, he wrote under the pen name 'Ghanshyam Vyas.' Munshi also wrote in Hindi and English, and most of his work focuses on historical and mythological themes. Munshi, in his book Akhand Hindustan (1942), observes that most of the books on Indian history were written by foreigners and thus lacked an Indian perspective.

In 1946, Munshi's various achievements made him an active member of 16 committees and sub-committees, including the Drafting Committee and SubCommittee on Fundamental Rights, where he presented his draft on Fundamental Rights that sought progressive rights. He was also part of the ad hoc Flag Committee that selected the Flag of India in August 1947.

But one contribution of Munshi that is not remembered enough, because of its contentious nature, is the rebuilding of the Somnath Temple. Located in the coastal town of Veraval in Gujarat, the temple houses one of the 12 Jyotirlingas of Shiva and was repeatedly destroyed by Muslim invaders and then rebuilt.

But the quest for rebuilding the temple suffered a setback when Gandhi and Patel died, in 1948 and 1950, respectively. Now, the responsibility rested on the shoulders of Munshi and Gadgil, who faced strong opposition from the then Prime Minister, Jawaharlal Nehru. He was totally opposed to Congress ministers being involved in a temple project. But Munshi was adamant. He saw the temple not only as an ancient monument but as a symbol of India's identity – one that had been battered and needed rebuilding

Before India's independence, Veraval was a part of the Princely State of Junagadh. But at the time of Independence, its ruler, Nawab Mahabat Khanji III, decided to accede to Pakistan, claiming easy access to the country via sea. India refused to accept his decision and on 12th November 1947, Sardar Vallabhbhai Patel, India's then Home Minister, NV Gadgil, Minister for Public Works, and Munshi, accompanied by the Indian Army went to Junagadh and got it to join the Indian Union. By then, the Nawab had fled to Pakistan.

Sir Syed Ahmed Khan was knighted with the title of "Sir"

Syed Ahmad was bestowed with the suffix of 'Khan Bahadur' and was subsequently knighted by the British government in the 1888 New Year Honours as a Knight Commander of the Order of the Star of India (KCSI) for his loyalty to the British crown, through his membership of the Imperial Legislative Council.

Ultra-Ashraf (ASHRAF, who claim foreign-origin descent), Syed Ahmed Khan was an opportunistic zealot who quickly morphed himself into a political huckster by crawling before the all-powerful East India Company despite owing an ancestral debt to the Mughal court which had richly patronized his lineage for at least five generations.

Syed Ahmed Khan was the original progenitor of nearly half a century-long Muslim collaboration with the British against the numerically and politically superior Hindus and the fledgling Indian National Congress. In return, he received the vacuous and degrading award given to a willing slave who helps the oppressive master – the Knighthood.

He also obliquely birthed and inspired two prominent leaders in his mould: Allama Iqbal and M.A. Jinnah.

Maulana Abul Kalam Azad was born on November 11, 1888

Maulana Abul Kalam Azad was born with the name Abul Kalam Ghulam Muhiyuddin on November 11 1888, in Mecca, Saudi Arabia.

From 1947 till his death in 1958, Maulana Abul Kalam Azad was India's Education Minister. Today (November 11), the entire nation observes National Education Day in his honour and discusses how he was instrumental in the development of independent India's education system, but no one seems to discuss how he began the process of negationism of history to cover up misdeeds of Islamic tyrants.[4]

Azad was born in Mecca on November 11, 1888, and spent his childhood in Mecca and Medina. His mother taught him Arabic, and his father taught him Urdu.

According to his own admission, he was home-schooled, and while he was taught a variety of courses, the emphasis was on Islamic studies, which he learned from his father three times a day.

Maulana Khairuddin did not value English education and wished for his sons to succeed him as Pirs (Muslim saints).

Today, it is because of his partisan curriculum that people engage in frivolous debates over how Indian principles are anti-humanity. People are aware of the practice of Sati, but they are not aware of atrocities such as triple talaq and Nikah halala.

We have always been taught in school that Babur, Humayun, Akbar, Jahangir, Shah Jahan, and Aurangzeb were the 'greatest' emperors of the Mughal dynasty. Our history books were replete with anecdotes of their bravery and valour. On the contrary, we found very few textbooks that spoke about India's rich dynasty and cultural heritage that was mercilessly decimated by these Islamic tyrants.

We had to, in fact, buy additional non-syllabus books to study this because all of this information was conveniently removed from school

---

4   https://www.opindia.com/2022/11/abul-kalam-azad-pir-education-minister-distorted-history-to-cover-up-misdeeds-of-islamic-tyrants/

textbooks after India gained independence and Maulana Abul Kalam Azad was chosen as the first education minister.

The 5ᵗʰ Marquess of Lansdowne is appointed as Viceroy of India on December 10, 1888

Lansdowne was the fifth Marquess of Lansdowne and the great-grandson of the previous Prime Minister, Lord Shelburne (born Henry Petty-Fitzmaurice in 1845).

He attempted to reform the army, police, local governments, and the mint. In 1890, there was an Anglo-Manipur War in which Manipur was conquered, with Lansdowne securing the death penalty for the initiator against strong opposition from Britain. His proposal to limit jury trials in 1893, however, was rejected by the home administration. In 1894, he returned to England. His policies heightened tensions between Hindus and Muslims.

The hill station Lansdowne (in Uttarakhand's Pauri Garhwal district) was named after Lord Lansdowne, the Viceroy of India from 1888 to 1894. However, the area was formerly known as Kaludanda, a combination of the words Kalu (Black) and Danda (hills) in Garhwali. The area underwent substantial development as the British utilised it as a recruit training facility for the Garhwal Rifles. Even now, the location serves as the command post for the Indian Army's Garhwal Rifles division.

Prof. Ramesh Chandra Majumdar India's Greatest Historian born on December 4, 1888

Prof. Ramesh Chandra Majumdar was born on 4ᵗʰ December 1888, at Kandarpada. District Faridpur, now in Bangladesh, to Haladhar Majumdar and Bidhumukhi Majumder.

R.C. Majumdar was influenced by Ishwar Chandra Vidyasagar in his school days and eventually became a great devotee of Sri Ramakrishna Paramahamsa and Swami Vivekananda. Till the very end of his life, R.C. Majumdar proudly displayed a life-size painting of Swami Vivekananda in his living room. From these and other inspirations, he developed an unshakeable conviction in the eternal genius of *Bharatavarsha* and distinguished himself as a great patriot. In fact, it was his attachment to India that led him to investigate our past and establish the fact that we were the greatest civilization in the world, uninterruptedly for over two thousand years.

R.C. Majumdar was also one of the pioneers in researching and writing on obscure or little-known topics of history; for example, in his time, there was little or no information about the enormous influence of Indian civilization on South East India.

R.C. Majumdar didn't write these volumes by merely consulting books. He actually travelled to these places and stayed there for months together, spoke to the locals, read inscriptions in their native languages, and deciphered obscure scripts...it was thorough, painstaking, boring work. But this is precisely why his books are authoritative and have become indispensable guides for future generations of scholars. Perhaps it was R.C. Majumdar who wrote the first comprehensive history of ancient Lakshadweep. As the proverb goes, a path is automatically carved wherever the elephant treads.

But above all, R.C. Majumdar was conscientious to a fault, honest to his own detriment, and fearless in the face of adversity. No matter who it was, he would not compromise on the truth. To quote his own words, "History is no respecter of persons or communities, and one must always strive to tell the truth." And the Majumdar told the truth and paid the price for it. India's first Prime Minister, Nehru ensured that R.C. Majumdar's career would never be the same again. Why? Because R.C. Majumdar openly wrote that he would tell the true story of the Indian freedom struggle including some stark truths about the role played by Gandhi and Nehru.

R.C. Majumdar represents the distinguished example of a committed scholar working alone and eventually publishing the exemplary three volumes of the history of the Indian Freedom Movement five years before the "official" Nehruvian version was published.

December 4, 1889 - Remarkable Death of Tantya Bhil - The Indian "Robin Hood"

Tantia Bhil -Indian Robin Hood

Tantya Bhil was one of the known revolutionaries, having fought an armed battle against British rule for twelve years and endeared himself to the public through his unwavering courage and desire to overthrow foreign control. Tantya Bhil became a symbol of tribal and general people's feelings.

Tantya Bhil used to raid the British government's treasuries and transfer the wealth of their sycophants to the poor and needy. He was, in fact, the Messiah of the have-nots. People of all ages affectionately referred to him as 'Mama.'

Tantya's address became so widespread that the Bhills are still proud to be addressed as Mama. He had a magical way of reaching out to folks in need of financial assistance.

Tantya Bhil's arrest was widely publicised in the November 10, 1889 issue of the New York Times. In the news, he was dubbed "India's Robin Hood."

Tantya Bhil was born in the village of Badada in the Pandhana tahasil of East Nimar (Khandwa) of the former Central Provinces. He wanted to teach the British a lesson and actualize Bhils' goal of a communist society. He was driven by a desire to liberate India from British colonialism. He repeatedly broke the jail. He was an expert in guerilla warfare. He was also an excellent shooter and skilled at traditional archery. His main weapon was *"Dava"* or *"Falia."* He had also learned how to use a gun. He spent his entire life measuring swords with the British and Holkar State soldiers in deep forests, valleys, ravines, and mountains. He inflicted reverses on the great British Empire's police and eluded them for many years. Thousands of individuals were detained, and hundreds of them were imprisoned on the charge of assisting Tantya.

Tantya was eventually caught due to the treason of Ganpat, his formal sister's spouse. He was imprisoned at the Central India Agency in the British Residency district of Indore. Later, he was transferred to Jabalpur under police protection. He was shackled and imprisoned at Jabalpur, where British officers tortured him inhumanely. He was subjected to a wide range of abuses. On October 19, 1889, the Sessions Court in Jabalpur sentenced him to death by hanging. The British government was so terrified that it is still unknown when and on what date he was executed. It is widely assumed that his body was thrown near Kalapani railway station on the Khandwa rail track near Indore after he was hanged. Tantya Mama's *Samadhi* is said to be the location where his wooden effigies were placed. Even today, all train drivers pause for a moment to pay tribute to Tantya Mama. Tantya Bhil is revered in tribal areas of Nimar, Malwa, Dhar-Jhabua, Betul, Hoshangabad, Maharashtra, Gujarat, and Rajasthan. The majority of his stories and songs about his life and actions were written in the Nimar region. Poems and songs in Malwi, Marathi, Gujarati, and Rajasthani eulogise him as well.

December 3, 1889 - Birth of Khudiram Bose

Bose was born on December 3, 1889, in Habibpur village of Midnapore District, West Bengal, to Nerajol's 'Tahsildar' Trailokyanath Bose and his devout wife Lakshmipriya Devi. It is said that his mother instilled in him a deep sense of karma by reciting religious scriptures to him every day as a young boy.

Khudiram was just six years old when he lost his mother; a year later, his father died. His elder sister, Apurba Roy, nurtured him. Amritlal Roy, Apurba's husband, got Khudiram into Tamluk's Hamilton High School. During that time, Khudiram was motivated by public talks given by Sri Aurobindo, the founder of the 'Anushilon Samiti.' Anushilon Samiti was an organisation that believed that the only way to eradicate the British from Bengal was through military confrontation.

The Hajo Raij Mel of 1890

The Hajo Raij Mel of 1890 was a form of peasant rebellion that took place in the Kamrup Metropolitan district of Assam against the unjust land revenue policies introduced by British rule.

As the British began establishing their rule in Assam, several new policies were put in place in relation to land revenue which caused widespread discontent among the people. This led to a series of peasant rebellions of which the Hajo Raij Mel was significant. Here, protesting against the increase in rents on land, the Raij Mels in Hajo tahsil resorted to non-payment of rents.

On June 12, 1890, those who were involved in the Hajo Raij Mel were put on trial and sentenced to six months of imprisonment. Nevertheless, the people continued to resist and challenge the social and economic injustices perpetrated by foreign rule.

On Sunday, June 10, 1890, India announced its first weekly holiday

The Indian staff were then required to work all seven weekdays without any breaks or rest time. Sunday is a day of religious observance and abstinence from labour for Christians. Friday evening until Saturday evening is a day of prayer and repose for Jews. Every Sunday, Christians attend Church services to pray. So, Sunday is a festival in Christianity, referring to it as God's Day. Christ, after his crucifixion, rested in the grave on the Sabbath and rose the next day, beyond the end of the week. As a result, the day following the Sabbath became known as "the Lord's day," which was Sunday, for Christians.

Rao Bahadur Narayan Meghaji Lokhande (1848-1897) fought hard to provide Indian labourers one day off per week with full compensation. He was a Dalit born as *Fulmali* (florist), a Hindu untouchable caste. He was a contemporary and renowned colleague of Mahatma Jyotirao Phule of Poona, who was yet another well-known revolutionary. Both belonged to the Mali caste, which is now known as Other Backward Caste (OBC). To fight for their rights, both joined the Satya Sodak Samaj movement and organised labour.

At that instance, Narayan Meghaji Lokhande, the mill workers' leader, presented a proposition for a weekly holiday in front of the Britishers.

"After working hard for six days, workers should be given a day to serve their country and society," he concluded. Sunday is dedicated to the Hindu god 'Khandoba.' As a result, Sunday should be declared a holiday."

Lokhande believed that labourers required at least one day of rest. This allows them to focus on their family concerns, for which they work diligently. So, in 1881, he addressed the British Government of India with a written request to allow labourers a day off once a week. However, the British government rejected his offer, and the Indian labourers continued to work seven days a week with no breaks. However, in the United Kingdom, Sunday had been declared a national holiday since 1843. When the British Indian Government declined to accept his proposal to make Sunday a vacation for Indian employees as well, he launched a campaign for the same. This campaign lasted for eight years. When Narayan Lokhande's fight for the rights of toiling Indian labourers gathered traction, the British government made Sunday a holiday in 1889. The success of the initiative was not only a huge relief for the workers, but it also encouraged

Indians to start additional such initiatives for mass benefits. Since then, protests, agitations, and non-cooperative movements became a tool in the hands of the Indian populace to obtain their human rights enforced by the British rulers. Lokhande was a labour movement pioneer in India. Meghaji Lokhande created the Bombay Mill Hands Association to organise mill employees (BMHA). He was also the country's first President.

Lokhande is recognised not only for improving the working conditions of textile mill workers in the nineteenth century but also for his brave initiatives on caste and communal concerns. He was the founder of the "Mumbai Kamgar Sangh."

In 1890, he was chosen as an associate member of the Bombay Factory Commission. Meghaji Lokhande is widely regarded as the "Father of the Indian Trade Union Movement," and the British Government bestowed the title of "Rai Bahadur" on him in recognition of his outstanding labour welfare activities.

Mill employees gained the following privileges as a result of Rai Bahadur Rao Narayan Meghaji Lokhande's efforts:

- On Sunday, mill workers were given their weekly holiday.
- Workers should be entitled to a half-hour break in the afternoon.
- The mill should have specified hours of operation, beginning at 6:30 a.m. and ending at dusk.
- He demanded that the workers' salaries be paid by the 15th of each month.

Jyotirao Phule and K. R. Bhalekar founded the Marathi-language periodical *Deenbandhu* in 1877. It was the first newspaper in India, produced from Bombay, to appeal specifically to the working class. It also functioned as a forum for Phule's Satyashodhak Samaj. Narayan Meghaji Lokhande took over as publisher of *Deenbandhu* from Bombay. He had been writing for it since 1880 and was selling over 1650 copies per week in 1884, making it the second-most distributed Marathi or Anglo-Marathi newspaper in the Bombay Presidency after Kesari, another Marathi paper launched in 1881 by Lokmanya Bal Gangadhar Tilak.

In 2005, the Government of India produced a postage stamp featuring his portrait.

Social Reforms by Tilak

Tilak thought that a true Indian social reformer should be a connoisseur of Indian civilization and culture. His concept of social transformation did not violate popular belief but rather gained legitimacy from historicity and rational cultural grounds. In his speech, on November 1, 1890, he remarked in favour of social reforms by quoting, "...In changing society, care should be made to avoid the construction of any distance between the people on the one hand and the reformers on the other. We must sway public opinion, which can be accomplished, among other things, by winning religious support for our reforms."

His reformist ideals emerged by embracing the foundations of Indian spiritualism and religion rather than opposing, maligning, and ridiculing them.

Here's another significant event in this period which might explain the hatred of the predominant Hindu leadership of the current Congress leaders towards this great Congress leader.

Tilak, who was always a supporter of modern education, helped Mrs Ramabhai, a Christian lady, establish a resident school for Hindu girls. His only requirement was that the curriculum be really secular. When it was discovered in 1889 that four of the school's kids were being taught Christianity, Mrs Ramabai encountered significant opposition from Tilak. As a result of this incident, he and his former colleague Agarkar parted ways in favour of Mrs Ramabai. They did return to Tilak, regretting their failure to discover the organization's evangelising and missionary nature by 1893, but by then the entire reform movement had been disgraced in the public eye.

Tilak becomes a member of the Indian National Congress in 1890

In 1890, Tilak joined the Indian National Congress. He was opposed to its moderate stance, particularly on the drive for self-government. He was regarded as one of the most prominent radicals of the time.

Many Indian National Congress leaders, including Bipin Chandra Pal, Lala Lajpat Rai, Aurobindo Ghose, V O Chidambaram Pillai, and Muhammad Ali Jinnah, allied with him.

Fellow Indian nationalists Bipin Chandra Pal in Bengal and Lala Lajpat Rai in Punjab backed Tilak. They were known as the 'Lal-Bal-Pal triumvirate.'

The Anglo-Manipur War of 1891

Manipur, which means "Jewelled Land," is a Meitei-dominated area inhabited by Meiteis, Nagas, and Mizos. The Empire, which formerly stretched from central Nagaland to the borders of Rakhine, is now embroiled in internal war among its own people.

The Meitei Land, which was dominated primarily by Hindus, was a joyous area. It was a location to visit because of its natural beauty and unique tribal traditions. The tribes did fight, but they had an agreement. Everything was fine until the British arrived.

The empire crumbled. The Anglo-Manipur War was fought between the British Empire and the Kingdom of Manipur. The war lasted from March 31 to April 27, 1891, and ended with a British triumph. They focused on what they were strong at. They were successful in inciting strife between Burma and Manipur through their 'Divide and Rule' agenda. Initially, the British solely controlled the Manipuri Empire's heartland. The dissolution of the peripheral states was permitted. They reverted to their barbaric ways. It also saw a number of Meiteis, Mizos, and Nagas convert. The British took over Nagaland, Mizoram, and Manipur with over 200 confirmed deaths, many unrecorded homicides, and sheer cunning.

For months, Australia, Singapore, the United Kingdom, and the United States discussed the Anglo-Manipuri War of 1891. The execution of Crown Prince Tikendrajit of Manipur was a highly contentious episode in the unfolding events of 1891. Patriots' Day is honoured in Manipur today, August 13th, the day of the execution.

Following the Sepoy Mutiny of 1857, native Indian newspapers denounced it as British colonialism, declaring the war to be part of India's wider struggle against foreign control.

Indian Constitution's Chief Architect was born

Ambedkar was born to a Dalit family on April 14, 1891 in the Mhow Army Cantonment, Central Provinces (modern-day Madhya Pradesh). He was his parents' fourteenth child. Because of his family's poor caste rank, his childhood was marred by prejudice, segregation, and untouchability.

Dr Ambedkar, a great democrat and a humanist who steered the drafting committee of the constituent assembly deposed with the responsibility of writing a newly independent India's constitution. In his essay 'Buddha or Marx,' he upheld the Buddhist path rather than the violent methods propagated in Marxist thoughts. Morality, love and compassion to him were the supreme values of humanity that could only be inculcated through the means of religion among the masses. He did not consider religion as the opium of the masses. This abiding belief led him to convert to Buddhism along with thousands of his followers at Diksha Bhumi in Nagpur on October 14, 1956. He clarified that converting to Islam or Christianity would have cut off his Indian root, which he did not want.

The Indian Councils Act of 1892 was enacted on June 20, 1892

The Indian Councils Act of 1892 was an Act of the United Kingdom Parliament that empowered legislative councils in British India by increasing their size, laying the groundwork for India's Parliamentary system. Before this ordinance, the Indian National Congress made various demands during its session in 1885-1889.

Although the Indian Councils Act of 1892 was the result of many protests and patient waiting, it did not provide the people of India with anything substantive. It's no surprise that critics point out numerous flaws. Elections were held in a roundabout way. The people who were elected to legislatures through this system did not truly represent the people. As a matter of right of election, they were not permitted to sit in legislatures.

Tilak and Vivekananda had an accidental encounter in 1892

Lokmanya Tilak was returning from Bombay to Poona from Victoria Terminus (CSMT) in 1892 (before the World Congress of Religions) when he first encountered Swami Vivekananda. Swami Vivekananda arrived and sat in the same cabin as well. Swami Ji and Tilak were acquainted by a few Gujaratis who had come to see him off. They hit it off immediately, and after arriving in Poona, Tilak invited Swami Vivekananda to stay at his home which Swami Ji gladly accepted and went to stay for 8-10 days.

Tilak and Vivekananda agreed that Tilak would promote nationalism in the "Political" arena, while Vivekananda would promote nationalism in the "Religious" arena.

September 17, 1892: the birth of Hanuman Prasad Poddar

Hanuman Prasad Poddar was born in 1892 in Shillong. Poddar was dedicated to the cause of a great Ram temple in Ayodhya throughout his life. He spent years organising garments and *prasad* (offerings) for Ram Lalla. Not only that, but he dedicated numerous pages in his journal, 'Kalyaan,' to the cause of the Ram Janmabhoomi *Andolan* (movement).

Poddar, a freedom fighter, litterateur, philanthropist, and above all, fervent promoter of a huge temple at Bhagwan Ram's birthplace in the ancient city of Ayodhya, founded the Gita Press which is, the world's largest publisher of Hindu scriptures. He was one of the major figures who served as the backbone of the Ram Janmabhoomi movement.

Hanuman Prasad Poddar was arrested and convicted at the age of 22 of giving arms to revolutionary Indian Freedom fighters of Anushilan Samihiti who aspired to liberate India by fighting a direct battle against the British.

Hanuman Prasad was rejected by his own community when he was arrested and released.

Nobody wanted to be associated with someone who provided arms to Indian revolutionary freedom fighters. Poddar's community was involved in the business. They didn't want to ruffle the British's feathers.

Boycotted and despised, Poddar fled to Mumbai from his hometown of Kolkata.

He moved in the quest of work! The amazing man who created India's largest publishing firm from the ground up was once unemployed!

Poddar, true to his name, continued to serve Shri Ram and other devotees but never revealed his true identity. He kept organising essentials for prayer and attire for Ram Lalla, with an eye on the Ram temple.

Govind Ballabh Pant, the then-home minister, nominated Hanuman Prasad Poddar for the Bharat Ratna. Pant was surprised when Poddar outright declined it. Poddar had spurned all honours during his life.

Nonetheless, Jawaharlal Nehru despised Gita Press and did everything in his power to shut it down. He even arrested Hanuman Prasad Poddar on suspicion of complicity in Gandhi's assassination.

Poddar was imprisoned. G. D. Birla declined to assist Poddar, accusing Gita Press of spreading "Shaitan Dharma."

The court ordered Poddar's release at the next hearing because "there was not a crumb of evidence of his involvement in Gandhi's assassination," according to the court.

In his newspaper, Kesari, Lokmanya Tilak praised the celebration of Sarvajanik Ganesh Utsav in 1893

Ganeshotsav was not designated as a *sarvjanik* or a communal celebration until 1892.

In 1892, Bhausaheb Laxman Javale of Pune, well known as Bhau Rangari, established the tradition of a community festival. This was a small-scale event designed to provide cover for independence fighters to congregate in one place while avoiding British scrutiny. Javale built a Ganesh deity battling a demon out of paper pulp. This three-foot idol is now housed in a temple in Pune's Budhawar Peth. Every year, it is painted and maintained, but it has remained intact since it was first worshipped in 1892.

At the time, Bal Gangadhar Tilak was developing the young Indian National Congress, an umbrella organisation at the time, in his own unique style. Tilak concentrated on connecting the freedom struggle with symbols and themes from Indian tradition, and lauded Javale's efforts in his newspaper, Kesari.

Following the 1857 war of independence, the British agreed to refrain from intervening in Indian religious affairs. At a period when political gatherings and meetings to support India's independence were being scrutinised by the British, Lokmanya Tilak regarded festivals as a way for people to come together (indirectly) for the cause of independence.

Until this period, the only religious processions recorded in Bombay were the Muharram processions (Tilak had participated in one or more such processions). Tilak saw Ganesh Chaturthi celebrations, which were previously restricted to Brahmin households, as an opportunity not only to bring people together for the cause of India's independence but also to foster a sense of pride among Hindus and break the shackles of casteism that plagued Hindu society at the time, leading to Hindu revivalism.

Following Lokmanya Tilak's request for public Ganeshotsav celebrations in 1893, his disciples, Raobahadur Limaye and Narahari Shastri Godse, began the festival in their *chawl* - Keshav Ji Naik Chawl – which was, perhaps, the city's first sarvajanik Ganeshotsav celebrations.

1893 - Matilda Joslyn Gage publishes her book, "Woman, Church & State"

In 1893, Matilda Joslyn Gage published her book, "Woman, Church & State". It outlines a history of oppression of women by the Church, citing as evidence the burning of accused witches.

Gage was one of the first writers to emphasize the ancient matriarchy and the witch trials as pivotal events in the history of women. Her claim that nine million people were slain during the witch trials has been often referenced, but this does not diminish the misery. However, the British wish to demonstrate that India used to engage in such horrible activities (Sati Pratha) and to conceal "Witch Hunting" in Western countries.

Sati Pratha

There was no mention of Sati in Parliamentary deliberations regarding the East India Company charter in 1793, even though it had been recounted numerous times, including by Company eyewitnesses.

Sati, however, was prohibited in all Company possessions by 1829. This turnaround was the consequence of a missionary lobbying campaign. The Christian lobby had to persuade British Parliamentarians that Christianizing India was beneficial and necessary, and, therefore, worthy of the Company's active or passive assistance, namely to liberate the people from savagery. Sati was the best eye-catcher for that purpose.

It is a myth that Sati was a common practice among Hindus.

Sati was a rare practice, mostly among the ruling class, in which the childless widow of the deceased king voluntarily ascended the funeral pyre with him.

The term "self-immolation of widows" was used in the first British report on the phenomenon. Contrary to current feminists' allegations of "murderous patriarchy" (who have the same stupid notions about Hindu culture as the ordinary western tourist), women selected this spectacular fate.

Those who believe that sati is a common practice among Hindus should remember that if it were the norm, Hindus would have died out in a few hundred years because there would be no one left to procreate. So, if every woman, without exception, actually dies on her husband's funeral pyre, it's a formula for demographic suicide, especially in the past, when most of today's curable diseases were lethal and took away a large portion of the population regularly.

The total number of Sati cases during the British Raj was small. In their story, a long-dead custom had to be resurrected.

The British spread propaganda about Raja Ram Mohan Roy's campaign against the evil practice of Sati.

Sati was a principle of "Death before Dishonor;" not a horrible behaviour. Hindu ladies performed Sati and ensured that a Muslim invader could not rape her dead body (Necrophilia).

In 1830, Ram Mohan Roy travelled to the United Kingdom as a Mughal Empire's ambassador, ostensibly to ensure that Lord William Bentinck's Bengal Sati Regulation, 1829, prohibiting the practice of Sati was not reversed. But his true motivation was to encourage the British government to boost the Mughal Emperor's stipend by £30,000! Roy also petitioned that the King double his allowance and perquisites! Mughal Emperor Akbar II bestowed the title 'Raja' on him in 1831.

Raja Ram Mohan Roy died of meningitis in England in 1833 and was buried in Bristol.

Why would the British give such an honourable burial to an Indian patriot in their own land, especially at a period when white colonial overlords did not even consider dark-skinned beings to be human?

In 1800, the Brahmanical Peshwas prohibited Sati in their realms; in 1801, Shri Swami Narayan began campaigning against Sati; in 1821, the Hindu Maratha kingdom Savantvadi prohibited Sati; and in 1829, the British/Ram Mohan Roy abolished Sati in their kingdoms.[5]

While the British/Ram Mohan are given sole credit, the Peshwas are remembered in history as Brahmanical tyrants.

---

5   "Sati: Historical and Phenomenological Essays" by Katherine Young and Arvind Sharma(1988) "Suttee A Historical And Philosophical Enquiry" by Edward Thompson

September 20, 1893, Swami Vivekananda's speech titled – 'Religion not the crying need of India'

Swami Vivekananda began his awe-inspiring lecture by bowing to Ma Saraswati, the goddess of wisdom. "America's sisters and brothers!" the saffron monk from India began his discourse with such words. As if the west had never heard these words! With such statements, Vivekananda received a three-minute standing ovation from a crowd of 7,000.

When the stillness was restored, Vivekananda responded:

"I thank you in the name of the most ancient order of monks in the world; I thank you in the name of the mother of religions; I thank you in the name of millions and millions of Hindu people of all classes and sects." Swami Vivekananda explained Sanatana Dharma and Indianness to the world audience in this discourse with amazing precision.

In his model speech, the saffron monk defined India and Hinduism precisely. *"I am proud to belong to a faith that has taught the world both tolerance and universal acceptance. We believe not just in universal tolerance, but also in the truth of all religions. I am delighted to be a citizen of a country that has provided refuge for the persecuted and refugees of all religions and nations."*

Unlike Abrahamic religions, which propose dividing the world into believers and Kafirs or believers and heathens, Hinduism adheres to the unrivalled concept of *"Sarve Bhavantu Sukhinah"* (May all become happy, May all see what is auspicious). While the other speakers focused solely on their own faith, Vivekananda emphasized the importance of interfaith understanding, religious tolerance, and worldwide fraternity. He taught the world that the basic message of all religions is the same, and that service to others is the most effective form of God's devotion.

Vivekananda's message is still applicable to today's world, which is plagued by religious chauvinism, one hundred and twenty-three years after he delivered his Chicago talk. Needless to say, both Western and Islamic societies could learn a lot from Vivekananda's 9/11 speech.

"Sectarianism, prejudice, and their dreadful offshoot, fanaticism, have long dominated our beautiful earth," Vivekananda told the Parliament of World Religions. *"They have filled the globe with violence, soaked it in human blood regularly, devastated civilisations, and driven entire nations to despair. Human culture would be a lot more advanced if it weren't for these dreadful demons."*

Vivekananda delivered India's traditional teachings in their purest form in that model speech. His address embodied the spirit and sense of the universality of the World Parliament of Religions.

"India, the mother of religions, was represented by Swami Vivekananda, the orange-monk who exercised the most remarkable power over his auditors," remarked Parliament President John Henry Barrows.

What the American Press said

Swami Vivekananda was described in the American press as a "handsome oriental," a "cyclonic monk from India," the "greatest figure" in the Parliament of World Religions, and the "most popular" and "influential" individual in the Parliament.

According to the New York Critique:

"By divine right, Swami Vivekananda was an orator, and his strong, intelligent face in its magnificent surroundings of yellow and orange was no less appealing than those sincere words, and the rich, rhythmical utterance he gave them."

According to a Boston Evening Transcript editorial, "Vivekananda was a top contender in Parliament... He is praised even if he simply crosses the platform."

According to the New York Herald, "Vivekananda is, without a doubt, the most important personality in the Parliament of Religions. We realise how ridiculous it is to send missionaries to this learned nation after hearing him."

Yes, Swami Vivekananda was a true missionary. He never converted individuals away from their natural faith.

Vivekananda's Chicago speech will always have an alluring appeal. The speech signalled the start of Western interest in Indian values. To commemorate the spirit of that speech, September 11 is also observed as World Brotherhood Day. Swami Vivekananda will be remembered for his unwavering commitment to making the world a better place filled with truth, beauty, and goodness.

Massacre of Patharighat: 1894

The British Government aimed to plunder India of her resources. They raised the land revenue and other agrarian taxes, so much so that the peasants starved. On January 28 1894, peasants at Patharughat (now Patharighat) in Assam assembled to protest against the raised land revenue demands. As its nature was, British forces opened fire at the unarmed peaceful peasants. Indian sources reported that at least 140 patriots were martyred.

Tilak made the household worshipping of Ganesha a grand public event in 1894. (Sarvajanik Ganeshotsav)

In 1894, Tilak held Ganesha festivities of his own, followed by the public festivities of Chhatrapati Shivaji Jayanti the following year. Tilak gave the liberation movement a boost by bringing to the general public the ideologies and messages articulated by the intellectual Indian National Congress lobby on these two occasions.

The Ganeshotsav was designed to last 10 days and included public participation in the form of dances, skits, and plays. During these ten days, anti-British sentiment could be built up using inventive tactics and the comparatively easy movement of freedom fighters to organise specific demonstrations and protests. Public engagement and cultural activities continue to this day, with children, music groups, and orchestras receiving an opportunity to demonstrate their skills to their communities around the country. Only the substance of cultural motifs has altered, from 'promises not to submit to raiding invaders' to the affirmation of *'aashiq surrender hua.'*

The marquee pandals have grown in popularity in Mumbai and Pune over time. Dagduseth Halwai, one of the rebels who gathered in Javale's house for the 1892 festival, established his own Ganeshotsav, today well known as the Shrimant Dagduseth Halwai Ganpati, in Budhawar Peth, Pune. The first Sarvajanik Ganesh Mandal in Mumbai was established in Girgaum's Keshavi Naik chawl, where regular Indians working in cotton textile factories lived with little comfort and delight in their hard manual-labouring lives.

The emergence of Punjab National Bank (PNB) on May 19, 1894

Lala Lajpat Rai founded the Punjab National Bank in 1894 – the first Indian bank to be founded completely in the Indian capital, and it is still in operation today.

PNB was founded by Swadeshi movement activists even before M.K. Gandhi arrived at the forefront of the Indian independence struggle. It was their conviction that if India was to grow and thrive after independence, it needed its own institutions, particularly financial institutions. The bank was established with such great objectives.

On April 12, 1895, PNB launched its first branch in Lahore, West Punjab. It then spread to Sindh and the NWFP during the next five years.

CHAPTER - VII

INDIA'S WHEREABOUTS DURING THE REIGN OF THE EARL OF ELGIN

On October 11, 1894, the Earl of Elgin was appointed as Viceroy of India

In 1894, Victor Alexander Bruce, 9th Earl of Elgin, was proclaimed Viceroy of India. His Viceroyalty was rather unremarkable. Elgin disliked the pomp and ceremony that came with the viceroyalty, and his conservative tendencies were not well adapted to a moment of economic and social upheaval.

During his tenure as Viceroy, a famine struck India, and Elgin acknowledged that millions had died.

Tilak establishes the Shri Shivaji Fund Committee in 1895

Tilak established the Shri Shivaji Fund Committee to commemorate "Shiv Jayanti," the birth anniversary of Chhatrapati Shivaji Maharaj, the Maratha Empire's founder. The project aimed at funding the renovation of Shivaji's mausoleum (Samadhi) at Raigad Fort.

Shivkar Bapuji Talpade flew an aircraft successfully in 1895

Shivkar Bapuji Talpade, a Sanskrit scholar, designed a rudimentary aircraft named Marutsakthi (meaning Power of Air) based on Vedic technology in 1895, eight years before the Wright Brothers, and had it take off unmanned in front of a large audience in Bombay's Chowpathy beach. The Wright brothers' significance stems from the fact that it was a manned flight at a distance of 120 feet, and Orville Wright became the first man to fly. However, Talpade's unmanned aircraft travelled to a height of 1500 feet before collapsing. Fortunately for Talpade, Maharaja Sayaji Rao Gaekwad of Baroda, a staunch proponent of Indian science, was eager to assist him, and Talpade proceeded with his aircraft design using mercury engines. One day in 1895 (unfortunately, the exact date is not mentioned in the Kesari newspaper of Pune that covered the event), in front of a curious scholarly audience led by the famous Indian judge Mahadev Govind Ranade and H H Sayaji Rao Gaekwad Talpade, his unmanned aircraft named 'Marutsakthi' took off, flew to a height of 1500 feet, and then crashed to the ground. Tilak, Kesari's editor, had submitted an editorial. Apparently, due to censorship by the British Raj, the success story never left Indian shores

However, the Imperial rulers were dissatisfied with the achievements of the Indian scientists. Following a warning from the British government, the Maharaja of Baroda ceased assisting Talpade. Talpade's wife died at this vital point, and he was unable to continue his studies. However, his efforts to spread the brilliance of the Vedic Shastras were recognised by Indian intellectuals, who bestowed upon him the title of Vidya Prakash Pra-deep.

Talpade died unrecognised in his own country in 1916.

Pune was hit by the bubonic plague in 1896, as part of the global third plague pandemic

The first documented incidence of bubonic plague in Pune (then Poona) was found on October 2, 1896, when two travellers from Mumbai arrived at the railway station. By December of that year, the city had shown evidence of local transmission, and the disease had begun to spread quickly - particularly in the heavily-populated Peth regions. Previously, after receiving reports of the plague from Mumbai in September 1896, the municipal corporation appointed a medical officer at Pune Railway Station to keep an eye out for people with plague symptoms and transport them to special shelters built at Sassoon General Hospital.

The plague wave that reached Pune was part of the 'Third Plague Pandemic,' which began in Yunnan, China in 1855 and entered India via the port city of Mumbai via Hong Kong. Between 1896 and 1918, the disease swept one city after another, killing around 10 million Indians.

Among the dozens of cities affected by the pestilence, none caused as much political controversy as Pune.

When the bubonic plague broke out in the Bombay Presidency in 1896, Bhikaji Cama jumped at the chance to aid the team attempting to save plague victims. Hundreds of people died in Bombay, and Bhikaji was also infected with a terrible sickness. Despite her recovery, she was in bad health as a result of her sickness.

The Epidemic Diseases Act of 1897 was passed in February of that year

To combat the outbreak of bubonic plague in the erstwhile Bombay Presidency in the 1890s, the British government enacted the Epidemic Diseases Act in 1897. The colonial officials, empowered by the Act, inspected homes and scrutinised travellers suspected of having the plague. Forcible segregation, evacuations, and demolitions of afflicted areas took place.

Crowd gatherings were prohibited, public meetings and festivals were prohibited, and pilgrimages were halted. Alleged humiliation (including public stripping) and violence against women sparked popular outrage, and riots were recorded in several locations.

Military forces were utilised in various places to ensure that precautionary measures were properly implemented. The abuse of the act drew harsh criticism from nationalist circles.

Bal Gangadhar Tilak was sentenced to 18 months in prison for criticising the imperial rulers' handling of the disease in his journals, Kesari and Mahratta.

In India, the Epidemic Diseases Act of 1897 has been consistently implemented.

The cabinet secretary declared on March 11, 2020, that all states and union territories should invoke Section 2 of the Epidemic Diseases Act of 1897. This made all advisories issued by the Union Health Ministry and state governments enforceable. On the same day, the World Health Organization declared the coronavirus epidemic to be a pandemic.

The Deadly Plague

Pune reported 308 cases of plague with 271 deaths by the end of February 1897. The fear of the sickness, which had such a high fatality rate, had driven the city's residents to evacuate. Municipal officials estimated that 15,000 to 20,000 residents had fled the city to avoid the pandemic and relocated to settlements on the outside. At the same time, residents and Englishmen were calling for the appointment of a "strong officer" to remedy the city's sanitary and health conditions, fearing that "things will never be repaired and will fall down from bad to worse."

The strongman appointed by Bombay Presidency Governor William Mansfield Sandhurst was 34-year-old Walter Charles Rand, an Oxford-educated officer of the Indian Civil Service stationed in Satara at the time. Rand was appointed as the Assistant Collector and Chairman of the Poona Plague Committee on February 10, 1897.

The scheme was vigorously enforced by British soldiers. When their homes were searched, their family worship-places were desecrated, their household belongings were scattered or destroyed, and their womenfolk were rough-handled; the public was subjected to a great deal of abuse. Rand, the plague officer, had little regard for public opinion, and his arrogant behaviour drew harsh criticism from the local newspaper.

Beginning of Famine: 1896-97 in Bundelkhand

The 1896–1897 Indian famine began in Bundelkhand, India, early in 1896 and expanded to many sections of the country, including the United Provinces, the Central Provinces and Berar, Bihar, parts of the Bombay and Madras presidencies, and parts of Punjab, as well as the princely states of Rajputana.

Emergence of Zionism

Zionism is a Jewish philosophy and nationalist movement that advocates for the re-establishment and support of a Jewish state.

Theodor Herzl (Austro-Hungarian journalist) instilled a fresh ideology and practical urgency into Zionism in the 1890s, leading to the First Zionist Congress in Basel in 1897, which established the World Zionist Organization (WZO).

Zionism promotes ethnic nationalism, or the idea of a national community based on religion, ethnicity, or blood.

During his detention in Ratnagiri jail in 1922, Savarkar penned his "Essential of Hindutva" which is no exception. He describes his Hindu nation's traits in terms of *matrubhumi, jati, Sanskriti,* and *punyabhumi.* This flattens not only all Hindu castes, but also other religions that originated in India, such as Jainism, Buddhism, and Sikhism.

Neither Zionism nor Hindutva called for the deprivation of other communities' civil and political rights to the extent that they did not contradict the national culture. Land possession, experience with civic nationalism, and pluralism distinguish Hindutva and Zionism from other nationalist movements.

Subhas Chandra Bose was born on January 23, 1897 – the actual Mahatma who got us independence

Subhash Chandra Bose was born in Cuttack (Orissa) on January 23, 1897, to Janakinath Bose and Prabhavati Devi. Janakinath Bose was a successful lawyer in Cuttack and was given the title "Rai Bahadur." He was later elected to the Bengal Legislative Council. Subhash Chandra Bose was a bright and diligent student who was uninterested in sports. He received his B.A. in Philosophy from Calcutta's Presidency College. Swami Vivekananda's teachings had a profound influence on him, and he was noted for his patriotic zeal as a student. He also held Vivekananda in high regard as his spiritual Guru.

In 2019, PM Narendra Modi inaugurated a museum at Red Fort, to commemorate the 122nd birth anniversary of Netaji Subash Chandra Bose. The museum contained digitised documents, narrating the childhood of Netaji and his efforts to form the INA.

On September 8, 2022, the Prime Minister also unveiled the statute of Netaji Subhash Chandra Bose installed at the India Gate hexagon. The jet-black granite statue has been placed under the Grand Canopy located at the centre of the Hexagon, between India Gate and the National War Memorial.

Putting up a 28-foot black granite statue in place of where George V once stood (unbelievably till 1968) is a considerable step in recognition of the role of Netaji Subash Bose in the fight for the freedom of India.

Swami Vivekananda founded the Ramakrishna Mission (RKM) on May 1, 1897

Swami Vivekananda, founded the Ramakrishna Mission on May 1, 1897, with dual goals of working for one's own emancipation as well as for the benefit of the world at large.

The organisation is philanthropic and volunteer-based. The mission is involved in a wide range of activities, including health care, disaster assistance, rural management, tribal welfare, elementary and secondary education, and culture. It relies on the united labour of hundreds of ordered monks and thousands of lay devotees. The mission's work is based on the ideas of karma yoga.

Diamond Jubilee of Queen Victoria's reign

The Diamond Jubilee of Queen Victoria's coronation was commemorated in Pune on June 22, 1897. Damodar Hari writes in his autobiography that he felt the jubilee celebrations would bring Europeans of all ranks to the Government House, allowing them to assassinate Rand. Damodar and Balkrishna Hari chose a location on Ganeshkhind Road (now Senapati Bapat Road) next to a yellow bungalow to shoot Rand.

They were each armed with a sword and a pistol. Balkrishna additionally carried a hatchet.

When they arrived in Ganeshkhind, they saw what appeared to be Rand's carriage pass by, but they let it go, unsure and decided to attack him on his way back. They arrived at Government House around 7.30 p.m., after the sun had set and darkness had descended. A considerable crowd had assembled at the Government House to witness the show. On the slopes, there were bonfires. Because the swords and hatchets they carried made it impossible to move without drawing suspicion, they stashed them behind a stone culvert near the cottage. Damodar Hari waited at the Government House gate, and as Rand's carriage approached, he trailed it by 10 - 15 yards. Damodar made up the distance and cried out "Gondya ala re," a preset signal for Balkrishna to act, as the carriage approached the yellow bungalow. Damodar Hari untied the carriage's flap, raised it, and fired from approximately a span away. It was originally planned for both to shoot at Rand in order to secure Rand's death, but Balkrishna Hari lagged behind and Rand's carriage rolled on, while Balkrishna Hari, suspecting the occupants of the following vehicle were whispering to each other, fired at the head of one of them from behind. Lieutenant Ayerst, Rand's military bodyguard, died on the scene, and Rand was transferred to Sassoon Hospital, where he succumbed three days later on July 3, 1897.

Alluri Sitarama Raju born on July 4, 1897: The Man who led the Manyam Rebellion

Sitarama Raju, fondly known as 'Manyam Veerudu' (hero of the forest) was born on July 4, 1897. He was born in the Mogallu village of West Godavari district to Venkata Rama Raju and Surya Narayanamma. Since childhood, Sitarama Raju was eager to fight British oppression. History has it that at the age of 13, when Sitaram Raju was offered a handful of badges with King George's picture on it, he threw all but one, pinned it on his shirt, and said, "To wear them is to flaunt our servitude. But I pinned it on my shirt near my heart to remind all of you that a foreign ruler is crushing our lives."

Alluri Sitarama Raju is known for his brief but emphatic 1922 Rampa Rebellion in the Eastern Ghats of Andhra Pradesh against the Britishers. Alluri, who is also referred to as Manyam Veerudu (Jungle Warrior), rallied thousands of poor tribals and kindled the spirit of freedom among them.

Alluri Sitarama Raju is one of the main characters portrayed by actor Ram Charan in the SS Rajamouli-directed epic action drama film RRR (Rise, Roar, Revolt). The other character played by Jr. NTR was another freedom fighter, Komaram Bheem. The movie was an adaption of the life story of two legendary revolutionaries and their journey away from home before they started fighting for the country in the 1920s.

On the occasion of his 125th birth anniversary and as part of the *Azadi Ka Amrit Mahotsav* celebrations, Prime Minister Narendra Modi, unveiled a 30-feet tall bronze statue of one of the greatest freedom fighters of his time, who laid his life fighting against the tyrannical British Raj for the rights of the tribal communities.

Lokmanya Tilak was appressed on charges of sedition

After a trial, Tilak was sentenced to 18 months in prison for inciting speech (Tilak had written about Chhatrapati Shivaji Maharaj killing Afzal Khan a week earlier), which led to Rand's assassination by the Chapekar brothers against the backdrop of the plague, which was cut short after the British realised that Lokmanya Tilak's arrest had made him a hero and gained momentum among the freedom fighters. Tilak's lawyer, Dinshaw Dawar, secured bail for him (with Dwarkadas Dharamsey who arranged a sum of Rs 50,000 for the bail bond, a large sum in those days within just 4 hours) a year later with appeals made by several Indian and European leaders including Rabindranath Tagore and Max Mueller to reduce his sentence.

This was a historic trial since it was the first case of sedition, and Tilak was the first freedom fighter to be convicted of sedition. During this time,

Tilak was confined to Dongri and Byculla prisons before being transferred to Yerwada.

September 12, 1897 - Battle of Saragarhi

If you believe that, until now, the Battle of Thermopylae was famous because of the courageous resistance of a small Greek force against the overwhelming Persian Army of Xerxes I in 480 B.C (movie 300), check out this last stand of 21 Sikhs battling 10,000 Afghans at Saragarhi.

Saragarhi is the remarkable story of 21 men from the 36th Sikh Regiment (now the 4th Sikh Regiment) who gave their lives in the service of their country. This battle, like many others fought by the Sikhs, displays the bravery of a tiny group of Sikh soldiers against overwhelming odds. This incident occurred on September 12, 1897, in the Tirah district of the North-West Frontier Province (now in Pakistan).

UNESCO (United Nations Educational, Scientific and Cultural Organization) has published eight accounts of collective bravery, including The Battle of Saragarhi. It has been named one of the world's five most significant events of its kind, alongside the Battle of Thermopylae. The British colonial rulers built a succession of forts to keep control of the NWFP (North West Frontier Province - now a state in Pakistan) and to protect troops against roving tribesmen and their *lashkars* (large bodies of troops). The majority of these forts were originally erected by Maharaja Ranjit Singh as part of the Sikh empire's consolidation in Punjab, and the British added a few more. Because the British had only partially succeeded in taking control of this territory, skirmishes and, at times, severe confrontations with the tribes were common. The NWFP, on the other hand, served as an excellent training ground for the Indian Army, allowing it to refine its abilities and techniques.

Fort Lockhart and Fort Gulistan were a few miles apart on the Samana ridge of the Hindukush and Sulaiman hills. Because these forts were not visible from one another, a signalling relay post called Saragarhi was built on a cliff halfway between them to allow heliographic communications (A heliograph is a basic mechanism for sending Morse code using a mirror capturing sunlight). This fortified post or picket had been built to provide safety and protection for the signalling detachment. In 1897, the Afghans orchestrated a mass rebellion in the NWFP as part of their programme, which became known as the "prickly heat policy," to direct tribal hatred against the British. Mullahs (Muslim religious leaders) played an important part in this rebellion. The 36th Sikh Regiment was tasked with occupying the forts of Gulistan and Lockhart.

Orakazai and Afridi Lashkars attacked Fort Gulistan between September 3rd and 9th, 1897. The attacks were repulsed on both occasions. A relief column was dispatched from the fort to aid in repelling these attacks. On the way back, the relieving column from Lockhart replenished the signalling detachment at Saragarhi, bringing its strength to 1 NCO (Non-Commissioned Officer) and 20 ORs (Other Ranks). On September 12, 1897, hordes of tribesmen laid siege to Fort Lockhart and Saragarhi, with the goal of overrunning the latter and blocking any assistance from the former. Lt. Col. Haughton, the Commanding Officer of the 36th Sikh, was at Fort Lockhart and communicated with the Saragarhi station through a heliograph. Under the tenacious and inspiring leadership of their detachment commander, Havildar Ishar Singh, the defenders of Saragarhi vowed to defend their station in the best tradition of their race and regiment. They weren't ready to hand over the post to the enemy and flee to safety. Havildar Singh and his men knew the post would fall because a handful of men in that improvised fort of stones and mud walls with a wooden door could not withstand the onslaught of thousands of tribesmen. These valiant guys were well aware that they would perish, but they were determined to do so by battling to death.

The tribes set fire to the post, while the valiant garrison lay dead or dying, their ammunition depleted. The next morning, the relief column arrived at the post, leaving the telltale signs of the epic battle for all to see. The tribes later claimed that a minimum of 600 - 1400 people were killed, with many more injured. When this story was recounted in the British Parliament, the members gave a standing ovation in honour of the Saragarhi's defenders. The narrative of these men's brave exploits was also told to Queen Victoria. The account was met with astonishment and admiration all throughout the world. The Indian Order of Merit Class III (posthumously) was presented to all 21 heroic warriors in this historic combat, which at the time was one of the greatest gallantry honours given to Indian forces and is considered equivalent to the modern-day Vir Chakra. All the Saragarhi heroes' heirs received 50 acres of land and 500 rupees. Never before or since has a troop received a single gallantry award for a single action. It is, undoubtedly, a one-of-a-kind action in Indian military history.

Saragarhi will be remembered as one of history's most incredible last stands. The Order of Merit was bestowed upon all 21 Sikhs, the highest honour bestowed upon Indian soldiers serving in the then-British Indian Army. Every year on September 12th, the units of the Sikh regiment observe Saragarhi Day as their regimental battle honours day. The battle is commemorated by two Gurudwaras, one in Amritsar near the Golden Temple and the other in Firozpur Cantonment. When the news of the battle arrived, the British Parliament observed a three-minute silence in honour of the engagement. Saragarhi is an event commemorating not the achievements of the British Indian Army, but the actual heroism displayed by Indian warriors under the harshest of conditions to defend their soil and maintain their country's honour. Their bravery can be immortalised in their attempts to safeguard the people they have vowed to and the country to which their names now belong forever.

> "It is not an exaggeration to say that armies containing valiant Sikhs cannot be defeated in a war."
>
> – Queen Victoria in the British Parliament in 1897.

'The Plague Manifesto'

When the plague first made an appearance in Calcutta in May 1898, Swamiji, along with other sannyasis such as Swami Sadananda and Bhagini Nivedita, wished to begin relief operations as quickly as practicable to assist the affected people.

The plague epidemic that engulfed Calcutta caused widespread panic. Relief efforts included caring for the sick in segregation camps and maintaining public cleanliness. When a plague epidemic struck Calcutta again the following year, a relief programme was launched on March 31, 1899. Bhagini Nivedita and Swami Sadananda led the relief effort.

Swamiji began by authoring a plague manifesto in Bengali and Hindi. Sadananda and Nivedita's tireless efforts ensured that the manifesto reached the majority of the public and greatly reassured them.

1898 - The Queen's Daughters in India - Book

"The Queen's Daughters in India" written by Elizabeth W. Andrew & Katharine C. Bushnell in 1898 uncovers a tragic truth of the British rule in India. The book exposes the British's exploitation of Indian women who were used as sex slaves for the soldiers of the British Military.

The book also says that the British established "Cantonments" after they gained control of India. These "Cantonments" were special British residences where Civil laws governing India did not operate but some arbitrary laws of the British prevailed. It was mentioned that about 100 such Cantonments were established. The purpose of these "Cantonments" was to guard against any rebellion or uprising and protect the British soldiers.

Cantonment Acts of 1864 enabled prostitution in these Cantonments and also regulated them. The rights of the Indian women were openly abused and the Britishers officially created brothels and called them *Chaklas* on the pretext of giving economic independence to the poor Indian women. Apparently, only 12-15 Indian women served an entire regiment of 1000 British soldiers. But the Britishers justified prostitution as a necessary precaution to protect the British Army from the evils of homosexuality.

The book noted, "The Raj was convinced that without sexual contact with women, the British army would verily become "Sodom and Gomorrah." The imposition of section 377 starting in 1860 punished sodomy, buggery, and bestiality as offences wasn't sufficient – reports stated that the military men were a willing market for homosexual acts on young boys, but were women not readily available.

"The Queen's Daughters in India" unearths shocking facts about the British Empire that often pretends to be the saviour of Indian Hindu women from socially fabricated myths of sati and child marriage. That the

British forcibly tortured Indian women and subjected them to prostitution and sexual slavery deserves much greater attention than it has received.

Abysmal sacrifices by Chapekar Brothers

The assassination of Mr Rand stunned the British Empire, and special officers were immediately appointed to investigate the crime. The British Government declared a reward of 20,000 rupees for anyone who would provide information on the whereabouts of the assassins, who in the real sense added a colourful chapter to the history of India's freedom struggle. To instil fear in the hearts of the people, the police resorted to merciless persecution. The Anglo-Indian press, particularly The Times of India, published suggestive pieces claiming that Lokmanya Tilak's remarks incited the killers to murder Mr Rand and that the Poona Brahmins had plotted to overthrow the British administration.

Meanwhile, Damodar Chapekar had been arrested in Bombay for Rand's murder. Chapekar confessed all culpability in the murder. People were astounded when they learned of his bold declaration in court. Damodar was found guilty and sentenced to death in the Sessions Court on March 2, 1898.

Tilak was confined in another ward of the Yervada prison while Damodar Chapekar was put in the ward for inmates to be hanged. Damodar Chapekar asked permission from the prison officials to meet with Tilak at least once. The authorization was granted. When Damodar met Tilak, he asked for a copy of the Bhagavad Gita and asked that his funeral rites be done according to Hindu tradition following his death. Tilak gave Damodar a copy of the Bhagavad Gita, and he proceeded to the gallows, quietly clutching the holy book in his hands. Tilak prepared for the deceased's funeral and the last rituals were to be carried out according to his preferences.

In December 1898, Bal Krishna Chapekar was arrested. The Dravid brothers, who were once members of the Chapekar Club, became informers, and the police arrested Damodar and Bal Krishna Chapekar as a result of the information they provided.

On February 8, 1899, the youngest of the Chapekar brothers, Vasudeo, and Ranade, another Chapekar Club member, shot the Dravid brothers near their home in Sadashiv Peth, Poona. The Dravid brothers died the next day as a result of their injuries, and Ranade and Vasudeo Chapekar were imprisoned.

In the second week of May 1899, Vasudeo, his brother, Bal Krishna, and Ranade were all hanged in the Yervada prison.

All three brothers believed they were dying for a noble cause and showed no fear or remorse as they approached the gallows. The three brothers' supreme sacrifice was one-of-a-kind and inspired awe in the hearts of the people. Tilak prepared for the last rituals to be performed for the three brothers and their associate, Ranade, who had given their lives for the honour of their nation.

Lala Lajpat Rai on Chapekar Brothers

The lion of Punjab, Lala Lajpat Rai, wrote, "The Chapekar brothers, who murdered the two officials who had made themselves unpleasant during the plague epidemic in Poona, were not seen as criminals by the people. The Chapekar brothers courageously accepted their fate. People admired the motivation behind the act, but not the act itself. The Chapekar brothers were, in reality, the pioneers of India's revolutionary movement."

The Chapekar Brothers' Impact on the young Savarkar

The assassination and subsequent execution of the Chapekars sparked outrage throughout the Bombay Presidency. Vinayak Savarkar was deeply touched by their stories of gallantry, trail details, and the manner in which they accepted the gallows with words from the Gita on their lips. He was enraged when some newspapers chastised the Chapekars for being impulsive and misleading young men. While their acts lacked strategy and meticulous planning, Vinayak simply could not accept the insult of martyrs who had laid down their lives for the country.

After that, he couldn't sleep for several nights. In a fit of rage, he dashed to the Ashtabhuja Bhawani idol in his hometown of Bhugur and poured his heart out to her. In front of his family goddess, he took a solemn vow to devote himself and his life to the liberation of the country through armed struggle. In her presence, he exclaimed, *'Shatrus maarta maarta mare to jhunjen!'* (I shall make war on the enemies and murder them until the day I die.)

Vinayak also penned a play about the Chapekars named *"Veershriyukta"* to promote the revolutionary spirit in Bhagur. Vinayak's poem *'Caapekarancha Phatka'* was popular until the 1910s and encouraged young people all over Maharashtra.

The Rashtrabhakta Samuha, or Club of Patriots, (a secret society of young revolutionaries) was founded around the end of November 1899, led by a sixteen-year-old Vinayak, and included Mhaskar and Paage as members.

On January 1, 1900, the trio established the 'Mitra Mela,' or Group of Friends, as a front-end organisation of the Rashtrabhakta Samuha. Vinayak inducted young patriotic men into the Mela, including himself. He urged Mela participants to strive for "absolute political independence for India."

January 6, 1899 - Commencement of the most Controversial reign of the era of the British

Lord Curzon, India's Viceroy from 1899 to 1905, was one of the most divisive and pivotal figures in the country's history.

Curzon famously stated in 1901, "As long as we dominate India, we will remain the greatest power in the world. If we lose it, we will immediately become a third-rate power."

Curzon was a virulent bigot who believed in Britain's "civilising mission" in India. He regarded Indians as having "extraordinary inferiority in character, honesty, and capacity" in 1901. "Why not appoint a notable native to the Viceroy's Executive Council?" he continued. "The explanation is that there isn't a single Indian on the entire continent who is qualified for the position."

In India, the despicable "Lord" Curzon is remembered for three things:

* Bengal's infamous partition in 1905.

* His "education policy," which wiped out Sanskrit education that had existed uninterrupted for hundreds of years, and

* His role in slowly allowing the victims of the Great Indian Famine of 1899-1900 to die of starvation.

The Man who avenged the Jallianwala Bagh Massacre born

Udham Singh was born on December 26, 1899, at Sunam, Sangrur district of Punjab, India to Sardar Tehal Singh Jammu and Mata Narain Kaur. His father was a farmer and also worked as the railway crossing watchman in the village of Upali.

After the death of his father, Udham Singh and his elder brother Mukta Singh were raised by Central Khalsa Orphanage Putlighar in Amritsar. In the year 1918, Udham Singh passed his Matriculation Examination and left the orphanage in the year 1919.

June 9, 1900 - The Incognito; Birsa Munda

Although Birsa Munda lived for only 25 years, he is regarded as a legend who had a long-lasting impact on India's fight against the British. A young revolutionary fighter and tribal leader whose late-nineteenth-century involvement is recognised as a strong indication of protest against the British authorities in India.

Birsa Munda was baptised and raised as "Birsa David" as a child at a Christian missionary-run school in Jharkhand. Many tribal people were forced to convert as a condition of receiving an education in missionary institutions at the time. This happened in the 1870s and 1880s, when Christian missionaries, explicitly supported by the British colonial administration, oppressed the Indians.

As he grew older, he abandoned the name "Birsa David" and opted to return to his previous beliefs. The Church demanded tribute from the public at the time, causing enormous hardship among the downtrodden and impoverished people. He decided to launch an insurgency.

The Mundas' rebellion was sparked by British agrarian policies. The Mundas have adopted the *Khunkhatti* system of communal landholding. The Zamindari System, introduced by the British, permitted foreigners to penetrate these tribal regions. The arrival of outsiders, aided by the British, resulted in the exploitation of the indigenous tribes. Mundas, who were previously landowners, were quickly reduced to forced labourers, resulting in even more poverty and hardship.

Things came to a climax on Christmas Eve of 1899 when Birsa Munda and his followers rose up against the Church and landlords supported by the imperial authorities. He was apprehended by the British administration and died soon after in the Ranchi jail, before the age of 25. Authorities say he died of cholera, but this is being challenged.

Surprisingly, some of the goals of Birsa Munda's "Ulgulan" insurrection were released after his death, when the British implemented the Chotanagpur Tenancy Act in 1908. The groundbreaking act was significant legislation for Jharkhand's tribal community because it prohibited the transfer of tribal land to non-tribals. The British administration also recognised tribes' *"Khuntkatti"* rights and prohibited *"Beth begari,"* or forced labour.

October 28, 1900 - Demise of Friedrich Max Müller

"India has been conquered once, but India must be conquered again, and that second conquest should be a conquest by education."

– Max Muller

On October 28, 1900, Friedrich Max Muller, one of the pioneers of the western academic area of Indian studies, died. Max Muller argued that if Christianity did not intervene, it would be the fault of Indians because India's old religion was doomed at the moment.

According to a letter written by Muller to his wife, he was specifically hired to interpret the Vedas in such a way that Hindus lost trust in them.

William Hunter, a British clerk, and Max Muller, a distinguished orientalist, used their words, sentences, and imagination to make an English translation of *Manu Smriti*. *Asthadhyayi* Panini Grammar was never read by either of them.

Max Muller, perhaps the most well-known early Indologist and Sanskritist, was the one who attempted to pit the narrative against the Vedas and the great Indian culture, as the British administration intended. He and other Indologists sought to dominate and convert Vedic culture adherents by spreading the myth that the Vedas were essentially mythology. They purposefully misconstrued Sanskrit scriptures in order to portray the Vedas as primitive, and they systematically attempted to make Indians ashamed of their own culture. The Aryan invasion theory was one of these Indologists' forgeries of history.

William Jones, Max Muller, and Hunter shared a single goal – to create a divided narrative and incite hostility in a segment of Sanatan society. And they might be able to successfully plant the seeds. They were on a mission to denigrate any religious value or tradition that was not their own.

Max Muller proposed an Aryan invasion dating back to 1500 BC in the colonial period, either purposefully or unintentionally, with no archaeological or scientific basis and only on linguistic grounds. Selective reading of the Vedas and Puranas/Upanishads led to the interpretation of the war mentioned between Deva and Asur as a conflict between Central Asian attackers and indigenous people. When further sites were uncovered, including Rakhigarhi in Haryana and Lothal in Gujarat, most historians rejected the Aryan invasion theory in favour of Aryan immigration.

Thus, it appears that the behaviour of these Indologists is motivated by their racial agenda. Despite this, Max Muller later praised the Vedas. He admitted the purely speculative nature of his Vedic chronology, and in his final work, "The six systems of Indian Philosophy," published shortly before his death, he wrote, "whatever the date of the Vedic hymns, whether 1500 or 15000 B.C.E., they have their own unique place and stand by themselves in the literature of the world."

CHAPTER - VIII

JANUARY 22, 1901 – THE DEMISE OF THE QUEEN[6]

When Queen Victoria died on January 22, 1901, at the age of 81; her family, court, and subjects were taken aback. The Victorian era came to an end with her death. She had already escaped many assassination attempts. Stewart Richards examined Queen Victoria's dying moments and the frantic preparations for her state funeral on February 2, 1901, and the hidden things in her coffin. The funeral was estimated to have cost £35,500 (£4.5 million).

During Queen Victoria's reign, the British Empire expanded dramatically, and her reign was marked by conquests, invasions, and conflicts.

She saw 10 prime ministers; five Archbishops of Canterbury and six commanders-in-chief; 18 presidents of the United States; 11 Viceroys of Canada; 16 Viceroys of India and France successively ruled by one king; one emperor and seven presidents of a Republic. She had also outlived all nine of her bridesmaids.

Lord Curzon, India's viceroy at the time, chose to erect a large marble monument in her honour in Calcutta, the colonial capital at the time. It took a decade and a half to construct the Victoria Memorial Hall. The museum, which first opened in 1921, has artefacts spanning approximately 300 years.

---

6   https://www.historyextra.com/period/victorian/queen-victoria-death-funeral-mask-cause/

Census in Colonial India and the birth of caste

H. H. Risley, who became census commissioner of India for the 1901 edition of the project, observed later that the report prepared by his predecessor provided only "a patchwork classification in which occupation predominates, varied here and there by considerations of caste, history, tradition, ethnical affinity, and geographical position," (Risley 1903: 538)

Risley-Gait Census Commission (1901-1911) vertically delineated an entirely Indian population into seven ethnic races. Herbert Risley conceded in the Preface of his book 'The People of India' that his observations to divide Indian populations into myriad ethnic communities were not based on any historical document but on the findings of the contemporary display of social behaviour. But his approach became the citadel of composite culture theory.

The census of India in 1901 witnessed the most comprehensive attempt made by any census commissioner yet to understand caste.

In the census of 1901, the British administration made it mandatory to brand the tribals as "Animists." This policy continued to be meticulously followed till the Census of 1931, although every single Commissioner of the Census during this period expressed, within the Census report itself, his clear disagreement with the policy that he was implementing: Sir Herbert Hisley, Commissioner of the Census 1901, clearly opined that Hinduism was itself "Animism more or less transformed by philosophy," and "no sharp line of demarcation can be drawn between Hinduism and Animism."

The 1901 census recorded 1,646 distinct castes, which increased to 4,147 in 1931.

Unravelling the facts about the demise of Swami Vivekananda

Vivekananda made a prophecy that he would not live more than 40 years, which later held true. According to sources, on July 4, 1902, he went to his room later that evening, asked not to be disturbed, and never returned. He is said to have died while meditating at 9:10 p.m.

Vivekananda's selfless service to man and God wore him down physically. Throughout his life, he suffered from a variety of ailments. His motto is, "One has to die… it is better to wear out than to rust out."

"Learn from my experiences," he advised his disciples near the end of his brief life. "Don't be so hard on your body that you end up ruining your health. I have harmed my well-being. What was the outcome of my torturous treatment of it? During the best years of my life, my body has been ruined! And I'm still on the hook for it."

Narendranath Datta, later known as Swami Vivekananda, was born in 1863, the year Alexander Duff left India, confident that Hinduism was on its way out and Christianity was on its way in, at least in Bengal. Macaulay's prediction appeared to be coming true, as there had been a surge in Christian conversions.

Narendranath attended Alexander Duff's General Assembly's Institution, later renamed the Scottish Church College. But a watershed moment in his life occurred in November 1880, when he met Sri Ramakrishna Paramahamsa. For the first time, he was confronted with a powerful expression of Hindu spirituality in the form of a simple man who had never attended a primary school. His travel throughout India after Sri Ramakrishna's death provided additional insights into how Hindu spirituality had permeated effortlessly to the lowest levels of Hindu society. As a result, he was able to process Christianity through the lens of a new perspective. In the end, he dashed Alexander Duff's hopes and skewed Macaulay and Temple's predictions.

Swami Vivekananda has been forgotten in India, and his memory is now confined only to the various *Mathas* and *Ashramas* that he founded, as well as some educational institutions that bear his name.

1903 - Invasion of Tibet

In 1865, Tibet was a great white blank on most western maps. There was no knowledge of the precise locations of even Lhasa or Shigatse, the biggest towns of Tibet. Tibet had closed its gates off to foreigners, especially the westerners. But the Great Game was heating up and the British officers in India already had eyes on Tibet.

By the 1890s Christian missionaries were making serious attempts at breaching Tibet and converting it. China, which held a very fragile diplomatic sway over Tibet, would regularly scare Tibetans by saying that the Russians and the British were Christian missionaries who were out to destroy the ancient religion of Tibet and convert them to Christianity.

The British, meanwhile, were increasingly wary of the Russians in Central Asia. By the beginning of 1903, they were almost convinced that the Dalai Lama and the Russian Tsar had a secret deal and thus, Tibet would also soon be gobbled up by the Russian Empire. Lord Curzon along with his friend, the already famous Great Game player Francis Younghusband was planning an invasion of Tibet. It was in principle just a friendly visit to ensure that the Russians were not already in Tibet, but on the ground, it amounted to nothing less than an invasion. In 1903, the British tried to negotiate with the Tibetans at Khamba Jong just three miles inside the Tibetan border, but the Tibetans did not agree.

As a result, another British force was sent into Tibet forcefully in the December of 1903. It was two thousand soldiers strong with modern weapons. But the contingent was more than 12,000 strong as around ten thousand coolies were needed to carry the armaments on the high Jelap Pass. The soldiers were the Sikh and Gurkha regiments. Maxim machine guns were also carried, which would be a game-changer in the engagement.

Tibetans, on the other hand, were armed with nothing but matchlocks and swords. But the British army passed over the Jelap Pass and then, the walls of Yatun and finally over the great fortress of Phari too without any confrontation. The Tibetans kept protesting but did not put up a fight. Just short of the village of Guru, the first bloody battle between the British and the Tibetans happened. This was the first engagement of the Tibetans with a European-led army. The conclusion was foregone. More than seven hundred Tibetans were massacred in a matter of minutes in the grim March of 1904.

There were many engagements between the British and the Tibetans later. In the run-up to Gyantse the great fortress town of Tibet, two hundred Tibetans once again died with no casualty on the British side. It was once again a rout. At Karo Pass, approaching the great forbidden city of Lhasa, the British once again met a Tibetan force commanding great heights. A great and courageous battle was fought in which the British too left five men but the Tibetans lost more than four hundred. This Battle of the Karo Pass would become immortal in military history as it was fought at a greater altitude than any other in the history of warfare.

By now, the British goal was to march to Lhasa itself and not just Gyantse. The Tibetans were resisting and so, it was thought to teach them a lesson by stepping foot inside the sacred city. It was a belief in Tibet that if even one great fortress of theirs is occupied by a foreign force, then it would bring bad luck and all would be lost. The Tibetans were losing heart in the battle. Very soon, the British-led Indian army commanded by Francis Younghusband entered Lhasa, the city which no foreigner had yet visited without getting discovered. Its golden roofs and domes were a sight which enthralled the British and the Indians.

1904 - Savarkar's revolutionary organization came into existence

Vinayak D. Savarkar founded *Rashtra-bhakta-samooha* in 1899, and it was renamed *Mitramela* in 1900. This would later pave the way for the Abhinav Bharat secret society. The main activities were organising public Hindu festival celebrations and inviting other freedom fighters and intellectuals to give lectures. Lokamanya Tilak maintained close ties with this organisation, whose secretary was Babarao Savarkar.

Vinayak Savarkar and Ganesh Savarkar (Babarao) established the 'Abhinav Bharat Society' in Nashik, Maharashtra, in 1904. The Abhinav Bharat Society was a Maharashtra-based secret society. Mazzini's Young Italy, an Italian secret society formed to unite Italy, served as inspiration.

Abhinav Bharat stated that India can not progress unless it achieves complete independence. They desired Swaraj (independence), not dominion status under the British Crown. Only in 1929, during the Lahore session, did the Indian National Congress adopt this as a resolution. Babarao was the leader of both the *Mitramela* and the Abhinav Bharat.

Babarao organised lectures to enlighten the public. There would be a charge for freedom sloganeering. Ganesh in Nashik and Vinayak in Pune organised the first public bonfire of foreign clothes in 1905. This was done to protest the partitioning of Bengal.

The *Mitramela* marched through the streets with loud "Vande mataram" slogans during a Dussehra procession. Babarao and other members were arrested after thrashing a police officer who had hit Babarao with a baton. They were trialled, found guilty, and sentenced to pay fines. This was known as the Vande Mataram trial in Maharashtra (then The Bombay Province).

The first Nupi Lan, 1904

The First Nupi Lan (which translates into Women's War) was a significant revolt led by women in the Imphal West district of Manipur. It was one of the earliest uprisings in India to be led entirely by women.

The cause of the rebellion was the reintroduction of the Lallup system by Colonel Maxwell in July 1904, which required men to perform ten days of free labour after every 30 days. Maxwell had temporarily reintroduced the Lallup System after the bungalows of two British officials were burned down, leading to widespread protests against forced labour. On September 3, 1904, thousands of women marched to Maxwell's official residence, demanding that the orders to reintroduce the Lallup system be taken down. The British authorities promised to retract the orders, but their promises were in vain. This triggered another meeting of around 5,000 women at Khwairamband Bazar on 5th October to protest and demand the abolition of the Lallup system. The British tried to violently suppress the protest, but the women continued their protest with great enthusiasm. Ultimately, the British had to retract the orders and rebuild the bungalows at their own expense.

This revolt sparked many more women-led uprisings in Manipur. The most significant among them was the Second Nupi Lan, which took place in 1939. 12th December, the day of the Second Nupi Lan, is commemorated as Nupi Lan Day.

The diegesis of the partition of Bengal

The decision to split Bengal was made in July, and by October 16, 1905, Bengal had been divided into Piston Bengal and Assam (with 31 million people) and the rest of Bengal (with a population of 4 million of whom 18 million were Bengalis, and 36 million Biharis and Oriyas).

The decision was made after Lord Curzon claimed that Bengal was too large to be effectively governed. The actual purpose, however, was to divide the region so that the western part is the abode of the Hindu majority and the eastern part is a mecca to the Muslim majority.

The Bengal Partition, described as the "crowning act of [Curzon's] folly" by Prof. R.C. Majumdar, directly unleashed the extraordinary Swadeshi movement, which spectacularly flummoxed the British. The Swadeshi Movement stands alone as one of the most significant episodes in recorded existence, far surpassing the American struggle for independence or even the Civil Rights Movement.

Obviously, the frightened British reacted in the only way they knew how: by unleashing a reign of terror across Bengal. When that failed, Curzon enlisted the help of the Nawab of Dhaka, Khwaja Salimullah, an Islamic zealot. Curzon had already persuaded Salimullah to support the Bengal partition in February 1904. Curzon's government granted him a loan of rupees 14 lahks at a very low-interest rate in exchange for his assistance in quelling the protests against Bengal's partition. In 1906, the same Nawab Salimullah became the founding Vice President of the All India Muslim League, which eventually succeeded in acknowledging Pakistan's "vision" that Syed Ahmed Khan had first formulated long before.

Nawab Salimullah swung into action with the full support of the British Government. The first step was to incite Hindu hatred among Muslims. The consequences were immediate and catastrophic.

A wave of heinous violence against Hindus has erupted in East Bengal. Comilla (now Cumilla, in Bangladesh's Chittagong Division) and Jamalpur (now in Bangladesh's Mymensingh Division) were strewn with the blood and dead bodies of Hindus. Comilla was witness to unspeakable Muslim atrocities against Hindus for four harrowing days beginning on March 4, 1907.

This partition enraged the Bengali people, resulting in a variety of organised protest movements. Memorials with hundreds of thousands of signatures were delivered to the Governor General of India in Council, requesting that the partition be rescinded.

It was unprecedented in Raj's history for so many of her subjects to literally take up their pen in an organised protest against a government decision.

However, organising such a large signature campaign against the reigning colonial power was a tough challenge. Reaching the households of hundreds of villages throughout Bengal, crossing rivers and forests, and overcoming seasonal difficulties such as those encountered during the monsoon season would not have been possible without organised and concerted efforts.

The 16th of October, 1905, was designated as the National Day of Mourning. People fasted and partook in a general strike. Many people sang Rabindranath Tagore's composition "Amar Sonar Bangla." Many people were seen singing Vande Mataram as they strolled barefoot to the Ganga.

Vande Mataram, penned by Bankim Chandra Chattopadhyay, bears a striking resemblance to the Indian Freedom Fight since, when the infamous viceroy Lord Curzon split up Bengal, ostensibly to bridge a communal divide, Vande Mataram became an epitome of unity and was sung by Hindus and Muslims alike to demonstrate the extent of their cohesion. There was nothing communal about the song back then, and there is nothing communal about it now.

The outrageous movements by the trio Lal-Bal-Pal

Lala Lajpat Rai of undivided Punjab, Bal Gangadhar Tilak of Maharashtra, and Bipin Chandra Pal of what was the united Bengal had joined forces to advocate the Swadeshi movement, which asserted the rejection of British goods in pursuit of national self-sufficiency.

On August 7, 1905, the Swadeshi Movement, now known as the 'Make in India' campaign, was officially declared at the Calcutta Town Hall in Bengal. Along with the Swadeshi movement, a boycott movement was launched. The movements stood for the usage of Indian-made goods and the burning of British-made goods. After the British government decided to partition Bengal, Bal Gangadhar Tilak encouraged the Swadeshi and Boycott movements.

In 1905, Lokmanya Tilak founded "The Bombay Swadeshi Co-operative Stores Co Ltd" with Ratanji Jamsetji Tata and Dwarkadas Dharamsey as Directors alongside him. Dadabhai Naoroji inaugurated the first store, which was located in what is now known as the Times of India building.

By 1909, the movement had spread throughout the country and immediately turned to the anti-partition and anti-colonial movements. The Swadeshi movement was also known as the Vande Mataram movement in Andhra Pradesh.

Aurobindo and Tilak: Two precarious personalities proved fatal to the Empire

The Indian National Congress INC anti-Hindu stance initially surfaced in August 1906, on the topic of who should be nominated for President of the Calcutta Congress in December.

The presidential election in 1906 took place in the aftermath of Lord Curzon's partition of Bengal in October 1905. Aurobindo, along with his brother Barin Ghosh, Bhupendranath Datta (younger brother of Swami

Vivekananda), and other Jugantar revolutionaries, launched the Swaraj, Swadeshi, and Boycott movement, which was hailed and supported by Lokmanya Tilak, the most towering political leader at the time, with an unrivalled mass following across the provinces.

It is no coincidence that both Aurobindo and Tilak began their efforts to Hinduize the INC in 1893. Aurobindo's defiant and magnificent political epistles, which began in 1893 with 'Old Lamps for New' in Indu Prakash and 'Bande Mataram', and Tilak's blistering political commentary in 'Kesari' and 'Mahratta', as well as galvanizing Hindus in a ten-day public celebration of Ganesh Utsav, which also began in September 1893.

Both Aurobindo and Tilak employed Hindu religious symbols and metaphors to instil a strong desire for political liberty among the masses. The British authorities saw Tilak and Aurobindo as the two most significant enemies of their authority because they instilled nationalism into the INC, therefore undermining the fundamental objective for which the INC was formed.

November 18, 1905 – Appointment of the new Viceroy followed by Lord Curzon

In 1905, Lord Minto was appointed Viceroy of India, with John Morley as secretary of state. The two men agreed that certain political reforms were needed to satisfy educated Indians, strengthen moderate leaders of the Indian National Congress Party, and control rising nationalism.

The reforms were commonly referred to as the "Morley-Minto Reforms" because both John Morley and Lord Minto collaborated on their creation. The Indian Councils Act was approved by the British parliament in 1909. Separate reservation for Muslims was declared by the government in 1909 under the guise of legislative improvements, in the name of Minto-Morley reforms.

Minto Park in Kolkata (formerly Calcutta) is named in his honour. After his substantial sponsorship for the construction of the new school buildings, the school from which Aligarh Muslim University emerged, was called Minto Circle in his honour.

Minto Ophthalmic Hospital, which is located in Bangalore, is also named after him. This is one of the largest and busiest eye hospitals in India, as well as one of the oldest.

When Savarkar reached London!

Lokmanya Tilak and Kaal editor Shivrampant Paranjpe recommended Savarkar for the Shivaji fellowship. Tilak made the first instalment payment of Rs. 400, as agreed. Finally, on June 9, 1909, Savarkar boarded the S.S. Persia and arrived in London on June 24, 1906.

In London, Savarkar engaged in the following activities:

- He began holding regular Sunday gatherings to discuss various issues concerning India's future. These quickly gained popularity among Indian students. Other revolutionaries from Egypt, Ireland, Russia, China, and Turkey voluntarily participated. One of them was Lenin. The "Future Constitution of India" was one of the themes of discussion.

- Savarkar conducted national hero commemorations such as Shivjayanti (the birthday of Chhatrapati Shivaji Maharaj) and holiday celebrations such as Diwali and Dussehra. In India House, he also commemorated the golden jubilee of the 1857 War of Independence against the British.

- While in London, Savarkar continued the work of the Abhinav Bharat. Copies of the bomb handbook were printed at London's India House. One copy was delivered to Lokmanya Tilak in Pune.

- In September 1906, Savarkar finished his biography of Mazzini in Marathi. In June 1907, his elder brother, Babarao, published it in India. A year later, the book was banned in the United Kingdom. He penned his famous book 'Indian War of Independence 1857' in Marathi. It was later translated into English by his friends at India House. It was secretly published in Holland in 1909 and was instantly prohibited in India. For the next 40 years, Indian rebels were inspired by Savarkar's book.

Sikhs played a vital role in Hindu society. Their proportion in the Indian Army was fairly significant. As a result, Savarkar studied Gurumukhi and the holy works of Adi Granth, Panth Prakash, and Vichitra Natak. While in England, Savarkar took notes for his book, 'History of the Sikhs,' which he completed in Paris.

July 23, 1906 - The day when the fiery Chandra Shekhar Azad's tiny feet pattered on the earth

Chandrashekar Sitaram Tiwari, the boy who endured the cane blows, was born on July 23, 1906, in Bhabara village, now in Madhya Pradesh's Alirajpur district. His father, Pandit Sitaram Tiwari, was from the Uttar Pradesh district of Unnao and worked as a clerk in the forest department. This is where Chandrashekar spent his childhood years, amid a dense wilderness surrounded by hills and valleys. Sitaram Tiwari was honest and never sought to gain money illegally, despite the fact that he was not affluent and had to suffer due to poverty. Chandrashekhar was raised by his mother, Jagrani Devi, who yearned for her son to become a Sanskrit scholar. He had a considerable rebellious inclination, even as a youngster. When his hand got burned during Diwali, he didn't even notice it until his buddies told him.

Chandrashekhar and his brother Sukhdev attended a rural school where Manohar Lal Trivedi taught. Chandrashekhar was nurtured with high values and a strong sense of justice – traits he got from his father. Trivedi went on to become Chandrashekar's tutor because his father could not afford to pay for his education. He was the one who brought Chandrashekhar to his house and educated him. Because of his family's financial situation, Chandrashekar began working at the age of 14 for a local tehsildar, Sitaram Agnihotri. However, Chandrashekar was disappointed with his vocation and desired to just see the world.

Chandrashekar's mother convinced his father to send him to Kashi to study Sanskrit. Varanasi was the epicentre of Sanskrit learning at the time, with students from all over India pouring into the city. The nicest part was that students from low-income families received free boarding and accommodation. Sitaram Tiwari, with this in mind, sent Chandrashekhar to Varanasi for additional study.

However, the restless Chandrashekhar was unable to acclimatise to his new surroundings and fled from Kashi to Alirajpur, where his uncle lived. During his stay in Alirajpur, he became acquainted with the Bhil tribals. They taught him archery. He often spent hours swimming in the

Ganga. He enjoyed hearing Ramayana and Mahabharata talks, as well as stories of independence wars and their brave warriors.

The Colonisation Bill, 1906

In 1906, Banke Dyal, the editor of the Jang Syal monthly, coined the title of a song to protest the British Raj's agrarian policies. *"Paghri Sambhal Jatta"* translates as "Mind your turban, peasant." The turban is an important religious symbol for Sikhs and is perceived as a symbol of resistance to tyranny. The loss of the turban is regarded as a sign of defeat and despair.

Ajit Singh, the revolutionary Bhagat Singh's uncle, led the movement.

A slew of laws, including the Punjab Land Alienation Act of 1900, the Punjab Land Colonisation Bill of 1906, and an increase in water tariffs the following year, following two consecutive crop failures, had incensed the peasantry.

The colonisation bill enforced a Doctrine of Lapse-like condition under which privately held land in agricultural colonies along the Upper Bari Doab canal fell to the State if the proprietor died without a male successor. The East India Company's takeover of princely territories under the Doctrine of Lapse led the dispossessed royals to assist or lead mutineers of the Bengal Army in 1857.

Ajit Singh, Bhagat Singh's uncle, and All India Congress Committee members Kishan Singh, Ghasita Ram, and Sufi Amba Prasad initially sang the song at a 1907 rally in Lyallpur, now known as Faisalabad in Pakistan's Punjab province.

Bharat Mata Society, 1906

The Bharat Mata Society, founded by Lala Lajpat Rai and Sufi Amba Prasad in 1906, played a significant role in India's struggle for independence. With members such as Sardar Ajit Singh from the Shaheed Bhagat Singh district in Punjab, Anand Kishore Mehta and others, the society aimed to promote patriotism and fight against British rule.

Sham Das Varma, as the editor of Bharat Mata, the official organ of the society, took on additional responsibilities for Swarajya. However, when Sufi Amba Prasad and Sardar Ajit Singh fled to Persia, Varma had to return to Lahore urgently, and Ladha Ram Kapur succeeded him.

Despite facing legal repercussions, the Bharat Mata Society continued to inspire and mobilise patriots in the struggle for Indian independence. The society's members, including young men from Uttar Pradesh and other parts of India, were committed to bringing about change and challenging British rule. Their efforts, along with those of other freedom fighters, eventually contributed to India's independence.

The establishment of the All-India Muslim League

When the British saw the entire country unified in the liberation movement, they decided to isolate the Muslims from it. The All-India Muslim League (often referred to as the Muslim League) proved to be the ideal tool in the process. When the League was founded in Dhaka in 1906, on December 30, one of its founding goals was to foster allegiance to the British overlords.

The British ensured that the leading members of the Muslim League were on the same page by using bribes, inducements, and the promise of a disproportionately large role for Muslims in free India. The Muslim elite paid crores of rupees for bribes, arsons, and riots, with the Nawab of Bhopal being the major funder.

The British were successful in dissuading many Muslims from the concept of independence. According to Pakistani social sciences scholar and author, Rubina Saigol, Pakistan was primarily established to preserve and promote the class interests of the League's landed aristocracy. "The League was formed at a meeting attended primarily by the landed elite, who feared that if the British left India and a representative government was established, the traditional power of the loyal Muslim aristocracy would erode, especially since the class composition of the Congress reflected the educated urban and rural middle classes seeking upward mobility and a share in political power.

The Muslim League heightened the tension. It took a violent turn in the 1920s and, quite severely, in the 1940s, culminating in the subcontinent's final partition into two states, India and Pakistan, in 1947. Partition-related riots killed up to two million people.

Calcutta in 1906

Moderates believed in the policy of settlement of minor issues with the government by deliberations. But the extremists believed in agitation, strikes, and boycotts. They wanted to extend the boycott to all over India and refuse cooperation so that the task of administration becomes impossible.

The main extremist leaders were Lala Lajpat Ray, Bal Gangadhar Tilak, and Bipin Chandra Pal. They were called Lal Bal Pal. They had become so popular that the British were alarmed. The slogan was "Swaraj is my Birthright."

The moderates did not like these new techniques of struggle. They even thought of using the Boycott in only special circumstances. Lokmanya Tilak and his followers held a separate conference and formed the Extremist Party. However, they decided to work as a part of the INC.

The difference between moderates and extremists widened in Congress' Calcutta Session of (1906) and attempts were made to elect one of them as the President.

It was at the 22nd Congress, again at Calcutta in 1906 that the nationalist Quartet asserted itself, and for the first time, resolutions in favour of Boycott, Swadeshi, Swaraj and National Education were pushed through.

Chhatrapati Shivaji Maharaj and Bengal Revolution

Chhatrapati Shivaji Maharaj was an inspiration for Bengali patriots from 1857 onwards and everyone from Tagore and Bipin Chandra Pal to Aurobindo Ghosh eulogized him.

The Shivaji Festival elicited a popular response in Bengal. On 4th June 1906, the Shivaji Festival and an exhibition of Swadeshi goods took off to a grand start in Kolkata, with Tilak himself, G.S Khaparde, Dr B.S.Moonje, Aswini Kumar Dutt in attendance. While inaugurating the Shivaji Festival, Tilak addressed a huge gathering and declared the celebration "a political festival." Tilak told the large gathering at the heart of Kolkata that the words 'Bande Mataram,' are now inscribed on the temple of Chhatrapati Shivaji Maharaj at Ratnagiri. The Shivaji Festival is an inspiring political festival which must spread all over India. The Goddess Kali is the presiding

Goddess in Bengal, the same Goddess was the protector of Chhatrapati Shivaji Maharaj. We cannot conceive of Chhatrapati Shivaji Maharaj without Bhawani.

Bipin Chandra Pal also spoke that day, where he celebrated Chhatrapati Shivaji Maharaj as a great inspiration for Hindus, "Shivaji was a Hindu. He symbolized the religiopolitical ideal of the Hindu people. In honouring Chhatrapati Shivaji Maharaj, we honour that Hindu ideal." Bipin Chandra Pal also started a festival to celebrate Raja Pratipaditya of Jessore – a king who had fought Islamic invaders.

Also, through the 1906 Shivaji Festival, the great Maratha was truly taken to the masses. He became a strong source of inspiration for the budding revolutionaries in Bengal. Biographies of Chhatrapati Shivaji Maharaj began making their way in large numbers into the hands of men with nationalist thoughts and a strong desire to topple the British Government.

Barindrakumar Ghosh received his education at Deogarh under Deuskar, where the ideal of Chhatrapati Shivaji Maharaj had a great influence on him. He was the younger brother of the more famous Aurobindo Ghosh. Rabindranath Tagore's more popular poem on Shivaji was written in 1904. Titled "Shivaji Utsab," it was part of Deuskar's twenty pages book which was distributed free at the Shivaji Festival of that year in Calcutta.

A play by Girish Chandra Ghosh – Chhatrapati Shivaji Maharaj – ran to packed houses before it was banned. It was a Bengali play with a Bengali cast! As mentioned earlier, the Jugantar and Swadhin Bharat regularly published pro-Shivaji articles. Apart from this, Swami Vivekananda is also known to have spoken on Shivaji on multiple occasions.

Bengali historian, Sir Jadunath Sarkar's quote on Chhatrapati Shivaji Maharaj:

"Shivaji proved, by his example, that the Hindu race could build a nation, found a State, defeat its enemies; they could conduct their own defence; they could protect and promote literature and art, commerce and industry; they

could maintain navies and ocean-going fleets of their own, and conduct naval battles on equal terms with foreigners. He taught the modern Hindus to rise to the full stature of their growth. He demonstrated that the tree of Hinduism was not dead and that it could put forth new leaves and branches and once again rise up its head to the skies."

Vande Mataram Movement in 1907

The Vande Mataram movement was started on February 11, 1907, in Andhra Pradesh following the announcement of the Bengal Partition of 1905. The period witnessed a national awakening among the people of Krishna district.

The prominent leaders of the movement in the district were Harisarvothama Rao, Pingali Lakshmi Narayana, Kasinadhuni Veera Mallayya, Bodi Narayana Rao, and others. In April 1907, Bipin Chandra Pal made a historical visit to Vijayawada and Masulipatnam and gave speeches on the origin and meaning of Swadeshi and Vande Mataram. He was welcomed with slogans like "Vande Mataram" and "Swadeshi Ki Jai."

Bhagat Singh was born on September 28, 1907, in Banga, Pakistan

Bhagat Singh was born to Kishan Singh and Vidyavati on September 28, 1907, in Banga, Lyallpur district (now Pakistan). At the time of his birth, his father, Kishan Singh, and uncles Ajit and Swaran Singh were imprisoned for protesting the 1906 Colonization Bill. Sardar Ajit Singh, his uncle, was a supporter of the movement and founded the Indian Patriots' Association. In mobilising the peasants against the Chenab Canal Colony Bill, he was warmly assisted by his friend, Syed Haidar Raza. Ajit Singh faced 22 accusations and was forced to flee to Iran. His family was a Ghadar party supporter, and the politically conscious environment at home helped instil a feeling of patriotism in young Bhagat Singh.

Bhagat Singh graduated from the National College Lahore which was founded by Lala Lajpat Rai.

The Surat Split

The Surat Split was the division of the Indian National Congress into two factions, the Extremists and the Moderates, during the 1907 Surat session.

Lala declared that India should strive for freedom by using swadeshi products created in India and boycotting foreign goods. He expressed these opinions at the 1907 Congress session in Surat City.

On May 3, 1907, Lalaji was arrested for causing "turmoil" in Rawalpindi. He was imprisoned in Mandalay, Burma, for six months with Ajit Singh, a relative of Bhagat Singh, and was released on November 11, 1907, as an outcome of demonstrations in India fueled by Bal Gangadhara Tilak's fiery columns in Kesari.

During the Congress schism in Surat, the moderates evicted the "extremists," including Bal Gangadhar Tilak. Following his expulsion, he was imprisoned for 6 years in Mandalay Jail for sedition.

1907 - Commemoration of 50 years of the first battle of independence

The British were practically in a state of dreadful psychosis. The authorities were afraid that a hundred thousand men were waiting for a signal from Lajpat Rai to launch another insurrection. According to the government report, the people of Punjab were "urged to band together to withhold payment of government income, water rates, and other dues; to refuse supplies, carriages, and other assistance to government officers on tour and Native soldiers." Police officers were labelled as "traitors" and ordered to resign from the government. The authorities assumed that the Arya Samaj, to which Lajpat Rai belonged, had a hidden committee that was in charge of coordinating the propaganda.

The authorities were informed through a cypher telegram:

"The movement's leader and focal point is Lala Lajpat Rai, a Khatri advocate who has visited England as the Congress spokesman for Punjab.

He is a revolutionary and a political fanatic who is motivated by a fervent dislike for the British government."

Lalaji was not a Khatri, but as an Arya Samajist. He was opposed to casteism, hierarchy, and untouchability. As a result, he was banished to Mandalay without a trial in 1907. Viceroy Minto enthusiastically consented. While being escorted away, he wrote to his father, "Whatever occurs should be manfully endured."

Savarkar picked the year 1907 for the publication of his book since it was the fiftieth anniversary of the great rebellion. As a result, the British forbade the book, and it became a must-read for all Indian revolutionaries, including Madame Cama, Lala Har Dayal, Bhagat Singh, and Netaji Subhas Chandra Bose.

British intelligence could only get their hands on one chapter of the book when Savarkar released it. And what they discovered astounded them. A report on this first chapter by an official with the Government of Bombay's Home Department states, clearly alarmed:

The [chapter] is only a small fragment of a book containing nearly 470 pages, each page redolent of the most inflammatory language with quotations from English authors describing the most pathetic and pitiably tragic scenes and so forth.

He was no idle armchair historian. The work was also outlawed by the government for the next forty years.

Savarkar to confront a painful fact from 1857 history

The colonial regime purposefully and systematically demilitarised Indians. Further rebellion was almost impossible unless that condition was reversed.

When British historians and their Indian adherents consistently referred to the 1857 rebellion as a "mutiny," Savarkar argued that it was a "revolution." He penned, *"The history of the tremendous Revolution that was enacted in the year 1857 has never been written in this scientific spirit by an author, Indian or foreign."*

Savarkar pertains to the spirit of science rather than the spirit of nationalism or patriotism. What historian Savarkar sought was history as it happened, not eulogy. Only through understanding the past rationally and objectively can it be used to comprehend the present and prepare for the future. Otherwise, one could be living in a lunatic's utopia.

If there are any doubts about Savarkar's attitude toward Muslims, his book on the 1857 insurrection, The First Indian War of Independence, should dispel them. He 'hailed the rebellion as a magnificent example of Hindu-Muslim cooperation' and 'showered lavish praise on the Muslim heroes of 1857, including Awadh monarch Wajid Ali and Rohilkhand rebel chieftain Khan Bahadur Khan.'

The Prevention of Seditious Meetings Act of 1907

The Prevention of Seditious Meetings Act 1907, an Act to make better provision for the prevention of public meetings likely to promote sedition or cause a disturbance of public tranquillity, was a 1907 act of the Imperial Legislative Council of the British Raj that empowered the government to prohibit political gatherings.

Shyamji Krishnavarma moved his headquarters to Paris in 1907

Shyamji Krishna Varma, a fervent patriot, formed the Indian Home Rule Society, India House, and The Indian Sociologist in London. The monthly Indian Sociologist became a forum for nationalist ideas, and he criticised British rule in India through the Indian Home Rule Society. Varma, the first President of the Bombay Arya Samaj, admired Dayanand Saraswati and inspired Veer Savarkar, a member of India House in London. Verma was also the Divan of a number of Indian states.

Varma was born in modern-day Gujarat in 1857 and completed his education in India before going on to teach Sanskrit at Oxford University. Varma was a barrister in London until the Inner Temple prevented him from practising law in 1905 on grounds of sedition for writing against the colonial authorities. The Honourable Society of the Inner Temple is one of London's four professional societies for barristers and judges. So, the transfer was significant. In response to British criticism, Varma relocated his base from England to Paris and resumed his movement. However, with the onset of World War II, he relocated to Geneva, Switzerland and spent the rest of his life there.

Shyamji Krishna Varma's health was often poor in the 1920s. Although he continued to publish The Indian Sociologist in Geneva, his ill health prevented him from doing so after September 1922. On March 30, 1930, he passed away in a hospital in Geneva.

The British government tried to keep the news of his passing secret. Although Shyamaji Krishna Varma did not live to see India become independent from British rule, he made pre-paid arrangements with Geneva's municipal government, Ville de Geneve, and St. Georges Cemetery to preserve his and his wife's ashes (*Asthis*) at the cemetery for 100 years and to send their urns to India whenever India becomes independent. His ashes finally arrived in India on August 22, 2003, 55 years after independence, when the then Chief Minister of Gujarat, Narendra Modi, received them from the Swiss government. A memorial called *Kranti Teerth* dedicated to him was built and inaugurated in 2010 near Mandvi.

Muzaffarpur – The Plot that Shook the Colonial Foundations

Anushilon Samiti proceeded in their efforts to neutralise Kingsford after the original unsuccessful assassination attempt by Hem Chandra Das. What happened next will go down in history as one of the greatest stories of bravery and the Indian freedom movement ever told.

Samiti dispatched a two-man reconnaissance party to Muzaffarpur in April 1908. Prafulla Chaki and Khudiram Bose were the two men. The police were suspicious of Barin Ghosh's activities. Calcutta Police were also notified that Kingsford's life was in danger, and the information was conveyed to the Superintendent of Muzaffarpur.

To conceal their genuine identity, the two guys adopted aliases. Prafulla Chaki was renamed "Dinesh Chandra Roy," and Khudiram was renamed "Haren Sarkar."

The CID officer sent from Kolkata to follow them had returned with a letter from Armstrong, the superintendent of Muzaffarpur Police, alleging that the couple had not arrived in Muzaffarpur at all, six hours before the freedom fighters struck.

Prafulla Chaki and Khudiram Bose were hidden in the trees on April 30, 1908, waiting for Kingsford's vehicle to pass them by. On that fateful night, Kingsford's carriage was just behind a very similar-looking carriage occupied by the wife and daughter of Pringle Kennedy, a famous Muzaffarpur Bar pleader.

It was a dark night with terrible visibility. As the single-horse pulled carriage approached the eastern gate of Kingsford's complex, two men went up to it and hurled bombs at it, mistaking it for the Magistrate's carriage. There was a huge explosion, and the destroyed cabin of the carriage, as well as the ladies who had been injured, were subsequently discovered.

Miss Kennedy, the daughter, died of her injuries within hours, and Mrs Kennedy survived until the morning of May 2nd; she also died of her injuries.

Khudiram Bose was apprehended at the Waini railway station. On the following day, May 2nd, 1908, he was brought to Muzaffarpur station. The journey began on May 21, 1908. It is important to note that all of Khudiram's defence attorneys were working for gratis. Khudiram was sentenced to death by the judge. On August 11, 1908, an order was issued to carry out the death penalty. He was 18 years and 8 months old on the day he was hanged.

Student protests erupted on Kolkata's streets but to no avail.

Khudiram Bose

CHAPTER - IX

TILAK BACKED KHUDIRAM BOSE AND PRAFULLA CHAKI'S EFFORTS

Khudiram Bose's incident jolted the entire nation, and it became a subject of debate all over, eliciting various opinions. Mohandas Gandhi condemned the violence and expressed his condolences for the deaths of two innocent women. Whereas on the other hand, Bal Gangadhar Tilak defended Prafulla and Khudiram and espoused swaraj.

Tilak faced his second sedition trial in 1908 for defending Khudiram Bose and Prafulla Chaki, who attempted to blow up and assassinate British Judge Magistrate Kingsford. This time, Lokmanya Tilak was protected by the young barrister Mohamad Ali Jinnah, who decided to prosecute his own case once the bail petition was rebuffed. Tilak lost the case and was sentenced to six years imprisonment by Justice Davar, the same man who had granted bail to Tilak ten years before (Burma).

Soon after Justice Davar sentenced Tilak to six years of imprisonment in Mandalay, Imperial Britain knighted Justice Davar. Dinshaw Davar was elevated to the rank of Sir Dinshaw Davar.

Bombay's first political strike took place in 1908

Bombay textile workers strike 1908 took place in Mumbai city, Maharashtra.

The mill and textile workers in Bombay had an active role in the freedom struggle. The Bombay textile workers' strike of 1908 is one of the most famous strikes that the country faced during the first half of the 20th century. It took place when Lokmanya Tilak was sentenced to imprisonment for "sedition." To show their resentment against Tilak's imprisonment, the mill workers went on strike. When Tilak was sentenced to 6 years of imprisonment, the city of Bombay shut down. On 22nd July 1908, the markets in Bombay were shut and remained so for a week. The strike by the mill workers continued for almost a week. The authorities felt so threatened by the strike that they called the army. The violence that was unleashed caused the death of sixteen people, while fifty were heavily injured. Other mill workers, such as those from Mulji Jetha Market, also joined the strike witnessing the violence.

Vinayak Damodar Savarkar's the Indian War of Independence of the 1857 revolt was first published in 1909

The month of May 1907 commemorates the 50th anniversary of the War of 1857. It was hailed as the tremendous crushing of the Indian rebellion in London. In London, a drama portrayed Rani Lakshmibai and Peshwa Nanasaheb II as bandits and butchers. In response, Vinayak Savarkar organised a meeting on May 10, 1907, to commemorate the 1857 rebellion as the first fight for Indian freedom. Around 200 Indian students from all around Europe attended. The participants fasted, pledged devotion to the nation, paid homage to the 1857 warriors, and wore a badge on their chests honouring the Indian warriors. This enraged several Englishmen, resulting in scuffles. When some Indian students wore the badges to class, the English students and lecturers chastised them.

After examining the history of the 1857 Mutiny, Savarkar wrote, "The History of the War for Indian Independence," and he was one of the first to refer to it as India's First War for Independence. Because of its inflammatory nature, the book was banned across the British Empire, but Madame Bhikaji Cama was able to get it published in France, the Netherlands, and Germany.

Vinayak spent the first six months of his stay in London translating the autobiography of the Italian revolutionary Giuseppe Mazzini into Marathi. The book quickly became a best-seller in Maharashtra, selling over 2000 copies in the first three months. It served as an inspiration to many future Indian rebels.

Vinayak then set himself on the task of writing a detailed history of the 1857 struggle for independence. In London, he had access to several original letters, documents, and hundreds of books and references, particularly at the British Museum. After more than a year of intensive investigation, he completed the manuscript for his famous book – "The First War of Indian Independence" in Marathi.

Vinayak anticipated a moratorium on the book because of its fiery nature. So, he sent a copy of his work to his brother in Nashik. The Crime Branch searched every printing factory in Nashik but was unable to locate the text. Vinayak's brother Babarao had mailed it to a friend in Paris, who had then forwarded it to Germany. However, due to the lack of certain Devanagari script blocks and fonts, it could not be published in either of the locations. It was, therefore, translated into English by W. B. Phadke under the supervision of Aiyer. Unfortunately, it failed to be printed in England or France due to the CID's strenuous efforts. The book's copies were sent to France and preserved in Sardar Singh Rana's home. With the launch of the book, the book's popularity grew steadily. The book was also distributed in India, Japan, China, and the United States. The book has been adapted and republished in several languages. Madam Cama and MPT Acharya translated it into French, whereas, E. Perion, a French revolutionary, wrote the prologue for the same.

Generations of subsequent insurgents have been inspired by the novel. It was a major source of inspiration for the 1914-15 Ghadar Revolution. The book had been examined by all of the leaders of the Komagata Maru revolt of the Ghadar Party. The more the British colonial government opposed the book, the more popular it became, and it became a kind of Bhagwad Gita among the revolutionaries. Its second and third editions were printed by Madam Cama and Lala Hardayal and were distributed among the Gadar Party members, which ignited the flame of revolution in them, and these soldiers revolted against the British government. Shaheed-e-Azam Bhagat Singh printed this book in Lahore in the year 1928 and widely publicized it; it was its fourth edition. The fifth edition of "Indian Independence Summer: 1857" was published in Japan by Shri

Rash Behari Bose and distributed amongst the members of the Indian National Army. It is said that the inspiration from this book lay behind the formation of the Rani Lakshmi Bai Regiment.

The book was banned for 38 years. Madam Cama was the possessor of the authentic Marathi manuscript. During World War I, it was given to D. Y. Coutchino, an Abhinav Bharat member. He later fled Portugal with the manuscript and arrived in the United States. For 38 years, he kept the text safe in Washington, where he was a professor. Following India's independence, he delivered the text to Ramlal Vajpayee and Dr Moonje, who, in turn, returned it to Savarkar.

Savarkar had also completed another work of his, History of the Sikhs, by 1909. It was dispatched to India, but the Indian Post Office suppressed it.

Morley-Minto Reforms

The Morley-Minto Reform was a different name for the Indian Council Act of 1909, which was named for the Secretary of State and the Viceroy. The membership of the national and provincial legislative councils was increased as a result of this act. The number of elected members on these councils, however, was less than half of the entire membership. It should also be noted that the elected members were chosen by landlords, groups of traders and industrialists, colleges, and local governments rather than by the general public. As part of these reforms, the British instituted communal electorates. This was done to sow discord between Hindus and Muslims. Some council seats were set aside for Muslims to be chosen by Muslim voters. As a result, Lord Minto became known as the father of the Communal Electorate in India.

By doing so, the British attempted to isolate Muslims from the nationalist cause by treating them differently than the rest of the country. They taught the Muslims that their interests were distinct from those of the rest of India. To undermine the nationalist cause, the British began to pursue a continuous policy of encouraging communalism in India.

We are well acquainted that the British adopted the "Divide and Rule" principle. How did they manage it? The following are excerpts from Durga Das's "Introduction to Indian Constitution." They accomplished this through the use of legal acts, statutes, and reforms. Morley Minto reforms and the Indian Councils Act were introduced by the British in 1909. This statute introduced the concept of distinct representation of Muslims for the first time. This provided impetus to the Muslim League, which later demanded the establishment of the state of Pakistan. The then-British Prime Minister, Mr. Ramsay MacDonald, issued the "Communal Award" in 1932-33, which provided for distinct electorates for not just Muslims, but also Sikhs, Indian Christians, Anglo-Indians, Europeans, and Dalits. They intended to continue their control by dividing the public on some or other subject.

Veer Savarkar organised armed revolts against the Morley-Minto reforms, which granted separate electorates for Muslims and other minorities in India, in 1909. He passionately opposed such suggestions, believing that democracy should not be harmed by having so many separate electorates.

The Hindu Mahasabha (formally Akhil Bharat Hind Mahsabh or All-India Hindu Grand-Assembly) is an Indian political party.

Following the founding of the All India Muslim League in 1906 and the British India government's creation of a distinct Muslim electorate under the Morley-Minto reforms of 1909, the organisation was founded to preserve the interests of the Hindu population.

Madanlal Dhingra, a Savarkar follower, shot Sir Wyllie

Curzon Wyllie, a British Army officer and political Aide-de-Camp to the Secretary of State for India, was assassinated by Madanlal Dhingra, a close friend of Savarkar in London. The event took place on July 1, 1909, at the Indian National Association's annual celebration. Dhingra's first target was Lord Curzon, the man responsible for Bengal's partition. Dhingra had pursued him a few days before, but his efforts had been in vain. Dhingra then decided to assassinate Wyllie. Dhingra attempted to shoot himself as Wyllie fell but was overwhelmed by several of the attendees.

He claimed that he did not regret killing Curzon Wyllie because he had played a role in freeing India from barbaric British rule. Dhingra was executed on August 17, 1909. At the execution, his executioner gave him an unreasonably and inhumanely brutal lengthy drop of eight feet three inches. The causes for this are unknown and may only be guessed upon.

Savarkar was going through a rough patch at the time. A few days before Wyllie's assassination, India House was closed down.

He then spent a few days at Bipin Chandra Pal's house. At the same time, he was under the CID's surveillance. The British intelligence knew very well that Savarkar was the brains behind the India House members' activities, although they lacked evidence. Throughout June 1909, the CID, the Bombay government, and the Home Department deliberated over Savarkar's extradition. However, because the case against him was weak, they decided to gather evidence in London for the case being prepared against him in India. Savarkar was already in a state of mental anguish. In June, his elder brother Babarao was arrested and condemned to transit to Andaman cellular prison. His entire estate was confiscated. It was a difficult moment. The issues came down on him all at once. Deprived of food, money, and rest, he travelled from door to door looking for a place to stay. He had to leave two places in one day. Finally, a German landlady offered him a place to stay for a few days. On the 22nd of June, a few days before the Wyllie assassination, Savarkar was also informed that his call for the bar had been postponed because of his "seditious behaviour." He filed an appeal and was subjected to a scathing cross-examination by skilled barristers. The allegations were eventually dropped, and Savarkar was allowed (as a member) to Grey's Inn.

Anant Laxman Kanhere shot Nashik's collector on December 21, 1909

Meanwhile, Abhinav Bharat's revolutionary operations in India persisted. K. G. Khare built and tested bombs at Pen, Maharashtra, using bomb manuals smuggled into the country. And he taught many young rebels to make explosives. The pistols sent with Chaturbhuj by Savarkar were handed over to Patankar and were concealed in Pen. Babarao Savarkar, Savarkar's elder brother, was imprisoned in 1909 for publishing a book of patriotic poems. The British administration of India was concerned about the secret societies run by Babarao in and around Nashik, and hence, arrested him at the first opportunity. Babarao was sentenced to transportation after a trial in Bombay. Jackson, the Nashik collector, was in-charge of Babarao's arrest. Jackson was already infamous, and the villagers held him liable for torturing one advocate, Waman Khare. There were also a few instances where villagers were beaten to a pulp by British officers. As a result, Nashik's political climate has become a hot potato. Jackson's assassination was already on the cards.

Anant Lakshman Kanhere, a 17-year-old teenager, had vowed to assassinate Jackson. Savarkar sent the pistols, which were brought in by Chaturbhuj. Kanhere assassinated Jackson at the Vijayanand Theatre on December 21, 1909. He then tried to shoot himself but was intercepted by deputy collector Khopkar and a man named Mr Jolly.

During the investigation, authorities discovered that the firearms had been sent by Vinayak Savarkar. "Thus, the chain of the Jackson assassination began with Kanhere and concluded with Savarkar in London," writes Dr V. M. Bhat in his book Abhinav Bharat. In Madam Cama's weekly Talwar, Savarkar published an article titled "Martyrs of Nashik."

The Act relating to the Press of 1910

The British Government's approach towards Indian Press varied from time to time. The period from 1908 to 1935 witnessed the enactment of numerous press legislation to curb the anti-British tone of the Indian Press. The resurgence of political terrorism made the British adopt a rigid stand towards the Indian nationalists. Lord Ridley, the Home Member introduced a Bill on 4th February 1910 to arrest the dissemination of anti-government literature. Lord Minto II, the Viceroy of India implemented the Indian Press Act of 1910 on 9th February, Section 12(1) of the Act empowered the Local Governments to issue warrants against any newspaper or book which contained seditious matters, were to be forfeited to his majesty. A large number of nationalist press and political literature were proscribed under the provision of the Indian Press Act of 1910.

Savarkar was appressed in London and hauled to India

For the residents of India House, the year 1909 was exceptionally turbulent. Curzon Wiley was assassinated by Madan Lal Dhingra (1883-1909). Savarkar was widely acknowledged as Dhingra's inspiration. It was the first political assassination of a British officer by Indian resistance outside of India. Savarkar openly endorsed Dhingra's actions and paid him a visit in jail. In August 1909, Dhingra was executed. The police maintained a strong watch on Savarkar. His elder brother, Babarao, had been sentenced to deportation to the Andaman cellular jails a month before. Later, his younger brother, Narayanrao, was apprehended in connection with the bombing of Lord Minto. Savarkar then relocated to Paris. Savarkar spent two months in Paris. He contributed to Madam Cama's Talwar and attempted to recruit people for Abhinav Bharat. By 1909, Paris had become Europe's epicentre for Indian revolutionaries. The Indian community in Paris included affluent pearl merchants, some of whom supported the Indians' revolutionary activities.

On March 13, 1910, he headed towards London. He was apprehended as soon as he got onto the Victoria Station grounds. His bail was denied on April 20th, and he was transported to Brixton jail. The Magistrate ruled on May 12th that Savarkar should be extradited to India.

In a daring escape from 'Morea', a British merchant vessel that was carrying him from Britain to India to start a trial against him for his revolutionary activities. He had jumped into the sea through a porthole and swam to Marseilles. This legendary jump into the Mediterranean Sea on July 9, 1910, is regarded as an act of extraordinary fortitude and conviction.

On the morning of July 7, the ship docked in Marseilles. When the ship docked in Marseilles, he dived into the sea via the porthole at the top of the water closet in the toilet. Despite the British pursuing him, he managed to swim to land. Sadly, his friends, Madame Cama and V. V. Aiyar were late, and Savarkar was detained by the authorities. Because he was detained by the British on foreign soil, it constituted a violation of international law. France strongly objected to this violation of the law, and the matter was heard by the Permanent Court of International Arbitration. The Court noted that because France and Britain were working together on Savarkar's case and his arrest was accomplished without any deception, the British authorities could extradite him to India for trial. However, stories of his bravery spread throughout India, inspiring millions to fight for the cause.

Savarkar landed in Mumbai in July 1910 and was imprisoned in Nashik; rumours of his attempted escape from Marseilles made him a sort of hero. He declined to testify in court, claiming that he was entitled to asylum and safeguards in France. He was eventually charged and sentenced to life in the notorious Andaman and Nicobar Islands' Cellular Jail. On June 27, 1911, Savarkar boarded the vessel *S.S. Maharajah* en route to the Andaman Islands. The Cellular Jail was the Indian replica of Devil's Island, a legendary prison with horrible stories of torture and cruelty.

Europe amidst Savarkar's rebuke

The news of Savarkar's escape was mentioned briefly in the Paris edition of the Daily Mail on July 11th. It created a stir, and the issue was taken up by Jean Jaurès, the French socialist leader. Various European media outlets chastised the British government. The French press, in particular, was emphatic in its condemnation of Savarkar's capture by the British on French soil. The two nations agreed to bring the case to the International Court of Arbitration. The prize was widely condemned in France and the rest of Europe. Furthermore, on the same day that the Hague judgement was issued, the Russian State Duma passed a measure that abolished the right to asylum!

The Valour of Gade Chinnapa Reddy

Gade Chinnapareddy was born in the village Kotha Reddy Palem, Chebrolu Mandal, Guntur district of Andhra Pradesh in the year 1864.

In 1907, he went to a market in Chennai and attended a meeting in which Bal Gangadhar Tilak was addressing the people against colonial rule. It had a great impact on Chinnapa Reddy. After coming back to his village, he gathered all the villagers and began the Non-Cooperation Movement. People of that area used to sing songs about the courage and the spirit of Gade Chinnapa Reddy.

On 18 February 1909, on *Shivratri* day, Gade Chinnapa Reddy decorated and brought a 60 feet Prabha to Kotappakonda, along with his bullocks. Bringing Prabha and bullocks to Kotappakonda on Shivratri day is a ritual followed by the nearby village people. The bullocks brought by Chinnapa Reddy were not found in that huge crowd. Everyone was searching for the bullocks. But the British police shot those bullocks very cruelly and arrested Chinnapa Reddy as he was participating in the Non-Co-operation Movement. People around him in that area shouted slogans against the British. The British police started firing. In that encounter, two young men and two policemen died.

As a result of this incident, the British government filed cases against Chinnapa Reddy and hundreds of his followers. Chinnapa Reddy appealed in the Madras High court and said, "If you want to hang me, hang me. But leave all others."

On 3 August 1910, the Madras High Court judge, Manro, declared for Chinnapa Reddy to be hanged and the other 21 people to be sent out of the country. He kissed the hangman's rope with a smile on his face for the sake of freedom. Even the villagers never lost their courage and sang about his Glory - "*Sai Sai Raa Chinnapa Reddy – Nee Peru Bangaru Kaddi.*"

This story hopes to inculcate the spirit of patriotism in future generations.

Batukeshwar Dutt was born on November 18, 1910

Batukeshwar Dutt was born on November 18, 1910, in Oari village, Burdwan district, West Bengal, to Goshtha Bihari Dutt. He graduated from Kanpur's PPN high school and was also known as BK Dutt, Battu, and Mohan. He was a close companion of independence fighters such as Chandrashekhar Azad and Bhagat Singh, whom he met in Kanpur in 1924 while working for the Hindustan Socialist Republican Association (HSRA).

Kashi – one of the oldest living cities in the world

In 1910, the British made Varanasi (also known as Kashi and Benares) a new Indian state, with Ramnagar (on the opposite bank) as headquarters but with no jurisdiction over the city of Varanasi. Under British rule also it remained a commercial and religious centre.

Varanasi had spearheaded the 1857 Mutiny. Kashi Naresh or the king of Kashi still resides in the Ramnagar fort, East of Varanasi across the Ganga. He is the scion of the Varanasi royal family and continues the traditions of his forefathers.

In 1947, after Indian independence, the Varanasi state became part of the state of Uttar Pradesh.

The Lord Hardinge of Penshurst was appointed as Viceroy of India on November 23, 1910

Lord Hardinge was India's Viceroy from 1910 until 1916. The following significant events occurred during his tenure: the 1911 Delhi Durbar, which forced the British to relocate the capital of their government in India from Calcutta to Delhi, and the partition of Bengal, which was finally reversed in 1911 by Lord Hardinge in the face of unrelenting opposition. The Delhi Conspiracy Case (1912), Mohandas Gandhi's departure to South Africa, the outbreak of World War I (1914), Tilak's formation of the Home Rule League, the establishment of Banaras Hindu University, the establishment of the Ghadar Party, the Komagata Maru incident, Foundation of Indian Independence League at Berlin, (1914) etc.

A statue of Lady Hardinge in a sitting posture can be found on the campus of the Lady Hardinge Medical College and Hospital, which was founded in Delhi in 1916, the same year the Hardinge Park, named after her husband, was launched in Patna in a lavish ceremony. The park was renamed 'Shaheed Veer Kunwar Singh Azadi Park' after the statue was removed, although it is still referred to as 'Hardinge Park' by old-timers and locals.

In late 2017, one of the remaining Raj-era relics, the pedestal on which Hardinge's renowned statue previously stood, was also dismantled. In April 2018, an equestrian statue of Veer Kunwar Singh, renowned for his valour during the 1857 Revolt, was relocated to the park from a nearby public roundabout.

Karl Marx's grandson fought for Savarkar against the British in the International Court of Justice

Vinayak Damodar Savarkar may have always been demonised by Marxists – including historians and the intelligentsia – for his views on the ideology of Hindutva, but it was none other than Karl Marx's grandson who defended him after his daring escape to France from British captivity.

Jean-Laurent-Frederick Longuet (1876–1938), a French socialist, politician, journalist and lawyer, not only stood in the International Court of Justice in The Hague to defend Savarkar but also praised him for his bravery, patriotism and intellect.[7]

Marx's grandson was born to Charles and Jenny Longuet, Karl Marx's daughter, in London. The family later moved to France, where Jean Longuet worked as a journalist and got trained as a lawyer. He was also the founder-editor of the French newspaper Le Populaire and was a prominent socialist leader in France.

Arguments in the case began on February 14 1911 and ended on February 17 1911. The decision was delivered on 24 February 1911 in favour of Britain. Savarkar was later imprisoned by the British at the Cellular Jail in Andaman, infamously known as 'Kala Paani.'

---

7   https://theprint.in/india/how-karl-marxs-grandson-fought-for-savarkar-against-british-in-international-court-of-justice/666966/

1911 - Savarkar awarded life transportation

Savarkar was notified of the Hague Tribunal's decision and that his sentence of 50 years had been confirmed. He was handed an iron badge with the year 1960 etched on it to commemorate his liberation. Savarkar requested that his two sentences be run concurrently. However, the application was turned down. He was sent to Madras by train in June 1911. And on June 27th, *S.S. Maharajah* set sail for Port Blair in the Andamans, popularly known as the 'Kala Pani.'

In the Andamans, Savarkar was the only person sentenced to double life imprisonment for a total of 50 years. Given the severe conditions in jail, it was difficult to stay for another 50 years. On this, Savarkar said to the British superintendent, "Good! At the very least, the British government has agreed to the Hindu theory of rebirth while rejecting the Christian doctrine of resurrection for this reason." The superintendent was at a loss for an appropriate response.

As he approached the Cellular Jail, his thoughts turned to how these islands may serve as outposts for a Free India.

It was also prophetic in a manner, for when Netaji launched his lengthy armed battle, he initially took the Andaman and Nicobar Islands, which he instantly called Shahid and Swaraj. The Cellular Jail was a true hell on earth, the kind of place you wouldn't even want your worst enemy to be in.

The jailor, Barrie, despised the revolutionaries and subjected them to the most heinous torture imaginable. They were chained to the oil mill like animals and forced to work all day. The horrors of the Cellular Jail were comparable to those of Auschwitz, Devil's Island, and Russia's Gulags.

Imagine experiencing a life of solitary confinement for not just one or two years, but for 12 years; indeed, that is how long Savarkar was imprisoned. Savarkar's hands bled when he was assigned the task of chopping coconuts with a heavy mallet. He was tethered to the oil mill and forced to work long hours. Despite all of these humiliations, Savarkar bore them with courage, tolerance, and character.

Savarkar not only endured the humiliations heaped on him, but he also boosted the spirits of his fellow inmates. Savarkar's mere presence raised the spirits of most of those who were living a life depleted of energy.

Meanwhile, Savarkar went on to teach political science, economics, and constitutional law to the convicts. He campaigned with the government to protect inmates' rights and provide them with basic necessities. He emphasised the importance of education, particularly in economics and constitutional law, to the convicts. *"Knowledge without action was lame, and action without knowledge was limited,"* he thought.

Strategic alliance Besant – Malviya

Annie Besant met Pandit Madan Mohan Malaviya in April 1911, and they resolved to work together to establish a common Hindu university in Varanasi. Besant and the trustees of the Central Hindu College, which she created in 1898, likewise consented to the Government of India's need for the college to become a component of the new university. In July 1911, the huge educational business was fully operational. The university's needs and goals were explained in a redesigned prospectus.

On July 15, 1911, Pandit Madan Mohan Malaviyaji appealed to the public for a crore (ten million) rupees for the creation of the university. Deputations were formed to raise cash, and they travelled to Calcutta and several locations in the United Provinces, Bihar, and Punjab. Over a few months, the public pledged almost thirty lac (three million) rupees in donations.

Delhi as new capital plan announced on December 12, 1911, during Delhi Darbar

The British first settled in Surat on the West Coast when the Mughal Emperor Jahangir let them start a factory in 1618. The British called their first acquisitions Western Presidency. When half a century later the British got control of the islands, which form the modern-day Mumbai city, the capital was moved. Thus came about the Bombay Presidency in

1687. In effect, this was also the capital of the East India Company (EIC), which leased these islands from the British Crown. Until 1753, Bombay was the de facto EIC capital, after which the control transferred to Calcutta for almost a century and a half.

During the Delhi Darbar on December 12, 1911, the British Emperor made an announcement. He declared that Delhi would be the new capital of the crown's Indian province. This unequivocal proclamation of intent to relocate the capital from Calcutta (now Kolkata) surprised the nation.

Delhi was a vital stop on the subcontinent's commercial routes and a coveted seat of government for various empires that ruled India in the past. The strategic location of Delhi, as well as the weariness that had set in from the escalating violence of nationalists against the British in Bengal, prompted them to rush at the opportunity to develop Delhi for the future. Lord Hardinge hoped that they would be able to undo the Partition of Bengal and flee.

As a result, during the Delhi Durbar on December 12, 1911, George V, Emperor of India, and Queen Mary laid the foundation stone for Delhi. Lord Hardinge, the Viceroy of India, commented on the need to relocate the capital in a letter addressed from Shimla to London on August 25, 1911. That infuriated Lord Curzon, the former Viceroy who had guaranteed that the Prince of Wales laid the groundwork for Queen Victoria's memorial in 1905. (As she had died in 1901).

In Delhi, construction on the new capital began. The work was allocated to British architects Sir Edwin Lutyens and Sir Herbert Baker. They chose the southern plains beyond Shahajanabad's historic walled city as their location. In contrast to the previous walled city, the new capital's roads were to be massive and wide.

The region was first designated as a district province of Punjab. Lord Hardinge hoped that "New Delhi" would be completed in four years. Then, all of a sudden, Britain was engulfed in World War II. WWI depleted scarce resources. With the coffers empty, it took more than 20 years to complete the construction of what became known as "New Delhi" (in 1927).

It was 1931 when the British could formally launch the new capital in New Delhi. On 13 February 1931, Viceroy and Governor-General of India Lord Irwin declared Delhi to be the capital of British India.

Bomb attack on Lord Hardinge at Chandani Chowk in Delhi in 1912

On the brisk morning of December 23, 1912, Delhi was decked out to greet then-Viceroy Lord Hardinge as the capital was transferred from Calcutta to Delhi. A small woman could be seen waiting with the crowd to meet the Viceroy at a building in Chandni Chowk, and then a bomb exploded. Basant Biswas, a 16-year-old boy, had disguised himself as a woman and hurled a rudimentary bomb at the elephant carrying the Viceroy. Hardinge escaped unscathed. Rash Behari was the mastermind behind the attack and assisted in the fabrication of the bomb.

Following this, the Ghadar Revolt in Punjab and the Hindu German conspiracy in 1915 [the two are so closely interwoven in actual action that it is impossible to separate the two, although they came from different locations and for different reasons]. Rashbehari Basu commanded the latter, assisted by Sachindranath Sanyal, Girija Babu (Hindu Bengalis), Vishnu Ganesh Pingley (Marathi), and Kartar Singh Sarabha (Punjabi).

Following the event, efforts were undertaken to eradicate the Bengali and Punjabi revolutionary underground, which had been under great pressure for a long period.

The Mangadh Hill massacre took place on November 17, 1913

Bharat appears to have forgotten the Mangadh Massacre, which occurred on November 17, 1913, nearly six years before the Amritsar Jallianwala Bagh Massacre. Theresa May, the British Prime Minister, expressed regret for the Jallianwala Bagh atrocity but said nothing about the equally horrible slaughter of 1500 Bhils in Mangadh.

The Mangadh hill in Rajasthan's Banswara district, on the boundary between southern Rajasthan and Gujarat, has become a symbol of tribal identity and historical sacrifice. The name "Mangadh Dham" was given to it by the locals.

Govind Giri was born in Dungarpur, Rajasthan, to a Banjara family. He began his career as a bonded labourer in the princely kingdom of Santrampur. He recognised that the socioeconomic situation and alcohol addiction were the primary causes of the Bhils' suffering.

In 1908, Govind Giri founded the Bhagat movement. Among the Bhils, he promoted vegetarianism and abstinence from alcohol and gambling. He urged the Bhils to oppose bonded labour, demand a fair wage, and fight for their rights. The kings of Dungarpur, Banswara, and Santrampur became highly concerned about the Bhagat movement and Govind Giri, whom the Bhils began referring to as Govind Guru.

In October 1913, Govind Giri and his followers began gathering at Mangarh. They were supposed to go to a religious fair in the Indian month of *Karthik*, organise a massive 'havan' (fire rites), and take the pledge. More than a million Bhils gathered in Mangarh for the holy event. Govind Giri (Govind Guru) raised awareness among the local Bhils about the need for improved wages from the rulers and the British. When the Bhils refused to surrender and disperse, the throng was actually shelled.

The social reformer, along with thousands of his followers, was apprehended at the 'havan' location in Mangarh. He was condemned to life in jail, but due to his good behaviour, he was released in 1919. He was barred from entering the princely territories of Dungarpur, Banswara, and Santrampur, where he had a significant following. In 1931, he passed away in Limbdi.

As a gesture of gratitude to the 1,507 tribals who were slain in the liberation movement against the British in 1913, Shri Narendra Modi dedicated a Govind Guru Smriti Van to the "social and religious reformist" with 1,507 trees, and a university named Govind Giri University was constructed in Godhra in 2015.

Mandalay jail release

In Mandalay, the man of action remained absorbed in reading, discovering new things, and pondering the true message of the Gita. The Geeta Rahasya was a beneficial result of this persistent reading and meditation. Tilak was notified that his exile had ended on June 8, 1914.

As the date of Tilak's release from prison approached in July 1914, the government of India became concerned about the political ramifications of his release.

Tilak was diagnosed with diabetes while incarcerated at Mandalay. On June 16, 1914, just as World War I was about to begin, he was liberated.

He then attempted to reconcile with Congress and persuade Mohandas Gandhi of the hopelessness of employing nonviolence as a weapon against such a vast empire.

Tilak and Sayajirao planned India's Independence in 1914[8]

Maharaj Sayajirao Gaekwad

---

8 https://timesofindia.indiatimes.com/city/vadodara/when-tilak-planned-indias-independence-with-sayajirao/articleshow/6423044.cms

While the first revolution against the British Empire occurred in 1857, a similar revolt against colonial control was planned for 1914. Only a few are aware that Maharaja Sayajirao Gaekwad, the former ruler of Baroda state, was involved. Gaekwad and freedom fighter Lokmanya Tilak had devised sophisticated preparations to launch an all-out war against the British.

The fact that Gaekwad and Tilak were close colleagues was also kept a closely guarded secret to avoid unwanted attention from the British. The Maratha emperor and Tilak wanted India's independence soon before World War I (WW-I) began in 1914, and Germany was asked for assistance. "In 1914, a huge battle for independence was planned, led by Tilak. The insurrection was conceived in Amritsar, and the objective was to catch the British administrators by surprise. Only 2,000 British men were present in India at that time and Tilak wanted to cash in on that opportunity.

Gaekwad used to travel around Europe frequently, giving the impression that he was engaged in leisure activities. Gaekwad's purpose in touring European countries, on the other hand, was to study the administration there.

Tilak, in fact, used to send Gaekwad to Europe and the United States for research facilities. Between 1897 and 1920, Gaekwad travelled to Europe on an annual basis, and he even visited the United States. The concept was intended to design India's administration and institutions after independence.

Gaekwad and Tilak had known each other since the early twentieth century, but they avoided public meetings to avoid undue attention. Gaekwad's movements and activities were closely monitored by the British. Gaekwad met numerous people in the United States and conducted extensive research into how Americans gained their independence. Such was their conviction that it was determined before WWI that the country would be named India after it gained independence.

If it had happened, Tilak would have been India's first prime minister, and Gaekwad would have been the country's first president.

However, the insurrection was thwarted when two traitors, Buta Singh and Mula Singh, reported the planned uprising to British officers. The government staged an army march in Amritsar as a show of force, which resulted in the postponement of the rebellion. Tilak died in 1920, shortly after WWI ended, putting the Independence War plan on hold.

The Mcmahon border line was created between India and China in 1914

For centuries, Tibet had been an independent territory with little or no Chinese influence or authority. In the 17th century, the Qing dynasty established Chinese sovereignty over Tibet. Tibet declared independence following the fall of the Qing dynasty in 1913.

A demarcation line between the Tibetan Region and British India, known as the 'McMahon Line,' was negotiated at the Shimla conference (October 1913–July 1914), which was attended by Sir Henry McMahon, the Foreign Secretary of British India, and Lonchen Satra, the representative of the government of Tibet.

Although it is currently the effective border between China and India, the Chinese government disputes its legal existence.

Interestingly, while China has acknowledged the McMahon Line as its border with Burma, it refuses to accept it with India because doing so would imply China recognizes Tibet as a separate and independent entity.

In March 2023, the US Senate passed a resolution recognising the McMahon Line as the boundary between China and Arunachal Pradesh and affirming that Arunachal Pradesh is part of India.

CHAPTER - X

1914 – THE FIRST WORLD WAR BEGINS

Germany commenced the First World War in 1914. The Indian revolutionaries were ecstatic. Finally, a strong power had developed which was capable enough of breaking the British backbone. In Berlin, expatriate Indian freedom fighters and patriots successfully petitioned and were granted assurance that Germany would provide finance and arms to freedom fighters and safe travel back home.

On the other hand, in India, one of the key persons entrusted with the task of receiving German money and weapons was the selfsame grandson. In 1914, he sailed to Java to obtain them. His actual name was Narendranath Bhattacharya, but he eventually renamed himself, Manabendranath Roy or M.N. Roy. He ultimately became India's first Communist terrorist, creating the Communist Party of India.

British India (now India, Pakistan, Bangladesh, and Nepal) contributed the most manpower to the war effort of any of the British Empire's colonies and dominions, with about a million and a half Indians serving in the war. As early as August 1914, Indians – not just infantry and cavalry, but also sappers and miners, labourers and followers – were making their way across the once-forbidden *Kalapani*, crossing the seas to join the battle.

According to a Times of India report, India recruited over 1.4 million soldiers and deployed more than 1.3 million of them overseas to fight for the British Empire between 1914 and 1918, saving Britain and her allies from an embarrassing defeat.

During this critical moment, the Indian National Congress publicly supported Britain. When the conflict broke out, Gandhi was in England, where he began forming a medical corps similar to the one he headed with the assistance of the British during the 1896 Boer War. Gandhi personally studied nursing, but he became ill with pleurisy and had to return to India by January 1915. So, in essence, the man who would go on to head India's freedom fight was denying the Dutch Boers the same freedom.

The Komagata Maru incident took place on May 23, 1914

Less than two decades after the historical Battle of Saragarhi, the British Empire's vaunted soldiers were pitted against them in the Komagata Maru event of 1914.

The significance of this event stems from the fact that it sparked an explosive scenario in Punjab. The Komagata Maru was the name of a ship transporting 370 passengers from Singapore to Vancouver, mostly Sikh and Punjabi Muslim would-be immigrants. After two months of suffering and uncertainty, they were sent back by Canadian authorities.

It was widely assumed that the Canadian authorities were swayed by the British government. In September 1914, the ship finally anchored in Calcutta. The convicts refused to board the train going to Punjab. 22

people were killed in the ensuing clash with the police in Budge Budge, near Calcutta.

The Ghadar leaders were enraged by this, and with the commencement of the war, they were determined to mount a violent attack on British control in India. They encouraged fighters to travel to India. Raghubar Dayal Gupta and Kartar Singh Saraba left for India. Rashbehari Bose and Sachin Sanyal, both Bengal revolutionaries, were approached and asked to lead the effort. Political scumbags were determined to raise donations.

The Punjab political feuds of January-February 1915 featured some fresh social content. Before fleeing with the cash, the raiders targeted money lenders and debt records in at least three of the five major cases.

As a result, an explosive situation developed in Punjab. The Ghadrites set February 21, 1915, as the date for an armed insurrection in the garrisons of Ferozepur, Lahore, and Rawalpindi.

Due to treachery, the plot was thwarted at the last minute. The authorities acted quickly, supported by the Defence of India Rules, 1915. Rebel regiments were disbanded, leaders were imprisoned and deported, and 45 were executed. Rashbehari Bose fled to Japan (where he and Abani Mukherji made numerous attempts to send weaponry), while Sachin Sanyal was imprisoned for life.

The nationalist reaction to British involvement in the war was three-fold:

(i)   As a matter of duty, the moderates, including Gandhi, supported the empire in the war.

(ii)   The extremists, like Tilak, backed the war effort on the misguided notion that Britain would reward India's allegiance with gratitude in the form of self-government.

(iii)   The revolutionaries were determined to take advantage of the opportunity to conduct a battle against British control and liberate the country.

The Indian backers of British war operations were oblivious to the fact that the imperialist nations were fighting to protect their own territories and markets.

Banaras Hindu University Foundation

Sir Hartcourt Butler submitted the Banaras Hindu University Bill to the Imperial Legislative Council in March 1915. The Bill was referred to a Select Committee, and it was brought up for final reading before the Imperial Legislative Council, along with the Select Committee's report. The Imperial Legislative Council passed the bill on 1st October 1915 and the same day, it received the assent of the Governor-General and Viceroy of India and became law.

The cornerstone for the University of Nagwa, located in the southern portion of Varanasi, opposite the Fort of Ramnagar, was laid soon after. The necessary property was secured at this location for the laying of the foundation stone, and extensive arrangements were made for the ceremony. On 4th February 1916, Lord Hardinge, the then Governor-General and Viceroy, laid the basic foundation of the University in the presence of a distinguished assembly of Governors, Princes, and the elite of India. This historic day will always stay remembered in our country's history.

Various spiritual rituals and ceremonies, such as *Vastu Puja, Rudra Yagna, Gayatri Japa, Puja to Guru Granth Sahib*, Jain ceremonies, and so on, were performed in the week preceding and four days after the 4th of February, 1916. On the 6th of February, Gandhi, who had recently returned to India from South Africa and had travelled to Benaras to attend the Foundation stone laying event at the invitation of Malaviyaji, addressed the gathering. The closing ceremonies took place on February 8, 1916, on the occasion of *Vasant Panchami* Day.

The Banaras Hindu University Act of 1915 was brought into action on April 1, 1916, by a notification published in the Gazette of India on March 25, 1916. Dr Sir Sunder Lal was appointed the first Vice-Chancellor.

Gandhi returned to India in January 1915

In the early 1900s, Indian politicians planned to depose the British by the 1920s, using ruthless armed force. However, Gandhi's arrival delayed liberation by more than two decades, allowing the cunning British enough time to divide the leadership, people, and, eventually, the nation.

Gandhi was greeted as a hero when he arrived at the Apollo Bunder in Bombay on January 9, 1915. Three days later, he was honoured by the people of Bombay at a lavish reception held in the opulent home of Bombay industrialist, Jehangir Petit. The government of India, along with the people of India, honoured Gandhi.

Who was this great Mahatma who was so revered and feared by the British that even the Prime Minister/King of the United Kingdom, as well as the racist South African government, allowed him an audience? The word about the newly arrived "messiah" was all over the papers.

Gokhale also urged Gandhi that, because he had been gone from India for so long, he should travel across the country to better comprehend it. He also asked Gandhi for a guarantee that he would not say anything about Indian issues for a year until his exploration of India was over.

Such was the curiosity sparked by the great Mahatma's never-ending promotion that multitudes lined up along railway tracks, doing *namaste*. It was a media frenzy.

Gokhale died on February 19, 1915

Gopal Krishna Gokhale died on February 19, 1915, at an early age of 49 due to excessive stress. Both Mohammed Jinnah and Mohandas Gandhi had Gopal Krishna Gokhale as their mentor in the field of politics.

Gandhi was taken aback. He mourned Gokhale's death by staying barefoot for a year, and out of respect for his mentor's memory, he made another attempt to gain admission to the Servants of India Society.

The Ghadar Mutiny (The Ghadar Conspiracy) was a plan in February 1915

The Ghadar revolutionaries, who were largely headquartered in the United States and Canada, had created an organisation to guarantee India's independence. The Hindu Bengalis sowed the seeds of the Ghadar revolt in the twentieth century. In 1907, Taraknath Das and Khagendra Chandra Das, among others, founded the Indian Independence League in the United States, and their first mission was to assist underprivileged Hindus and Sikhs on the West Coast of the United States [in San Francisco] 1907. This was going to be the first step in the Ghadar Revolt's destiny.

Sachindra Nath Sanyal was a prominent player in the Gadar party conspiracy. It was an anti-British revolt modelled after the 1857 Great Uprising. The scheme began to take shape with the outbreak of World War I, between the Ghadar Party in the United States, the Berlin Committee in Germany, and the Indian revolutionaries underground in British India. Large quantities of weaponry and ammunition were expected to be smuggled into India in order to spark a pan-Indian anti-British revolt. However, because of organised intelligence input and a spy network, the British learned of the movement and repressed it in February 1915.

Central figures were apprehended, as were revolts in local units and disturbed armed organisations within India. Sanyal went underground in order to avoid British intervention and to continue the liberation movement.

Sanyal, on the other hand, was apprehended and sentenced to prison in Andaman and Nicobar Islands Cellular prison. He penned his well-known book, *Bandi Jeevan*, (A Life of Captivity, 1922) there. He had been released from jail on several occasions since then. His misery in prison did not prevent him from continuing his subversive operations after he was released.

Lala Hardayal, Ramchandra, Bhagwan Singh, Kartar Singh Saraba, Barkatullah, and Bhai Parmanand were the driving forces behind the Ghadar Party. The Ghadrites planned to incite an uprising in India. Two events in 1914 fueled their plans: the Komagata Maru incident and the onset of World War I.

Rash Behari arrived in Tokyo in June 1915

During World War I, he organised a significant attempt to dislodge British rule from Indian soil, which is now officially recognised as the Hindu-German Conspiracy. It failed, and Rashbehari Bose was compelled to flee to Japan as P N Thakur, a relative of the great poet Rabindranath Thakur. He attempted to send weaponry and ammunition to his revolutionary companions from Singapore, but his machinations were discovered and foiled by the British. Rashbehari evaded Japanese authorities with the help of Toyama Mitsuru and the Soma family of Nakamuraya when the British forced the Japanese to issue a deportation order.

He married Toshiko, the eldest daughter of the Soma family, and managed to withstand the agony of several years of relentless hide and seek, becoming naturalised and, for the first time, affording the safety of a permanent home.

He arrived in Japan penniless in 1915, with a Japanese vocabulary of 3-4 words, and mastered Japanese in four and a half months. Subsequently, he tirelessly built up contacts among the highest echelons of Japan, became a soft power there, kept himself abreast of developments in India, and continuously organised and assisted the Indians living in Japan, particularly students and freedom fighters.

As a result, he served as India's unofficial ambassador in every position. These non-military initiatives, which he carried out in Japan over a two-decade period, laid the groundwork for his last onslaught during WWII.

Bagha Jatin died on September 10, 1915

Bagha Jatin is a nickname given to Bengal's great revolutionary, Jatindranath Mukhopadhyay. His name is associated with an armed insurrection against the British government.

In the aftermath of the First World War, in 1914, the revolutionaries got a huge opportunity of getting a cache of arms. This is known in history as the Rodda Company arms heist. Shrish Chandra Sarkar used to work in the Rodda Company in its Dalhousie branch. He got the news that the company was supposed to import 202 boxes of arms on the ship called *S.S. Tactician* on 26th August 1914. Shrish used bullock carts to carry the arms and absconded with the cart containing 50 Mauser pistols and ammunition. This heist became sensational at that time and police tried in vain to recover the arms. The arms were used for carrying out several assassination bids and daylight robberies for procuring arms. The person who drove the bullock cart was Haridas Dutta of Mukti Sangha. The Statesman described the heist as the "greatest daylight robbery." Haridas Dutta was arrested and put behind bars.

Bagha Jatin devised an armed uprising strategy in 1915 after consulting with members of other secret groups. Attempts were also made to smuggle weaponry and ammunition from Germany, which was Britain's adversary during the war.

In fact, a man called Narendranath Bhattacharya was dispatched to Batavia to contact German officials via their consulate. In fact, Narendranath travelled to Batavia (in South-East Asia) under the alias 'C. Martin.'

Jatin set off for Balasore, in present-day Odisha, with four young revolutionaries called Chittapriya Raychaudhury, Nirendranath Dasgupta, Manoranjan Sengupta, and Jyotish Chandra Pal, where two German ships – Annie Larsen and Maverick – were to arrive with ammunition. To continue their connection, a business called 'Universal Emporium' was established in Balasore, while they relocated to two hideouts between Mahuldiha and Taldiha, mingling with the locals and assisting those in need.

The plan, however, was leaked, and a British police unit led by Charles Target arrived in Balasore to seize the revolutionaries.

On September 9, 1915, the five men laid their final combat ground in a lonely stretch of field near Chashakhand in Balasore. They huddled in the trench, righting their Mauser pistols with the detachable wooden shoulder-stocks to make them look like long-range rifles.

Because of the trench's technical advantages, the injuries began with the police, who clambered up the mound assuming the opponents only possessed revolvers. A bullet struck Chittapriya's chest after nearly an hour of police battalion attempts. Jatin drew him onto his lap, injured in the right hand but still firing with the left. Chittapriya was the first martyr in "The Battle of Budi Balam."

Ammunition was running low, Jyotish was already injured, and Jatin was shot in the abdomen. He told his disciples to surrender and told them, "You are to stay… and convince our brothers that we were not dacoits."

Jatin was brought to the Balasore Government Hospital, where he died the next morning at the age of 35. Before his death, he issued a statement in which he accepted full responsibility for his actions and called for fair treatment of his innocent followers. Two months later, Nirendranath and Manoranjan, who were 23 and 16 at the time, were condemned to death. They delivered a speech from the gallows, announcing their mission and fulfilling their leader's dying request.

Jyotish scribbled their tale on the cell walls with a piece of charcoal before dying in prison in 1924.

The Indian Home Rule League was established by Tilak

During World War I, while Indian soldiers were bleeding to death for Britain's cause, presumably to save democracy, some nationalist leaders in India decided to demand the same for India from Britain. They eventually began an uprising against their countrymen's political servitude. This agitation, known as the "Home Rule Movement," thus served as a daring precursor to many daring political upheavals in subsequent times.

Mrs Annie Besant, an independent-minded Irish lady, and the great nationalist leader, Lokmanya Bal Gangadhar Tilak, were the driving forces behind this movement. She was in England from 1908 to 1914 and was deeply moved by the Irish people's campaign for "Home Rule" against the

English. While in England, she founded the Home Rule League and held its first conference at Queen's Hall in London. The purpose of the Home Rule movement, as often emphasised by Mrs Annie Besant and repeated by other leaders, including Lalaji and Tilak, was to achieve a kind of self-rule along Irish lines.

The Home Rule League was formally established on April 28, 1916, in Belgaum with the intention of "achieving self-government within the British Empire by all constitutional methods and educating and organising public opinion in the country towards the same."

Tilak immediately launched a large membership drive and formed branches in Bombay, Karnataka, and the central provinces following the foundation of the League. Tilak's activities were primarily limited to Bombay and the Central Provinces, whereas Annie Besant traversed the length and breadth of India, establishing branches in a variety of locations. Her passionate speeches almost electrified the Indians.

A large number of women joined this movement in South India as well. As a result of Tilak and Besant's tireless work, a new consciousness emerged, and "Home Rule" became a "Mantra" for the people.

In 1915, two prominent moderate politicians, Gopal Krishna Gokhle and Pherozeshah Mehta, died, and with their deaths, Annie Besant's long-standing push to reintroduce nationalist leaders like Tilak into the Congress was successful. The Congress Constitution was revised at the Lucknow session to allow militant nationalists like Tilak to return home after being ousted from the party in the Surat Session (1907) due to ideological differences.

A more positive outcome of this session was the agreement reached between the Congress and the Muslim League, which met in Lucknow at the same time as the Congress. An accord and agreement were reached to take coordinated action against the British government, which became known in history as the 'Lucknow Pact.'

The Lucknow Pact was an agreement signed between the Indian National Congress and the Muslim League in December 1916 at a joint conference of both parties in Lucknow. The two parties agreed to provide religious minorities with participation in provincial legislatures through the alliance.

The leaders of the Muslim League agreed to join the Congress movement calling for Indian independence.

Tilak rousing's infamous slogan "Swarajya Is My Birthright, And I Will Have It"

On June 14, 1916, Tilak paid a visit to the Shivanand Theatre in Belgaum. When he was released from prison, a meeting was held at the theatre. At the Bombay State Political Conference in Belgaum in 1916, he declared his famous phrase, *"Swaraj ha maza janmasidha adhikar aahe ani to mi milavinach"* (Swaraj is my birthright, and I shall have it). At this convention, Tilak met Mohandas Gandhi for the first time.

Tilak's Swaraj notion is based on Vedanta philosophy. Almost every leader at the time was infatuated with this notion.

It has been extensively written and spoken about by leaders such as Aurobindo, Bipin Chandra Pal, and Gandhi. They were promoting this notion to the nation as a cure for all of the ills brought forth by British control. Tilak articulated the concept and devised techniques to achieve the aim.

Lord Chelmsford has been appointed Viceroy of India on April 4, 1916

When the First World War broke out in 1914, Lord Chelmsford rejoined his regiment and was sent to India. He was named to the Privy Council on February 29, 1916. (PC). In March 1916, he was appointed as the Viceroy, succeeding Lord Hardinge. Nonetheless, he collaborated with Edwin Samuel Montagu, the secretary of state for India, on a study of the subcontinent's political conditions known as the Montagu-Chelmsford Report, which was delivered to Parliament in 1918 and served as the foundation for the Government of India Act of 1919. The number of

Indians on the viceroy's seven-member executive council was to be expanded from one to three.

However, before such measures could be implemented, Chelmsford, concerned about the burgeoning nationalist movement in India, supported the passage of the Rowlatt Act in early 1919, which was meant to continue the executive branch's wartime emergency powers.

The activities met with significant Indian protest, leading to the deadly Amritsar Massacre (April 13, 1919), in which hundreds of unarmed Indians at a meeting in Amritsar (now in Punjab state) were killed or injured by British soldiers. Martial law was swiftly implemented in the Punjab province, and Chelmsford's ability to handle the crisis was called into question. The reforms enacted under the Government of India Act were eventually implemented by the end of 1919. However, by the time the first elections to the reconstituted councils were held in late 1920, Mohandas Gandhi had already launched the noncooperation movement (1920–22), the first of his prolonged peaceful protest (satyagraha) campaigns, and the Indian National Congress had risen to prominence and boycotted the polling.

Promulgated the Defence of India Act in 1915

The Defence of India Act 1915, also known as the Defence of India Regulations Act, was an emergency criminal law created by the Governor-General of India in 1915 to curb nationalist and revolutionary actions during and after World War I.

The purpose of this act was to demolish the Ghadar movement.

Lokmanya Tilak sedition trials

Tilak had another run-in with the authorities in 1916 when he was charged with sedition for a series of lectures he delivered.

Barrister Mohammad Ali Jinnah, who was no longer a rookie and was now a known leader of the Home Rule League's Bombay chapter, appeared for Tilak again, and this time, won the case for Tilak.

Subhash - The emergence of the opposition to the British

Subhash Chandra Bose allegedly attacked and thrashed one of his British professors, E F Otten, in 1916. The professor made a crude joke about Indian students. Subhash was expelled from Presidency College and barred from Calcutta University as a result. Subhash was added to the list of rebel-Indians as a result of the incident.

From a young age, Netaji was quite influenced by the teachings and lives of Sri Ramakrishna Paramhansa and Swami Vivekananda. Netaji was spiritual and ever-committed to Dharmic ideals throughout his life. Just like Sri Ramakrishna Paramhansa, Netaji was an ardent follower of Ma Kali and kept a pictorial representation of the deity in his pocket. He believed that Swami Vivekananda preached the purest form of Hinduism, in which caste and creed had no relevance and bearing at all. Netaji highlighted the role Swami Vivekanand played in inspiring nationalism and encapsulating the very spirit of India in his writings. While Netaji was a student at Presidency College in 1913, he even considered joining the Ramakrishna Mission as a sanyasi. To that end, he met Swami Brahmananda, a direct disciple of Sri Ramakrishna Paramhansa and the then-president of the Order. It is said that the prescient Swamiji told Netaji that he was not meant to be a sanyasi.

His parents then sent him to the University of Cambridge in England to study for the Indian Civil Service. He passed the civil service exams in 1920. However, after learning of the nationalist upheavals in India, he dropped his candidacy and returned to India in April 1921.

The Justice Party was established (1917)

In 1917, the Justice Party was established in the then Madras by T M Nair, C N Mudaliar and P T Chetty. It was a political party also known as South Indian Liberal Federation. It was a Caste-based party of non-Brahmins. It was anger at the higher education level among Brahmins of the Madras Presidency that culminated in disproportionately higher and better socio-economic opportunities for the Brahmins under British rule.

During its initial period, the Justice party tried to convince the British government and the public to support communal representation for non-Brahmins in the presidency. Annie Besant's Home Rule League based in Madras was dominated by Brahmins and Justice Party took a stand against Annie Besant too. Gradually, the rift between Brahmins and non-Brahmins in Madras Presidency widened under a demand from Justice Party for proportionate caste-based representation in jobs and legislature, which the party ultimately extracted from the British government.

The Government of India Act 1919 implemented the Montagu-Chelmsford reforms, instituting a Diarchy in the Madras Presidency. The Justice Party opposed the non-cooperation movement of Gandhi in 1919. The Diarchy period extended from 1920 to 1937, encompassing five elections. Justice Party was in power for 13 of 17 years, save for an interlude from 1926 to 1930.

However, increasing nationalist feelings and factional infighting caused the Justice Party to shrink steadily from the early 1930s. After it lost to Congress in the 1937 election, it never recovered. The Party came under the leadership of E. V. Ramaswamy Periyar. In 1944, Periyar transformed the Justice Party into a social organisation called Dravidar Kazhagam and withdrew it from electoral politics. The party was dissolved in 1944. The majority group joined Dravidar Kazhagam and a minority group gradually joined the Congress.

Mrs Besant appears as the congressional president

Mrs Annie Besant, who was detained in June 1917, was later released by the British government due to rising national indignation. It was a moment when her celebrity status and the Home Rule movement were at their peak. As a result, she was elected President of the Congress at the Calcutta Session in 1917. This event marked the culmination of the Home Rule movement. This movement is remembered for two significant contributions. For instance, it gave cohesiveness to the ranks of the Congress. Mrs Besant brought together many moderates and some extremists, bringing the two wings of Congress closer together.

As a result, she was able to undo what had occurred in Surat in 1907. Furthermore, it had a significant impact on the character of the Congress. It effectively compelled Congress to learn the tactics of 'demand' and 'agitation,' forsaking its previous methods of 'petition' and 'prayer.'

When Lala Lajpat Rai observed, "India of 1917 was unlike the India of 1907," he was referring to this transformation. "We were fighting for crumbs in 1907. We are no longer pleading for concessions in 1917, but rather, for rights."

Even the apostle of peace, Gandhi, wanted Indians to fight in World War I

The ultimate irony was that Mohandas K. Gandhi, a staunch advocate of nonviolence, encouraged Indians to enlist as warriors in the British Army. During World War I, he set up camps to enlist Indians under the slogan "20 Recruits from Every Village."

Although the Indian Muslim troops were uneasy battling Turkey, and some of them revolted, British predictions of a general insurrection were unfounded.

Mohandas K. Gandhi had played such a remarkable role in quelling Indian rage against the colonial administration that even those planning a last battle with British security forces were swayed by his peacenik overtures.

He was awarded the Kaiser-i-Hind (Caesar of India) for his achievements, British India's highest civilian honour. Other Indians were opposed to his military attempts. Among them was Jinnah, who stated that before being asked to fight, Indians should be placed on the same footing as European British nationals. Second, they stated that Britain must ensure independence after the war. Gandhi, on the other hand, dismissed all such conditions.

The Indian liberation struggle was enormous in scope. Armed revolutionaries were not only fighting guerilla conflicts at home, but they also brought the fight to England, assassinating British leaders.

Gandhi, on the other hand, harshly rebuked such activities, labelling the Indian revolutionaries as "misguided individuals." "Our resistance should be free of hatred and vindictiveness," he stated.

Indian revolutionaries were upset by Gandhi's delay in demanding full freedom. His nonviolence infuriated these leaders because it protected the British from the Indians' wrath.

Gandhi extended unconditional support to the British initiatives from the start. He was adamant that this was not the time to disgrace Britain or utilise her precarious condition to help the Indian liberation cause.

The Russian eyes were on India

Actually, it was nearly three centuries before Russia was stained with Soviet blood. Tsarist Russia in the 18th and 19th centuries, like every other fledgling colonial state, had its sights set on the global economic titan known as India.

Tsar Peter the Great greatly sought to establish direct economic links with India in the late 18th century, and he trained in shipbuilding and maritime trade with the Dutch East India Company and the British East India Company.

Following that, Tsar Paul-I reached a contract with Napoleon Bonaparte to jointly attack India, and he dispatched an army of Don Cossacks in that direction. It was a catastrophe. In 1801, during a court intrigue, Paul was assassinated.

Almost a century later, in 1900, Russia established a military pact with France to invade India from Tashkent with combined soldier strength of 3,000,000. The railway connection connecting Tashkent was not built on time, and the Tsarist regime's domestic problems were rising rapidly. The invasion of India had to be postponed.

In just seventeen years, the Bolsheviks led by Vladimir Lenin won ultimate political power through large-scale brutality and abundant bloodletting of innocent Russians, transforming Russia utterly, irreversibly, and for the worse. This was the reality of 1917's so-called

October Revolution. The Tsarist royal family was cruelly exterminated, including children as young as 13 years old. The same "revolution" would be reproduced later by Mao and elsewhere.

The Bolshevik revolution begins on November 7, 1917

On November 7, 1917, a revolution occurred in Europe that altered the fate of humanity as a whole. It was known as the Russian Revolution. It gave birth to the World's first Communist state, the Soviet Union.

In 1917, Russia had two revolutions. The FIRST revolution was a constitutional revolution that brought an end to the centuries-old Tsarist monarchy. Tsar Nicholas-II abdicated in the face of widespread agitation on March 12, 1917 (27th February in the old Russian calendar), and Russia became a republic. The kingdom was taken over by a Provisional Government led by Prince Lvov as Prime Minister. This government was made up of elected members of the Russian Imperial Parliament's lower body, the State Duma. It represented, albeit a small, electorate and had 'empirical' credibility. In July 1917, Lvov was succeeded at the helm by Alexander Kerensky, a member of the Socialist Revolutionary Party.

The SECOND revolution, which gave rise to communist Russia, was a coup. It was on the night of November 7, 1917, (25th October as per the old Russian calendar) when the Bolsheviks, supported by sailors from a naval base on the island of Kronstadt and their own militia, the Red Guards, seized possession of the government buildings in St. Petersburg (then known as Petrograd). The following day, they drove legal Russian Premier Kerensky and his cabinet out of the Winter Palace, the seat of the Provisional Government, completing the so-called "Bolshevik Revolution."

During the Bolshevik Revolution, from 1918 to 1922, Russia undertook the first significant attempt to impose communism. During World War I, Russia was in turmoil, and Lenin capitalised on the instability by promising the people peace, food, and land. However, what transpired on the ground during the march is a truly terrifying scenario. Individuals who opposed or disagreed with them were executed during this campaign, which included violent methods like brutally beating and shoving people into furnaces by "chekas" (Bolshevik secret police).

Along with murders, the Bolsheviks began obtaining crops from peasants for little or no price, causing society to descend into a devastating famine (remember, food and land were "promised" by Lenin), killing thousands of people!

The 1917 revolution, which we in India commemorate as a huge victory for the world's proletariat and workers, was essentially a small and limited attempt by a few hundred Bolsheviks who had next to no presence in the vast rural expanses of the tsar-ruled Russia.

The Russian Revolution of 1917, on the other hand, enthralled the Indian educated class and revolutionaries by demonstrating a way to overturn a cruel tyranny. From the outside, it appeared that the Soviet Union had a lot going for it. The Soviet Union implemented the eight-hour working day, which is now standard in all developed countries, on the fourth day following the revolution, capturing the world's imagination.

Before the revolution, labourers in the West typically worked 12–15 hours each day, with only a 15-minute lunch break. Soviet achievements included the five-day work week and equal rights for women.

As a belief system, Communism was misanthropic as it inherited the political brutality found in its two Abrahamic cousins, Islam and Christianity. The concept of annihilating the "class enemy" was fundamental to communism's success, just as Islam and Christianity both try to convert non-conformists first through peaceful preaching, then by cunning or deception, and finally, if these two techniques fail, by offering them conversion or death.

The Red Terror began in August 1918, as a result of an attempt to assassinate Lenin. While recovering in his hospital bed after the attack, Lenin began the Red Terror, which was aimed at eliminating "enemies of the revolution." Capitalists, landowners, and everyone else who was wealthy were among them. Someone's occupation, as well as the size or value of their home, may be enough to cement their fate.

CHAPTER - XI

THE FIRST WORLD WAR CAME TO AN END, IN 1918

World War I had a profound impact on the entire world. It was one of the most significant geopolitical milestones in twentieth-century history. While the war lasted only from 1914 to 1918, it remained to determine the state of world politics until the Second World War.

From 1914 to 1918, it engulfed nearly all of Europe, the Middle East, and Russia. during the early 1917s, even the United States of America was engulfed. The "allies" France, Great Britain, Russia, Italy, Japan, and the United States defeated Germany, Austria-Hungary, and Turkey (the Ottoman Empire).

"History is written by the victor," says Winston Churchill, who served as First Lord of the Admiralty during World War I.

Churchill, a military historian and prolific writer who had served in the British Indian Army with the Sikh battalions, was less liberal in recognising Indian contributions to the First World War (or the Second World War, for that matter).

When we think of the First World War, we usually picture white men fighting on the battlefields, although nearly 4 million imperial non-white combatants fought on the battlefields.

An interesting anecdote tells us about Lokmanya's incredible vision and his evocative leap

Tilak was in London in 1919 to work for the Indian cause in England and post-war Europe. Tilak went on a walk with a friend one evening.

Tilak's companion laughed mockingly as he noticed numerous individuals eating out with their families.

Tilak informed him. "Without any need to laugh at these people; when access to education for women becomes popular in India, women will come out of the house and begin to work," Tilak said, surprising his companion, before adding, "Due to this, sooner or later, even in India, frequently going to restaurants would be a standard occurrence."

The scene described above is now prevalent throughout many localities.

Overcome jail atrocities in Mandalay, lobbied in the UK for Indian freedom

Lokmanya Tilak is quite well-known for igniting the Indian liberation fight in its initial phases. He is also credited with initiating the Ganeshotsav and Shiv Jayanti festivals in Maharashtra and Gujarat, which permitted the assembly of those nationalists whose intensions were to resist British directives against the legislature. Bal Gangadhar Tilak (in collusion with Maharaja Sayajirao Gaikwad of Baroda) also engaged in covert activities such as sponsoring (influencing) England's (then fledgling) Labour Party members so that they remained supportive of Indian independence if and when they got to power.

Tilak not only engendered revolt through the publications he published, using the motto 'Freedom (Swaraj-or self-rule) is my birthright and I shall have it,' but also actualized a legal matter to reach England and gain access to Labour leaders.

Tilak wasn't a gullible, uneducated individual. He had been paying close attention to what was going on in Europe. 1918 was a watershed moment in history. Emmeline Pankhurst, the 60-year-old pioneer of the Suffragette movement steered by the Women's Franchise League, had a successful year. In England, the Representation of the People Act of that year granted women over the age of 30 the right to vote.

England had won the First World War but at a high cost. Soldiers were retreating from the front lines, exhausted by the war. The country was beset by a lack of raw materials. Worker dissatisfaction arose as a result of poor wages, and unemployment threats loomed big. The Bolshevik Revolution occurred in Russia. The 1917 Russian Revolution demolished the Tsarist regime, paving the way for the formation of the Soviet Union. The reigning Conservative Party administration in England was experiencing a credibility crisis, while the Labour Party, which had been in power for nearly 17-18 years, was growing in strength.

Tilak seized the opportunity to put his plan into action. He seized the opportunity to file a libel suit against British journalist Vincent Chirol, who had named Tilak the "Father of Indian Unrest" in his book "Indian Unrest."

Chirol 'blamed' the Brahmin community (particularly the Chittapavan Brahmin fold to which Tilak belonged) for instilling rebellion in the minds of British imperial subjects in India. Tilak sailed off to the English coast to contest this in court.

He, of course, lost the case. How could a man whose newspaper headlines screamed "Freedom is my birthright" and who uttered the same "seditious" (according to the colonisers) things in public forums win a case that questioned the same reality, on the colonisers' native soil? The world knew that he had been imprisoned for sedition from 1908 to 1914 in Mandalay, Burma, and had developed diabetes as a result of the atrocities. But winning that libel case was not the only reason why Tilak had come to England. In 1918-19, he travelled to England to make contact with Labour Party leaders Arthur Henderson and Sidney Webb (also the founder of the London School of Economics or LSE).

Tilak intended to discuss the potential of Indian independence with Labour leaders if their party won power. He was holding a donation of £2000, which he gave to Labour funds. Arthur Henderson personally signed the receipt, which has now been housed in England's national archives. The £2000 was a significant sum in an era when the cash-strapped party was barred from accepting donations from any public sector union in the country under the Osborne Act, and 10gm gold could be purchased for £1.5. So here comes Tilak, armed with £2000 handed to him by Sayajirao Gaikwad, Maharaja of Baroda, and numerous nationalists. Henderson signed the receipt, which is dated December 6, 1918. Tilak went back home in 1919, a year before his demise.

Tilak's estimate proved right in 1922 when the Labour Party won 142 seats to become the dominant opposition party. With 191 seats in the Labour Party's kitty, Ramsay McDonald became Prime Minister in 1924, but this government was dissolved after 9 months. In 1929, the Labour Party won 287 seats, and McDonald was re-elected Prime Minister. Nevertheless, the worldwide economic downturn that year cost this government dearly. The Labour Party's fortunes declined from 1930 to 1940, and its credibility suffered.

During WWII, Winston Churchill appointed Labour Party leader Clement Attlee as Deputy Prime Minister to his War Cabinet. Following the war, the Labour Party won re-election in 1945, and Attlee became Prime Minister. That's when the Labour Party leaders fulfilled a vow they made to Lokmanya Tilak in 1918. We must not dismiss the efforts of the INA, the Royal Indian Navy Mutiny, Bose, Savarkar, and other revolutionaries for freedom. And on August 15, 1947, India attained independence.

England's archives, on the other hand, proudly keep all of these records.

The Anarchical and Revolutionary Crimes Act of 1919, (Rowlatt Act) passed on March 18, 1919

Following the First World War, the government saw the need to amend the Defence of India Act, which was enacted as an emergency measure to quell activist parties in India that could have impeded the war effort. The Government of India appointed Sir Sidney Rowlatt of the King's Bench to recommend measures to prevent sedition in December 1917. He proposed two bills, known colloquially as the "Rowlatt Acts." One of these was made into law. All Indian members of the Imperial Legislative Council voted against this Bill when it was passed by the Imperial Legislative Council. Three of the members resigned: Pandit Madan Mohan Malaviya, Mazarul Haque, and M.A. Jinnah.

The Congress leaders' anticipation that the British would grant India independence after the war did not come true. On the contrary, in March 1919, the government enacted the draconian Rowlatt Act.

This law gave the government the authority to detain and search individuals and properties without a warrant, to hold anyone without a trial, and to try people in special courts with no right to appeal.

The Act provoked a maelstrom of dissent unprecedented in Indian history. The law was succinctly stated, "*Na appeal, na dalil, na vakil.*" The opposition was strongest in Sir Michael O'Dwyer's Punjab.

The Rowlatt Act of 1919 (also termed the Anarchical and Revolutionary Crimes Act of 1919) was adopted by the colonial British government to detain political leaders seen to be "threats" for an extended timeframe. It gave the government the authority to arrest people without a warrant and incarcerate them for up to 2 years without a trial.

The convicted were not to be provided with any evidence used against them during the trial, nor were they to know who the accusers were. People were prohibited from engaging in any religious or political activity. The Act was intended to put a stop to revolutionary nationalist groups that had begun to acquire traction in India and threatened the Imperial Government.

Jallianwala Bagh Tragedy and the Great Amritsar Massacre, April 13, 1919

April 13, 1919, on the occasion of Baisakhi, more than 20,000 innocent unarmed men, women, and children assembled in Amritsar's Jallianwala Bagh. Most had simply wandered into the park to relax after attending the city's annual fair; some had come to hear protestors condemning the arrest and expulsion to the Andaman Islands of nationalist leaders Satya Pal and Saifuddin Kitchlew, who had led an agitation against the draconian Rowlatt Act; and very few in the vast crowd were aware that the British colonialists had declared a prescription on public gatherings in Punjab.

Brigadier-General Reginald Dyer, the commander of the British Army's 48 Infantry Brigade, was told of a big crowd amassing in the park at 4 p.m. Dyer led a team of 50 soldiers who "would have no qualms about shooting Punjabi civilians."

Jallianwala Bagh was a 6-7 acre park with a sole narrow exit going into a narrow bylane where only two individuals could walk side by side. Dyer issued the command to fire just before 5:00 p.m. The command was reiterated by a British captain called Gerry Crampton, whistles were blown, and the troops instantly began the fire.

Some in the throng attempted to shelter behind a well, but when the soldiers opened fire on them, many jumped into it, knowing they would almost likely drown. This well later yielded the discovery of nearly 100 bodies. The forces were also instructed to open fire on some of the horrified bystanders in the residences surrounding the Bagh.

The British counted 397 fatalities, while the Indians claimed 1,600 perished, including 44 children. The 'unofficially official' total was 1,800. The youngest of the dead was only eight years old, while the oldest was 80 years old. Jallianwala Bagh was somewhat mercy in the context of British atrocities and genocide in India (particularly the British-engineered Bengal Famine that would occur in 1943, killing 4-7 million Indians). Jallianwala Bagh, on the other hand, became a symbol of British colonialism since it was the first time the full amount of British cruelty and callousness towards Indian life was observed and recorded in excruciating detail.

Tilak's health began to deteriorate after the heinous tragedy of the Jallianwala Bagh slaughter. Tilak, despite his illness, issued a call to the Indians not to give up the movement, no matter the circumstances. He was eager to lead the movement, but his health wouldn't allow it.

Gandhi's writings reveal how he found it was morally right to forgive Dyer for the heinous crimes he committed in Amritsar by killing innocent and unarmed people. In an article titled "Religious Authority for Non-cooperation," authored by him and published in Young India on August 25 1920, Gandhi wrote, *"It would be sin for me to serve General Dyer and co-operate with him to shoot innocent men. But it will be an exercise of forgiveness or love for me to nurse him back to life if he is suffering from a physical malady."*

A trust was founded in 1920 to build a memorial at the site. A memorial, designed by American architect Benjamin Polk, was built on the site and inaugurated by President of India Rajendra Prasad on 13 April 1961. A flame was later added to the site.

The bullet marks remain on the walls and adjoining buildings to this day. The well into which many people jumped and drowned attempting to save themselves from the bullets is also a protected monument inside the park.

The President of the Indian National Congress was a permanent member of the Jallianwala Bagh Memorial Trust until 2019. This representation was skewed by the Congress Party gaining a prominent position in the Trust.

The Jallianwala Bagh National Memorial (Amendment) Bill, 2019 was then passed by the Parliament in November 2019 marking an end to the automatic nomination of the Congress President as President of the Trust.

Prime Minister Narendra Modi on August 28, 2021, dedicated the renovated monument of Jallianwala Bagh Smarak to the nation through a virtual conference.

Dyer's challenging final days

Dyer was struck with arteriosclerosis shortly after the incident. In December 1919, he had jaundice, which led to a slew of health issues, very doubt exacerbated by the extreme stress generated by the criticism of his actions and the potential of discharge from the army.

Dyer requested a six-month sick leave to travel to England to recover from his illness, but the army stated it could only be granted if he resigned from his position. The army speculated that he would not be promoted to Major-General due to his ailment. Dyer ended up feeling so acutely unwell after hearing it that he could no longer be looked after by his wife and had to be transferred to a hospital in Jalandhar. Things were about to get a whole lot worse.

Dyer was told to report to the army commander in chief in Delhi in March 1920, when he was requested to quit his job and informed that he'd never be re-employed in the army. He was given half a salary. Dyer arrived in Jalandhar in a vulnerable state and was immediately hospitalised. His health had deteriorated to the point where he could no longer compose his own letters. Dyer and his wife were crushed and disheartened when they returned to England.

Despite being sentenced to death by the army, Dyer gained worldwide support from people of British descent and Christians. Dyer had a stroke that rendered him unable to walk. The everyday mental torment was accompanied by physical pain. The demons of Amritsar tormented him at all hours of the day and night, and he tried to push them away by continually reading literature. But he never admitted that he had made a serious mistake.

Dyer suffered another stroke on July 10, 1927, leaving him mute after five years of nightmares. He passed away two weeks later. Annie, his wife, lived a hollow existence until her death.

Tilak died on August 1, 1920

Even in death, Lokmanya Tilak ignited and bequeathed behind an unprecedented nationalistic ferocity on August 1, 1920. Perhaps, it is not an exaggeration to say that the enormous success of the non-cooperation movement and the birth of Gandhi hinged on Tilak's funeral procession, as the Bombay citizenry was drawn into the vortex of the nationalist movement that day without any special effort on the part of the leaders. It was a watershed event in Indian history when an urban colonial city finally roused the locals to rediscover their entombed nationalism.

On the first day of the non-cooperation movement, Balgangadhar Tilak bequeathed "Swaraj" by his own death.

Lokmanya Tilak was the first (and last) person to be allowed (forced by his followers) to have a public funeral in Bombay. Following Tilak's untimely death, when word spread, thousands from Bombay and beyond flocked to Sardar Gruha to have one last look at their glorious leader.

Initially, it was planned that Tilak's body would be cremated at the nearby small Chandanwadi Crematorium, but due to the large crowd of people who were filled with rage, disappointment, and grief as a direct consequence of their revered leader's untimely death, and lobbying by influential Mumbai residents, the administration capitulated and granted special permission to have the cremation at Girgaum Chowpatty, but with restrictions. However, Vithalbhai Patel (Sardar Patel's brother) and Barrister KF Nariman (after whom Nariman Point is named) were able to persuade the Bombay Municipal Corporation to provide permission for the construction of a memorial. To generate funds for the Tilak memorial, a committee was formed in 1925, with Sarojini Naidu as its chairman. On August 1, 1933, 13 years after his death, Lokmanya Tilak's statue was unveiled at Girgaum Chowpatty.

A million people were believed to have participated in the last journey, including famous figures such as M.K. Gandhi, Jawaharlal Nehru, and Maulana Shaukat Ali, a prominent leader of the Khilafat Movement.

The Tilak era ends; the Gandhi era begins

Lokmanya Tilak, Congress's tallest leader, died on August 1, 1920. It marked the emergence of the Mohandas Gandhi era in the Congress. The Treaty of Sevres, signed in France on August 10, 1920, officially ended the Ottoman Empire. Mohandas Gandhi perceived this as an opportunity to bring Hindus and Muslims together in the Khilafat campaign, thus integrating Muslims into the national struggle. This would have bolstered his position within the party.

We were taught as children that Mohandas Gandhi linked the Congress to the Khilafat effort to speed up the non-cooperation movement. However, according to Dr Babasaheb Ambedkar, "the non-cooperation agitation had its origin in the Khilafat agitation and not in the Congress movement for Swaraj: that it was started by the Khilafatists to help Turkey and adopted by the Congress to help Khilafatists: that Swaraj (self-rule) was not their primary object, but Khilafat was, and that Swaraj was added as a secondary object to induce the Hindus to join it".

The Congress issued the British a one-year ultimatum to meet its demands on the Jallianwala Bagh massacre and the Khilafat at the Nagpur session in December 1920 and warned of a statewide non-cooperation movement.

Mohandas Gandhi promised that nonviolent civil disobedience, withdrawal of children from government schools, the boycott of foreign goods, withdrawal from British courts, and other such tactics would result in Swaraj within a year.

Swaraj did not specify if he wanted independence or more autonomy. However, the Congress indeed became a mass movement under Gandhi's leadership. Whatever the rationale for the Congress's support for Khilafat, it was successful in growing Muslim participation in the national movement as well as organising a substantial number of Hindus in support of Khilafat. The goal of Hindu-Muslim unification, however, remained a mirage. Many Hindus who supported the Khilafat were unfamiliar with Islam and its political doctrine. The Khilafat movement, on the other hand, fostered the seeds of dual nationality among Muslims. Supporting the Khilafat movement meant acknowledging that the ambition of Indian Muslims to establish an Islamic Caliphate in Turkey was as vital, if not more important, than the independence of their ancestral motherland.

The Khilafatists refute the charge of dual nationality by stating that India is their motherland and Turkey is their fatherland, emphasising that their support for Khilafat does not influence their love for India.

However, it left crucial questions unanswered, such as whether it is permissible to request Muslim countries' assistance for India's independence; whether India should be a constitutional democracy based on people's representation or a Hindu majority country to be ruled by Muslims, as these leaders considered necessary. Similarly, Islam does not encourage nonviolence (Ahimsa), which Mohandas Gandhi strongly supported as an integral component of the non-cooperation movement.

The Khilafat leaders read Quranic verses urging for Jihad and supporting the execution of Kafirs at the Congress' annual session in Nagpur in 1920.

When Mohandas Gandhi was pointed out, he smiled and clarified, "They're alluding to British bureaucracy." As a result, the Khilafat movement began to lose its orientation from the start.

Some Khilafat chiefs referred to India during the British Raj as Dar-ul-Harb or the "country of war." During the summer of the 1920s, several local committees of the Central Khilafat organisation urged Indian Muslims to sell their property and goods and immigrate to Dar-ul-Islam (a Muslim country). As a result, thousands of Muslims from Sindh, Punjab, and central India embarked on a journey to neighbouring Afghanistan. 30,000 people immigrated to Afghanistan in August 1920. As their numbers grew, Afghanistan closed its doors to newcomers. Many of them were forced to return to India in shambles. Mohammad Ali is said to have sent a message to Afghanistan's Amir asking him to invade India and pushing him not to make peace with the British. As part of the non-cooperation campaign, the Ali Brothers issued calls for violence.

The Khilafat Movement

The origins of the Khilafat movement may be traced back to the cornerstone of Islam and its introduction in India. Political and ecclesiastical authority was vested in the Prophet Mohammed throughout his lifetime. His successors were known as Caliphs, which means "leader or guide" in Arabic.

Although the Caliph's position was not as powerful as the Pope's in Catholicism, the Caliph had appeal among the Muslim world. Although Mughal emperors referred to themselves as Caliphs of India, the Ottoman Sultan, who ruled over an empire spanning Central and West Asia, North Africa, and parts of Eastern Europe for nearly five centuries and was the custodian of the holy sites of Mecca, Medina, and Jerusalem, was perceived as the Caliph of India. Following the fall of Mughal power, elites among Indian Muslims became more reliant on the Ottoman Sultan for political and religious assistance. Sultan Abdul Hameed II (1842-1918) promoted the Caliphate or Khilafat concept in order to protect the Ottoman Empire against European aggression and fragmentation. He dispatched Jamaluddin Afghani to India as his messenger. Afghani-inspired Muslim Umrao (nobles) and Ulema (clerics) in India who wielded power over the Muslim masses.

In 1914, the First World War began. The Ottoman Empire sided with the Central Powers, including Germany and Austria and Hungary, against the Allies.

With devastating reverses on the Western Front at the outbreak of war, the British government decided to mobilise Indian soldiers into the battle. The war council resolved that four Indian divisions, known as Indian Expeditionary Force A, would be dispatched as reinforcements to the battlefields of Europe.

Simultaneously, smaller Expeditionary Forces B, C, and D were assembling for deployment in East Africa and Mesopotamia. The religious implications of the battle were heightened by Sultan's role as Khalif. Anticipating a violent reaction from Indian Muslims, the British authorities took a conciliatory approach to the Empire's future at the end of the war.

Indian soldiers played a pivotal role in Ottoman Turkey's defeat. As World War I continued, fears of the Muslim world (Ummah) banding together against the Allied Forces proved exaggerated.

While this was going on, Mustafa Kemal Pasha's battles kept modern-day Turkey from being dismembered and a disempowered Sultan imposed on it. As a result, at the end of the war, the British were unconcerned about the wishes of several Indian Muslim leaders about the Ottoman Empire. As the empire began to fall apart by the end of 1918, the Khilafat movement – which sought to restore the Caliph – began to take root.

On February 9, 1919, the first meeting in this regard was conducted in Kolkata. On October 17, 1919, the inaugural Khilafat Day was observed. On November 22-24, 1919, Delhi hosted the first Khilafat Conference. More than half of the delegates at this conference came from what is now Uttar Pradesh. Resolutions were passed at this conference to abstain from triumphant celebrations, boycott British goods, and send a delegation to England to find a righteous alternative to the Khilafat conflict.

This meeting featured leaders like the Mohammed and Shaukat Ali brothers, Maulana Abul Kalam Azad, and Dr Ali Hasrat Mohani.

On November 24, Mohandas Gandhi proclaimed at a well-publicized combined Hindu-Muslim convention that Hindus were united with Muslims in their grievances against the Caliphate because it was a worthy purpose.

Under Mohandas Gandhi's leadership, the Indian National Congress held joint conferences with Khilafat leaders and embraced the Khilafat Committee's call for non-cooperation with the British.

In his book, Pakistan or the Partition of India, Dr B R Ambedkar stated that "Swaraj was not its fundamental purpose; it was Khilafat, and Swaraj was introduced as a subsidiary object to entice Hindus to join."

In 1919, proponents of the 'Khilafat', 'Caliphate,' or 'Islamic State' movement went so far as to invite Afghanistan's Amir to invade India.

The India government was established on December 23, 1919

The Montagu-Chelmsford (or Mont-Ford) Reforms were proposed by Edwin Montagu, Secretary of State, and Lord Chelmsford, Viceroy, in 1918, and resulted in the passage of the Government of India Act in 1919.

Montagu-Chelmsford Reforms, which came into operation in 1921.

This Act's main objective was to assure Indians' representation in the government. The Act instituted reforms at both the federal and provincial levels of government.

Bal Gangadhar Tilak called the Montford reforms "unworthy and disappointing – a sunless morning." The reforms, according to Annie Besant, were "unworthy of England to propose and India to embrace." Veteran Congress stalwarts, led by Surendranath Banerjea, backed the government's ideas.

Session of the Nagpur Congress, 1920

The irony of Jinnah's life was that he battled for a united India for the first sixty years of his existence. Jinnah's problems started after Gandhi returned from South Africa in 1915. Jinnah and Gandhi came into conflict during the Nagpur Congress session in 1920. Jinnah was loudly booed in front of his young wife, Ruttie, and Gandhi did not intervene.

Gandhi introduced the Non-Cooperation Resolution, and Jinnah resigned from the Indian National Congress.

The Non-Cooperative movement came into existence on September 5, 1920

MK Gandhi initiated a non-cooperation movement against the British Raj on September 5, 1920, demanding full independence and self-government. By backing the Khilafat movement of Indian Muslims, he was able to successfully combine Hindu and Muslim communities in civil disobedience against the British.

While Gandhi was super-violent, he blended Khilafat and the Non-Cooperation Movement and exhorted Congress officials to make their voices heard in defence of Turkey. Was it a war between Turkey and India?

Gandhi is well renowned for combining the Non-Cooperation Movement and the Khilafat Movement.

Muslim parties were quite thrilled regarding Turkey's Khilafat than Indian independence.

Sardar Bhagat Singh and Chandrashekar Azad during Non-Cooperation Movement

Sardar Bhagat Singh, a 12-year-old Sikh kid who witnessed the British's ghastly crimes of the Jallianwala Bagh massacre and martial law horrors, viewed Gandhi as a saviour and joined the non-cooperation campaign.

Chandrashekar was enraged by what had happened at Jallianwala Bagh and the British crimes in Punjab. The Congress, led by Lala Lajpat Rai, had a session in Calcutta (now Kolkata) in 1920 and passed a resolution calling for non-cooperation. In 1921, the non-cooperation movement spread like wildfire throughout India under Gandhi's leadership. Varanasi became embroiled in the movement as well, with students boycotting classes and participating in anti-government protests. Chandrashekhar dropped out of college to join the national struggle. During an agitation, Chandrashekar witnessed police brutally beating up demonstrators. He couldn't stop himself and flung a stone, hurting a sub-inspector. Despite his ability to flee, the cops tracked him down and detained him. He was only 15 years old when he was chained and placed in a dark, damp cell. However, rather than shattering his spirit, the incident strengthened his resolve.

The courage with which he survived the cane lashes and the resistance he displayed in the police station made him a hero in Varanasi. People flocked to witness this valiant son, whose intentions the British could not break. His picture was featured in the *Maryada* tabloid with the description "Brave Child Azad," along with a write-up about his brave actions. Chandrashekar Sitaram Tiwari, a 15-year-old Sanskrit student, was transformed into the great revolutionary Chandrashekhar Azad. His father, on the other hand, was concerned and pleaded with him to return home. Azad had already made up his decision to serve the nation and had dedicated his life to the occurrence.

The Imperial Bank of India (IBI) was established in 1921

The Imperial Bank of India (IBI) was the Indian subcontinent's oldest and largest commercial bank until it was merged with the State Bank of India in 1955. Before the foundation of the Reserve Bank of India in 1950, it served as the central bank for British India under its royal decree.

The Earl of Reading was appointed as Viceroy of India on April 2, 1921

Rufus Daniel Isaacs, 1st Marquess of Reading, resigned his position as Chief Justice in 1921 to become Viceroy of India. He was adamant about carrying out the requirements of the Government of India Act 1919. He personally greeted Mohandas Karamchand Gandhi and Muhammad Ali Jinnah and made a rapprochement visit to Amritsar. He did, however, use force on many occasions, including the suppression of the Malabar insurrection in 1921 and the repression of Sikh disturbances in Punjab in 1922. Gandhi was convicted for disobedience the same year.

Moplah Rebellion - 1921

The 1921 Moplah riots were a concerted Jihad campaign against Hindus. The genocide, orchestrated by people like Variankunnath Kunhamad Haji, Ali Musaliar, and others, caused the deaths of an estimated 10,000 Hindus in Kerala. Approximately 100,000 Hindus were compelled to flee Kerala as a result of the carnage. It is adjudged that a hundred Hindu temples were destroyed during the massacre. Forcible conversion of Hindus was widespread, and horrible crimes were committed against Hindus.

The barbarous Jihad against Hindus in the Malabar region can hardly be described as the "Moplah Rebellion." Even isolated episodes of burning, abduction of British officials, seizure of police stations, and so on, would not excuse this heinous cruelty as an ordinary "rebellion." The background is simple: the real, on-the-ground cruelty in Malabar was the gruesome culmination of a six-month-long build-up. In support of the so-called Khilafat Movement Expressed in different words, every single word written and spoken reeked of violent Islamism, often known as Jihad. In this heinous enterprise, pro-Khilafat Jihadists already saw the British and Hindus as Kaffirs screaming for slaughter or conversions.

Mohandas Gandhi exhorted Hindus not only to support but also to cheerfully die for this "phenomenon."

The Moplah riots were described in published works by Annie Besant and Babasaheb Ambedkar, among others.

In her book 'The Future of Indian Politics,' Annie Besant recounted the events as follows, "They slaughtered and pillaged lavishly, and killed or drove out those Hindus who would not apostatize." Approximately one lakh individuals were pushed from their houses with nothing except the clothes they were wearing, and they were deprived of anything and everything. Malabar has shown us what Islamic rule still entails, and we do not want to see another Khilafat Raj in India."

In his book, Pakistan or the Partition of India, Babasaheb Ambedkar writes, "The blood-curdling crimes committed by the Moplas in Malabar against the Hindus were terrible." A wave of appalled feeling had spread throughout Southern India among Hindus of all stripes, which was exacerbated when several Khilafat officials were so ignorant as to pass resolutions congratulating the Moplas on the valiant war they were undertaking for the sake of religion. Even after 100 years, the wounds of the genocide resurface in the Hindu conscience.

The Indian Council for Historical Research (ICHR) under the Ministry of Education would remove Variamkunnath Kunhamed Haji and Ali Musaliar, the leaders responsible for the Moplah Massacre of Hindus, from the Dictionary of Martyrs of India's Freedom Struggle in 2021.

The rebellion was sectarian in origin, intending to establish a Caliphate in the region rather than freeing India from British rule. The Moplah insurrection, also known as the Mappila revolt, was an uprising led mostly by Muslim landowners against Hindus. It also coincided with the birth of the Malabar Khilafat Movement.

The Khilafat movement, the Moplah insurrection, and Congress's muddled response all had a significant impact on Hindu nationalist leaders. When these incidents occurred, Veer Savarkar, who was serving two life sentences in the Andamans and Ratnagiri at the time, referred to Khilafat as Afat. In Marathi, he wrote the novel *"Mala Kay Tyache Arthat Moplyanche Band"* (The Moplah Revolt: I don't care) and Essentials of Hindutva, which is regarded as the first attempt to analyse political Hinduism.

CHAPTER - XII

VINAYAK SAVARKAR AND HIS BROTHER WERE TRANSFERRED FROM THE ANDAMANS TO THE INDIAN MAINLAND ON MAY 2, 1921

On February 28, 1919, the Government of India issued a letter to Superintendent Port Blair stating its intent to grant clemency to inmates. In response, the Chief Commissioner of the Andaman and Nicobar Islands and the Superintendent of Port Blair forwarded the case history of the Savarkar brothers.

Following WWI, the struggle to free political prisoners gained traction in India, particularly during and after 1919. Many petitions were sent, and conferences were conducted in its support. In a letter to the Viceroy, Maharashtra's District Home Rule Leagues demanded the release of the Savarkar brothers.

Sardar Patel's elder brother, Vithalbhai Patel, championed the issue of political prisoners' release in the Central Assembly. In light of the anticipated Royal Clemency, the Administration of India issued a telegram to the Bombay government on December 4, 1919. The Bombay government had denied the Savarkar brothers' request for Royal Leniency.

Gandhi published an article titled "Savarkar Boys" in Young India, appealing for the brothers' release.

After inspecting the conditions of the cellular jail, the Cardew Committee submitted its report to the government, and the decision was made to close the cellular jail.

In March 1921, KVR Iyengar, a member of the Council of State, proposed a resolution to free the Savarkar brothers. On May 2, 1921, the brothers were eventually placed on the *Maharaja* bound for Bombay.

The most prominent criticism levelled at Savarkar is that he wrote mercy pleas to save his life while other revolutionaries did not. This is completely untrue. There are numerous examples of revolutionaries convicted in various situations who filed petitions. Writing petitions was the norm, a legal option, and Savarkar was not the first or last to employ it. Damodar Hari Chaphekar, Mahadev Vinayak Ranade, the Dravid brothers, Lokmanya Tilak, Rajendranath Lahiri, Ram Prasad Bismil, Jawaharlal Nehru, and others have signed petitions.

Sitaram Goel: Modern India's Greatest Intellectual Kshatriya born on 16 October 1921

Sita Ram Goel

On October 16, 1921, in the Haryana village of Chhara, Sita Ram Goel was born. Though belonging to the merchant Agarwal caste, his family was quite poor but found sustenance in Vaishnavism and especially the devotional poetry of the local 18th-century Sant Garib Das.

Sitaram Goel was one of India's most important and original thinkers in the post-independence era. His writings are central to the Hindu awakening worldwide over recent decades which is now growing rapidly. While his guru and colleague, Ram Swarup, laid the spiritual and philosophical basis for the movement, the detailed analysis and in-depth articulation for it was supplied by Sitaram.

He realized the necessity of challenging and countering the forces seeking to destroy Hindu culture, exposing their wrong ideologies and biased theologies, as well as the misguided actions that their thoughts and beliefs must eventually result in.

While Hindu dharma is regularly denigrated and distorted by missionary, leftist and Marxist forces (which often have foreign funding and are well entrenched in the media and academia), Hindus are expected to be kind and tolerant in return and not criticize anyone in their defence, should they speak out at all. Such a defeatist attitude is what Sitaram reacted against and provided a clear alternative for.

Goel took up difficult issues like the massive Islamic destruction of Hindu temples, which others preferred to ignore or gloss over. He warned of the danger of Islamic terrorism long before it erupted on the world scene after 9/11, which type of attacks he predicted.

He challenged the Christian missionary assault on India, exposing its agenda of conversion in the guise of social service, and its exclusivist dogma using Hindu tolerance to hide its aggression. Whatever subject he examined, he dealt with directly, thoroughly and rationally, letting the facts speak for themselves.

Sitaram Goel deserves heartfelt appreciation for the tremendous service that he has rendered to Hindu society and the cause of truth. But no Bharatiya scholar, journalist, or student wrote one. Neither in their lifetime nor after he passed away. Our media did not even bother to take note of the demise of Sita Ram Goel in 2003. The chief reason for this unfortunate state of affairs is that his work remained largely unknown to the general public of our country. He was an original and non-conformist thinker. Our governments as well as the academic class felt quite at ease in ignoring him. The media happily followed suit.

Chauri Chaura, Incident - February 4, 1922

It was February 1922, and the non-cooperation movement had reached its zenith, sparked by Gandhi and the Khilafat movement; innumerable volunteers had joined in Chauri Chaura rallies.

On February 4, 1922, police opened fire on a huge throng of Chauri Chaura demonstrators, killing three and injuring many more. The mob became enraged and set fire to the police station, trapping 23 officers inside. On February 12, 1922, Gandhi discontinued the Non-Cooperation movement in the aftermath of the Chauri Chaura incident.

According to one account offered in Shahid Amin's book 'Event, Metaphor, Memory: Chauri Chaura,' "the real agents (asli log) involved in the riot are, again, other people altogether in the tale from Madanpur, a Pathan-trader dominated market village twenty miles south-east of Chauri Chaura."

Thousands of young people across India, including the young teenager Sardar Bhagat Singh, were disillusioned with Satyagraha and other Gandhian beliefs after his precipitous abandonment of the Non-Cooperation movement.

And, to quote Dr B R Ambedkar, "Mr Gandhi was anxious to preserve Hindu-Moslem unification and did not mind murdering a few Hindus for the sake of it. This mentality of excusing Muslims for any wrongdoing, lest it harms the goal of unity, is well illustrated by what Mr Gandhi said about the Mopla riots."

Mrs Annie Besant and Dr Ambedkar were correct in their concerns about the Khilafat being an extremist form of Islam.

As we stand in the twenty-first century, a century after the 'Caliphate' and non-cooperation movement, we can see some of the most catastrophic events of the previous century pass through the hourglass, proving beyond a doubt that collaboration with Islamic extremists has time and again proven to be detrimental.

Gandhi is long gone, and his message is admired around the world, but in his homeland, his Satyagraha and Khadi have become political symbols, since Khadi has lost its primacy.

The radical ideology of the Islamic State's 'Caliphate,' on the other hand, is here to stay. A dominie wants Kerala to become an Islamic state over the next ten years. One of the Islamic State's first Indian recruits came from Kerala. According to a recent UN report, there are "large numbers of ISIL operators in Kerala and Karnataka states."

Azad, like many others, was deeply upset when Gandhi suddenly and unexpectedly terminated the non-cooperation movement following the Chauri Chaura event in 1921. An enraged populace had burned down a police station in Chauri Chaura village near Gorakhpur, prompting Gandhi to call a halt to the movement. Azad believed that a violent revolution was the only way to gain independence, and he began to form alliances with Bengali insurgents.

Veer Savarkar was released from Yerwada prison and interned in Ratnagiri On January 6, 1924

Savarkar was placed under house confinement in Ratnagiri in 1921 and was unconditionally freed by the Bombay Governor in 1937. During his time in Ratnagiri Prison in 1922, he wrote "Essentials of Hindutva," which defined his Hindutva doctrine.

He interpreted 'Hindutva' as a commitment to Hinduism. It was a *sandhi* (joint) of the words "Hindu" and "tatva," which meant the core of Hinduism. Its purpose was to defend Hinduism. He claimed that a Hindutvavadi would know what it took to live a Hindu life in the real sense.

He believed that Hindus were too soft and open-minded to see these individuals as menaces and foes and that anglicised Hindus such as Gandhi, Nehru, and Radhakrishnan worked hand in hand with them. In fact, Muslims had become very strong and riotous after Gandhi launched the Khilafat Movement to mobilise Indian Muslims against the British following the Sultan of Turkey fiasco and the eventual abolition in 1924 of the office of the Sultan of Turkey/Caliph, whom Muslims considered the Spiritual and Political Head of Muslims worldwide.

Mr Savarkar presumed that the activism of Hinduism's spiritual values by Nehru, Gandhi, Radhakrishnan, and others had a debilitating effect on Hindus and was intended to subdue and weaken Hindus, to make them ignorant of their oppression by Muslims and Christians, and instead, welcome them with great enthusiasm, forgetting the generations of torture at their hands in the form of the rule of the Aryans, Greeks, the Delhi Sultanate, and Mughals.

Mr Savarkar emphasised Hindu identity, solidarity, and unity. He admired Hindu rulers such as the Mauryas, Guptas, Cholas, and Marathas. Mr Savarkar opined that these and other leaders such as Puru, Prithviraj Chauhan, Rana Pratap, Shivaji, Maharani Laxmi Bai, and others had fought a victorious war against foreign invaders and would tremendously act as role models.

The Khilafat Movement and the Non-Cooperation Movement both played a role in the emergence of Hindu nationalism. The Moplah Riots of 1921-1922, in which Moplah Muslims of Malabar targeted innocent Hindus and killed lakhs of them, influenced Hindu nationalists such as Vinayak Damodar Savarkar, Keshav Baliram Hedgewar, and Madhav Sadashiv Golwalkar.

When Veer Savarkar was imprisoned in Ratnagiri, he brought all the untouchable families to his home and fed them. The Pan-Hindu canteen and the Patit Pavan Mandir are surviving relics of Savarkar's reformist struggles. He also attended Mahar conferences in Ratnagiri to hear their complaints and fight for their welfare.

The Hindustan Socialist Republican Associations were formed in 1924

The Hindustan Republican Association (HRA) (later renamed the Hindustan Socialist Republican Association) was founded in October 1924 by a group of Indian National Congress youngsters dissatisfied with Mohandas Gandhi's unexpected appeal to end the non-cooperation movement. Ram Prasad Bismil, Yogesh Chandra Chatterji, Sachindra Nath Sanyal, and Shachindra Nath Bakshi founded the HRA in 1924.

Bhagat Singh, who the Communists 'appropriated,' was not a member of the Communist Party of India (CPI). He continued his activity by establishing the HSRA (Hindustan Socialist Republican Association).

While propagandists will tell you that he read Lenin, they will not tell you about his admiration for Swami Vivekananda. They also won't inform you that he covertly published Veer Savarkar's book in India. Savarkar's book, "The Indian War of Independence," was prohibited by the British. They also won't tell you that Bhagat Singh wrote positively about Savarkar in an article published in the *Matwala* Hindi periodical in 1924, calling him 'veer' and praising his philosophy. He also mentioned a meeting between Savarkar and Madanlal Dingra in England, where Savarkar tested Dingra's courage and they hugged each other with tears in their eyes.

Alluri Sitarama Raju Was Killed by the British on May 7, 1924

Sitarama Raju led the Rampa Rebellion (1922-24) against the Madras Forest Act, which prevented the free movement of tribals in the forests and impacted their livelihoods. Under his leadership, the tribes fought a gruesome guerilla war by attacking British armouries and police stations. Komaram Bheem led a rebellion against the feudal Nizams of Hyderabad and the British Raj in the eastern part of the princely state during the 1930s which culminated in the Telangana Rebellion of 1946.

The Rampa administrative area was home to many tribes who followed the '*podu*' method of shifting cultivation. The Madras Forest Act, of 1882 forbade them from engaging in podu farming and limited their freedom of movement so that the forests might be cleared and exploited for wood. Under the Rampa rebellion, which went on from August 1922 to May 1924, many tribal residents led by Sitaram Raju, attacked the British army.

He won a few battles using traditional weapons such as bows and arrows. He prepared tribals against the oppression of the British Officials, Christain Missionaries, and the Police. Later, Sitarama Raju led attacks on police stations to steal their firearms to support their uprising. The British government offered a prize of Rs 10,000 for Sitarama Raju's capture, and a large number of personnel and resources were mobilised to quell the uprising.

Despite announcing a cash reward, when the British failed to crush the uprising, it sent TG Rutherford in April 1924, who resorted to unprecedented violence in tribal villages to find his coordinates.

Finally, in 1924, Raju was taken into police custody. chained to a tree and executed in front of the entire community, effectively putting an end to the armed uprising. For his bravery, he received the title of '*manyam veerudu*' or 'forest hero.'

Kohat Genocide of Hindus in 1924

After Ranjit Singh's death and the British takeover, the Hindus of Kohat had to face daily what the Hindus of Pakistan continue to face since 1947: forced conversions to Islam, depopulation, and abduction and rape of women and young girls. But the Hindus did not give up, did not convert, and did not abandon their ancestral Karma Bhoomi. They formed the Sanatan Dharma Sabha, registered at Kohat, to safeguard and preserve their Dharma.

After the Khilafat movement began to fade, communal tension brewing underneath the facade of 'Hindu-Muslim unity' surfaced. On the fateful days of September 9th and 10th of 1924, radical Islamist mobs unleashed mayhem in Hindu *mohallas* (neighbourhoods) in Kohat town of North-West Frontier Province (now known as Khyber Pakhtunkhwa) in present-day Pakistan. It is just over 300 Km from Srinagar and about 750 Km from Delhi.

Kohat had a Muslim population of 12,000 while the number of Hindus and Sikhs stood at a mere 5,000 (Census 1921). The Hindus were prosperous even though they were outnumbered. The Hindu community lived in urban areas and controlled large businesses. Despite this, a large number of Hindus were converted to Islam (about 150 conversions each year between 1919 and 1924).

There was widespread resentment amongst the Muslims for the minority Hindus and the Kohat riots were a manifestation of long-standing friction. A fertile ground, conducive to riots, was being created by giving a communal twist to each incident.

Muslim mobs, particularly young boys, stormed into Hindu colonies and began wielding sticks and pelting stones. Shops, temples and houses were set on fire and destroyed. Properties belonging to the Hindus were vandalised and looted.

The fear and panic created by the riots prevented the return of Hindus, who were forced to leave their homes. The Hindu victims of the riots did not get any compensation but were offered loans of 5 lakh rupees for damages.

The Genocide of Hindus at Kohat would eerily repeat itself all over again sixty-five years later in the summer of 1989 in Kashmir. This time, the genocide and forced displacement of Kashmiri Hindus was on an industrial scale. Scripted, produced, directed, and executed with clinical brutality by the state Government in "independent" India.

Peasant massacre in Alwar, 1925

The peasant massacre in the Alwar district of the state of Rajasthan is one of the horrendous incidents of the brutal suppression of the agitation by the British government.

Committed on May 14 1925, the peasant massacre in Alwar exposed the inhumane approach of the British government towards the Indian population. Against the backdrop of the massacre lay the oppressive land settlement policy of the Alwar rulers and the financial crisis created by the first world war. To compensate for the demand for "war funds" by the British government, the ruler of Alwar increased the land tax causing distress among the peasants of Alwar and forcing them to protest against this move. On May 14, 1925, the peasants organized a meeting at Neemuchana village of Alwar district. Although the meeting was peaceful, the armed British troops, without any prior warning, opened fire on the agitators. Along with this, the whole village was attacked by the state troops.

The peasant massacre in Alwar resulted in the loss of many lives and properties and was compared to the Jallianwala Bagh tragedy. Although the inquiry committee established to investigate the tragedy reported only 13 deaths and 12 wounded, the actual numbers were estimated to be as high as 95 and 250, respectively.

Vinayak Savarkar meets Dr Hedgewar in 1925. Later, he found the RSS subscription

Hedgewar was a senior Congress leader in the Vidarbha region, he was on the organising committee when the National Convention of Congress was organised in Nagpur. Hedgewar was jailed for one year during the Non-Cooperation Movement. Bal Gangadhar Tilak's and Veer Savarkar's literary works had a significant influence on him. Hedgewar had formerly been a member of the Anushilan Samiti organisation, which advocated violent revolution against the British administration and had been detained repeatedly for defiance of British authority.

Dr Hedgewar was a devout Congressman who deserted the party after Mohandas Gandhi resurrected the Non-Cooperation Movement and became linked with Mr Savarkar.

At the same time, when the Abrahamics continued to commit atrocities against Hindus, Mr Savarkar persuaded Dr Hedgewar to establish a *sangathan* that would look after the needs of Hindus and shield them in all circumstances.

Several members of the Hindu Mahasabha led a procession through Nagpur's streets on the auspicious occasion of Lakshmi Pooja in 1923. The procession passed through an area with a mosque as it marched on with banging drums and intoxicating music.

Enraged by the bhajans, the local Muslim youth attacked the procession that was moving from the area in front of the mosque. Several Hindus were injured and a few died as a result of the communal fight. What followed was a near-massacre of Hindus in Muslim-majority parts of Nagpur, which prompted Dr KB Hedgewar to take the next steps.

According to Dr Hedgewar, the primary causes for Hindus' suffering during riots were divisiveness and a lack of organisation. Unlike Muslims, who operate as a single entity, Hindus are divided into numerous sects, faiths, castes, and philosophies. As a result, Hindus were particularly vulnerable to harm during communal confrontations at the time.

Despite being the majority in Nagpur, Hindus were lynched and persecuted by Muslim mobs. There was no communal solidarity to defend themselves from the rioters, but Muslims were able to fund, protect, and mobilise to attack Hindus.

The episode of 1923 made Dr Hedgewar think deeply about the status of Hindus in Nagpur, and it played a significant influence in his decision to establish the Rashtriya Swayamsevak Sangh in Nagpur to unite the Hindus together. After establishing the RSS in 1925, Dr Hedgewar established shakhas in every suburb of Nagpur and trained Hindus to act as a unified body.

The 'Kakori Conspiracy' happened on August 9, 1925

The Kakori Train Robbery, also known as the Kakori Conspiracy, was an armed robbery on a train in central Uttar Pradesh on August 9, 1925, and the subsequent court trial instituted by the government of British India against more than 20 Indian revolutionaries accused of involvement, directly or indirectly, in the brave act.

Members of the newly founded Hindustan Republican Association, a revolutionary organisation that was later renamed the Hindustan Socialist Republican Association, were among the revolutionaries. The revolutionary organization's purpose was to free India from British colonial control through a revolution that included armed revolt.

The major goal of the Kakori conspiracy was to obtain finances for the HRA by forcefully obtaining funds from the British administration. The HRA's other goal was to build a favourable image of itself among Indians by assaulting a high-profile British government target while causing as little collateral damage as possible. Revolutionaries Ram Prasad Bismil and Ashfaqullah Khan plotted the Kakori robbery. Bismil Khan, Chandrashekhar Azad, Rajendra Lahiri, Shachindra Bakshi, Keshab

Chakravarty, Murari Lal Khanna (Gupta), Banwari Lal, Mukundi Lal Gupta, and Manmathnath Gupta were among those who carried it out.

An HRA meeting on August 8, 1925, decided to plunder the national coffers to purchase armaments. The following day, August 9, rebels halted the Number 8 down train near Kakori on its way from Saharanpur to Lucknow and looted Rs. 8000 from the guard cabin. The train was allegedly transporting money-bags pertaining to the British Government Treasury.

The objective was a guard cabin that was transporting money from several railway stops to be deposited in Lucknow. Despite the fact that no passengers were targeted by the revolutionaries, one passenger, Ahmed Ali, was murdered in the crossfire between the guards and the revolutionaries. As a result, the case was classified as manslaughter. Following the tragedy, the majority of the revolutionaries fled to Lucknow.

Following the heist, the British government initiated a manhunt to apprehend all rebels. More than two dozen HRA members were detained a month after the attack. More than 40 people were arrested in the United Kingdom for plotting and carrying out the plan.

Ram Prasad Bismil was detained by British police on September 26, 1925. The other heist plan masterminds, Ashfaqullah Khan and Shachindra Bakshi were detained a year later.

Kakori Kand's final judgement was issued in July 1927. The court exonerated around 15 people due to a lack of evidence. During the trial, five people escaped. Ram Prasad Bismil, Ashfaq Ullah Khan, Thakur Roshan Singh, and Rajendra Lahiri were all sentenced to death by the court.

Sachindra Bakshi and Shachindra Nath Sanyal were sentenced to deportation to the Andaman and Nicobar Islands' Cellular Jail in Port Blair.

Formation of the Communist Party of India

Following the success of the Bolshevik Revolution in Russia during 1917-1923, a new dawn arrived on the political horizon of modern human society. The world saw with astonishment, a bloody revolution and civil war in Russia that physically overthrew the Russian monarch and established the government of the proletariat. With the establishment of the Communist regime in Russia, the Marxist theory entered its practical application phase.

A section of educated Indians got sucked into the new ideology which promised to end all socio-economic disparity between haves and have-nots.

The Communist Party of India (CPI) was formed on 26 December 1925 at the first Party Conference in Kanpur, under the guidance of Soviet Socialists. The founder, MN Roy, lived a disenchanted man through Indian independence and died in 1954. Another founder Abani Mukherji died in Russia, under Communist rule, in a strange twist of time during the Great Purge by Joseph Stalin in the late 1930s.

It's not surprising that one of the founders of Communism in India fell victim to the Communist state he held as his ideal. The independence of India in 1947 not only saw religious bloodletting across the country; it also witnessed a slowly-simmering discontent among the farmers being used by the Communists lamenting having been reduced to "mere appendage to the Congress" to leverage themselves into a prominent role, often failing due to internal conflicts.

In its early years, CPI was harshly suppressed through legal prohibitions and criminal prosecutions by the British government of India. CPI was legalized in British India in 1942 after the USSR allied with Britain in WW II. CPI also supported the Pakistan cause of the Muslim League.

CHAPTER - XIII

LORD IRWIN WAS APPOINTED VICEROY OF INDIA ON APRIL 3, 1926

On April 3, 1926, Lord Irwin was proclaimed the 30th Viceroy and Governor-General of India. This was the most turbulent moment in Indian politics. The following significant events occurred in the course of this period: the Simon Commission visit (1928), the Nehru Report (1928), the Murder of Saunders in 1929, the Bomb thrown in the Assembly Hall in Delhi by Bhagat Singh, the Death of Lala Lajpat Rai, the executions of Bhagat Singh, Rajguru and Sukhdev (1931), the Chittagong Armoury Raid (1930), the Civil Disobedience Movement, Dandi March (1930), the First Round Table Conference in London and Gandhi-Irwin Pact, Demand for Poorna Swarajya in Lahore session.

Establishment of Tablighi Jamaat

Tablighi Jamaat established in 1926 by Muhammad Ilyas al-Kandhlawi in the Mewat region of India has roots in the Deobandi reformist tradition. It was developed as a response to the perceived deterioration of moral values and the supposed neglect of aspects of Islam.

Soon, Ilyas and his band of Tablighis began touring the Mewat region giving out da'wās to the half-Hindu Mewatis – all scripted and directed from the modest structure of the Banglawali Masjid, now the sprawling skyscraper better known as the Nizamuddin Markaz, the global HQ of the Tablighi Jamaat, an Ivy League school of Jihadi theological indoctrination.

The Tablighi Jamaat also drew first blood almost overnight. On December 23 1926, a member of the Tablighi hired goon squad barged into the room of an ailing Swami Shraddhananda and stabbed him to death in cold blood. The warrior Swamiji was 70 years old.

Muhammad Ilyas' fanatical project of heartlessly isolating the Mewati children in his dingy Madrassa of bigotry was generously financed by the psychotic Nizam of Hyderabad, other major and minor Nawabs and landed Muslims.

Gandhi called on Savarkar at Ratnagiri in 1927

Gandhi wrote to Savarkar, expressing his desire to see him. On March 1, 1927, Gandhi arrived in Ratnagiri. The stage was prepared for two long-time adversaries to finally meet, some eighteen years after their last meeting in London. The Congressmen asked Savarkar to share the platform with Gandhi at a Ratnagiri Municipality public meeting. But Savarkar was adamantly opposed. Instead, Savarkar welcomed Gandhi to his home. After the public assembly, Gandhi went to meet Savarkar at his home. The two epic ideologists had a friendly meeting and discussed a variety of political matters.

While leaving, Gandhi told Savarkar that while they disagreed on several issues, he hoped the latter would not object to him conducting experiments to address the issues at hand. "Mahatmaji, you will be conducting these experiments at the heavy cost of the nation," replied Savarkar sternly.

The 10th anniversary of the October Revolution

"Welcome to the Land of Lenin" (V Strane Lenine) is the subtitle of a documentary commissioned by the Soviet trade unions to mark the first jubilee of the October Revolution

On the international stage, the USSR proclaimed itself as the leader of all the anti-imperialist and anti-colonial forces of the world and extended generous patronage to the leaders of various freedom movements in colonised countries. King-size patronage presented itself in November 1927 when the Soviet Union hosted its decadal celebration to commemorate the Great October Revolution of 1917. Accordingly, the Soviet Society for Cultural Relations sent an invitation to the Nehru family to witness firsthand the magic that the Communist Revolution had created in Russia.

Thus, in November 1927, Motilal Nehru, Jawaharlal Nehru and Vijayalakshmi Pandit visited Moscow. The four days that he spent there introduced him to lifelong Communist addiction to the eternal doom of Bharatavarsha. He was so thoroughly brainwashed by the elaborate charade that the USSR had erected for him that he became a champion-apologist for every excess that Russia inflicted both on its citizens and on the world.

Ram Prasad Bismil was hanged on December 19, 1927

Ram Prasad wrote under several pen names, including Ram, Agyat, and Bismil. However, he is best known as "Bismil," the man who popularised the immortal lines, *"Sarfaroshi ki tamanna ab hamare dil mein hai, dekhna ki zor kitna baazu-e-qatil mein hai"* (We shall see how much resilience lies in the arms of the murderer).

In 1916, Bhai Parmanand was sentenced to death for his role in the Lahore conspiracy. Ram Prasad had grown to admire Parmanand after reading his books, and the death sentence enraged him.

He made a vow to fight against the British government right then and there. On the evening of August 9, 1925, Ram Prasad, along with 9 other revolutionaries, pulled the chain at Kakori station in the evening and pillaged government funds from the guard's cabin.

Bismil and others made appeals and petitioned the Governor, Viceroy, and Privy Council for mercy. They were all turned down.

On December 19, 1927, at Gorakhpur Jail, Bismil was executed. Moolmati, Bismil's mother, went to see him before he was hanged. Bismil couldn't control his emotions and burst into tears when he saw his beloved mother, but his mother remained unswayed and told him that she was fortunate to have a son like him.

In turn, he told his mother that he cried not because he was afraid of death, but because he would never see her afterwards.

Moolmati's reverence for the cause of her beloved country can be understood by the fact that she addressed a public gathering days after her elder son's death and offered her other son to the freedom movement. Independence would have remained a distant dream if not for the sacrifices made by these great mothers. Ram Prasad Bismil might not have had the resolve to pursue the path he had chosen if it hadn't been for her unwavering support and conviction.

The Bangalore disturbances of 1928

The Bangalore disturbances of 1928 were a series of Hindu-Muslim clashes which took place in the city of Bengaluru in June - July 1928 over the construction of a niche on a Ganesha idol in school premises. These were the first major communal disturbances in Bengaluru.

But in those days, the incident in question evoked widespread outrage against the then-Mysore government. It is still alive in the memories of old timers, especially in Bangalore, and others in the Old Mysore region. In Kannada, they recall it as the *Ganapati Galabhe* or Ganapati clashes. To fourth and fifth-generation Bangaloreans, the incident will emerge as wisps of vague recollection of an important milestone of their city's history.

The Government School (formerly known as S R Nanjundayya School) on Arcot Srinivasachar Street in Sultanpet, Bangalore (today, AS Char Street) housed a small Ganesha idol on its campus since time immemorial. When the school underwent renovation in 1928, the contractor built a small mandap for the Ganesha idol.

Overnight, the government decided to focus its attention on this development which had gone unnoticed by the general public. The officials of the education department objected to the presence of this Ganesha idol inside the mandap. The reason? The house of Abbas Khan, the then head of the (Bangalore City) Corporation was located right opposite the school. A mosque stood next to his house.

The government, instead of rationally resolving the issue, decided to use brute force. It arrested student leaders who formed a significant and influential chunk, which only heightened tensions. The unrest only intensified. Now, the government had two problems on its hand instead of one: the demand for reinstating the Ganesha idol and the protest against the government's haughtiness. Thousands of protesters took out their processions in front of Diwan's home and the Bangalore Central Jail. Things reached such a dangerous pass that the army was called in to restrain the protestors.

Finally, the government backed down and released some student leaders on bail. Ramlal Tiwari, Subramhanyam, and Bhima Rao became instant heroes – they were paraded in a massive victory procession, which eventually reached the school. The Ganesha idol was reinstalled and Arati and Puja were performed.

Even as the Arati was being performed, a barrage of stones and footwear came flying from the opposite buildings. This was followed by the sound of a gun going off. Within minutes, an army of Muslims armed with sticks, swords, and other deadly weapons descended on the worshippers. Hundreds were grievously wounded.

That the nature and the aftermath of this unprovoked attack were so gruesome can be gauged by the fact that it not only made national headlines but was also reported in faraway London by the Times and other prominent papers.

Simon Commission, 1928

According to the provisions of the GOI Act 1919, the Simon Commission visited India in 1927 to continue investigating the progress of the governance scheme and propose additional reform steps. After 10 years of the GOI Act, such a commission was to be made official in 1929, but the conservative government in England advanced its date due to India's tumultuous political situation. This commission had no Indian representatives, and its seven members were drawn from three British political parties. This provided the Congress with an excellent opportunity to develop an agenda.

They staged a protest that the Simon commission was there to denude them of their chance to engage in the formation of their own country's constitution. The Madras session of the Congress passed a resolution advocating a boycott of the Simon Commission at all stages and in all forms.

The commission was met with black flags bearing the slogan "Simon Go Back" wherever it went in cities across India. The Indian press voluntarily came forward to report the Simon report's flaws and freely repudiated the commission's anti-Indian bias. The report's findings were dismissed as an "eye wash" in the political press. Simultaneously, the Muslim League was divided on the commission.

While Mohammad Ali Jinnah advocated a boycott of the commission, Mohammad Shafi backed the government. As a result, all parties, except for the Muslim League's Shafi cohort and the Justice Party of Madras, were opposed to the Simon Commission.

Nehru's Report

The Simon commission visited India twice, in 1928 and 1929, and issued a report in 1930. The Indians were uninterested in its discoveries. The secretary of state for India, Lord Birkenhead, challenged these congressmen to draught an Indian constitution. In February and May 1928, the elected elites took up the challenge and convened an All-Party Conference. To prepare the draught constitution, all political parties formed a committee led by Motilal Nehru. It was known as the Nehru Committee Report, and it was presented on August 28, 1928, at the Lucknow conference of all parties.

Lala Lajpat Rai's Death

It was October 30, 1928. A large number of Indians had accumulated in Lahore's streets in a silent, peaceful march to protest the Simon Commission. The British officers decided to use force against the peaceful protesters. And they had a specific target in mind – "the man with the umbrella." The turbaned man was frail and old, but he was the one who was restraining the crowd, keeping it orderly and completely non-violent in the face of the police's provocative actions. So, the Senior Superintendent of Police decided to assault him, with the help of one of his sidekicks, Mr. Sanders.

While he was invincible in spirit, the blows had wreaked havoc on his frail body. On November 17, 1928, he died as a result of his injuries.

And what a life he'd had!

The people of Kanpur pledged to commemorate his demise by observing "Lala Lajpat Rai Diwas." The students of the city came out to the streets and organized demonstrations and processions on the streets. The young freedom fighters organized a spontaneous strike in schools and colleges and did not attend their classes for the day. The role played by the young volunteers of D.A.V College, Bishambhar Nath Sanatan Dharam College, and Guru Narayan Khatri High School were at the forefront of the agitations.

Lala Lajpat Rai was a firm believer in the power of the youth and hoped that the young generations of the nation would overthrow the yoke of colonialism once and for all. This belief was amply borne out by the response of the youth of Kanpur to his death.

In response to the killing of Lala Lajpat Rai, J. P. Saunders was killed in Lahore in 1928

Lala Lajpat Rai suffered serious injuries as a result of the lathi charge and died of heart failure.

This incident shocked Bhagat Singh, and he planned to avenge his death by killing James Scott, who ordered the lathi charge, together with his companions, Chandrashekhar Azad, Sukhdev, and Rajguru. They assassinated J.P. Saunders based on a misunderstanding. This act was condemned by Gandhi and other leaders who saw nonviolence and non-cooperation as the only ways to free themselves from British atrocities.

As the investigation began, they left Lahore to hide in a safe location and wait for the matter to be resolved. He disguised and donned himself in western clothing, had his hair cut as he ditched the turban, and shaved his beard to attain an English appearance. Durga Bhabhi famously helped HSRA member Bhagat Singh flee Lahore after he was accused of being involved in the Saunders murder.

Bhagat Singh and Batukeshwar Dutt bombed the Central Assembly in 1929

The HSRA leadership has now decided to inform the public about their future initiatives and the need for a mass revolt. On April 8, 1929, Bhagat Singh and B.K. Dutt was asked to throw a bomb into the Central Legislative Assembly in protest of the passage of the Public Safety Bill and the Trade Disputes Bill, both of which would restrict citizens' civil rights.

Bhagat Singh and Batukeshwar Dutt drew the attention of deafeningly aristocratic British ears to a youth uprising that altered the course of India's freedom struggle. Political handouts and smoke bombs were thrown at the Delhi Central Legislative Assembly by them.

The bombing was intended to show opposition to the passage of two draconian bills: the Public Safety Bill and the Trade Dispute Bill. Following the objectives, Singh and Dutt were successful in stopping the Assembly meeting and surrendering to the police. Singh was later sentenced to death, while Dutt was sentenced to life in prison. One of several reasons for our country's independence was the courage of these two freedom fighters.

Batukeshwar Dutta had to face brutal colonial atrocities as did other Kala Pani inmates. He began a hunger strike against the abusive treatment of political prisoners and the discriminatory and inhumane prison conditions. He contracted tuberculosis soon after he was released from prison, having an adverse effect on his health. Although, this could not deter his spirit to fight for the cause of freedom.

The Purna Swaraj Declaration, or the Declaration of India's Independence, was signed on January 26, 1930

In 1927, Bhagat Singh was the first to raise the call for "Total Independence," or Purna Swaraj. Until 1929, the Indian National Congress fought for dominion status under the British monarchy. A Congress session was held in Calcutta in December 1928, and Mohandas Gandhi proposed a resolution calling for the British to grant India complete independence in under two years.

At its Lahore session on December 19, 1929, the Indian National Congress passed the historic "Purna Swaraj" (total independence) resolution. On January 26, 1930, a public declaration was made, which the Congress Party urged Indians to commemorate as "Independence Day."

Due to a malfunction in negotiations between the leaders of the freedom movement and the British over India's complete independence, the declaration was passed.

Lord Irwin, the then Viceroy of India, announced in 1929 that India would be granted dominion status in the future (known as the Irwin Declaration). Indian leaders were ecstatic, as they had been pushing for full independence for quite some time. They now wanted to concentrate all future negotiations with the British on formalizing India's dominion status.

The Irwin Declaration sparked an outcry in England, with politicians and the general public opposing India's claim to dominion. Under duress, Lord Irwin told Indian leaders Jinnah, Nehru, Gandhi, and Sapru that he couldn't promise dominion status anytime soon. The Indian National Congress became irritated and happened to change its stance – it abandoned its demands for dominion status and instead, passed the "Purna Swaraj" resolution, which called for complete independence, at its Lahore Session in 1929. The resolution signalled the start of a large-scale anti-colonial political movement.

The resolution was only 750 words long. It lacked a legal or constitutional framework and read more like a manifesto.

It demanded the dismantling of British affiliations and declared "Purna Swaraj," or "complete independence." It was a scathing indictment of British rule, and it succinctly articulated the economic, political, and cultural injustices inflicted on Indians as a result. The document spoke for Indians and stated clearly that the civil disobedience movement would be launched.

During the 1946–1950 constitution-making process, members of the Constituent Assembly chose January 26, 1950, as the date for the Constitution of India to take effect to commemorate the public declaration of Purna Swaraj.

Salt Satyagraha (Dandi March) was started by Gandhi

During the liberation movement, Gandhi organized the Dandi March, or Salt March, as a non-violent protest against the British monopoly on salt production. The March took place from March 12th to April 6th 1930. To defy the British diktat on salt, Gandhi produced salt after arriving in Dandi. He then relocated to the Dharasana Salt Works, where he was apprehended on May 5.

Aside from the Dandi March, none of Mohandas Gandhi's best-laid plans or agitations succeeded for the same reason – there was no clear definition of intent or actual result.

Gandhi's status as the Saint of the Masses was cemented with the Dandi March. With holiness came unchallenged suzerainty over not only the Congress party but also the entire freedom movement. In this grand monopoly, a non-Congress (synonymous with non-Gandhian) freedom fighter had little prestige or power.

Gandhi organized the Dandi March to disperse the Purna Swaraj movement, which Bhagat Singh had started in prison through his court trial speeches because Gandhi realized that the British would gladly pay the media to give him as much publicity as he wanted to disperse the Purna Swaraj Movement.

Take into account the following dates:[9]

Date	Events
08-Apr-1929	Butukeshwar Dutt and Bhagat Singh detonated a bomb in the Assembly.
07-May-1929	The trial of Bhagat Singh begins. They decided to use the court system to promote Indian independence-related speech and ideas. In prison as well as during his trial, Bhagat Singh raises the demand for Purna Swaraj.
24-Jun-1929	Begin hunger strike by Bhagat Singh, Dutt, and Jatindra Nath Das.

---

9   http://rahulmehta.com/301.htm

13-Sep-1929	Jatindra Nath Das dies after 65 days of starvation and inhumane treatment. There was no such thing as a *Gandhivaadi* who died by fasting. Some true fasters do perish.
	Bhagat Singh and Dutt have become enormously more famous in India than Gandhi. When Gandhi notices that everyone is praising Bhagat Singh and he is losing his number one position, he develops a fever and depression.
12-Mar-1930	The Dandi *Namak* (Salt) March was initiated by Gandhi.
	Salt March receive a lot of attention in the British paid media, but Bhagat Singh's expectation for Purna Swaraj gets lost in the concoction.
01-May-1930	The viceroy takes advantage of the fact that citizens' attention has deviated towards Bhagat Singh and declares an emergency and a secret court hearing started.
10-Sep-1930	Bhagat Singh is sentenced to death by a court of law.

Overall, the timeline demonstrates that the true goal of the Dandi Salt March was to derail the Purna Swaraj issue. If all Gandhi wanted was a march, why didn't he lead the march on the issue of Purna Swaraj, which was already a hot topic due to Bhagat Singh's trial speeches? Why did Gandhi take on such a minor issue as the salt tax?

Even as late as 1930, Congress and Gandhi did not fully believe in Total Independence and were only using it as a bargaining chip to gain dominion status. Bhagat Singh (and his HSRA) desired "Purna Swaraj," or complete independence. In 1931, Bhagat Singh was hanged and became a great statesman. Only after the public was moved by Bhagat Singh's execution and after Bhagat Singh became a hero for all of India did Congress recognise the opportunity and issue a call to unambiguously support Purna Swaraj.

It is possible that if it had not been for Bhagat Singh and the HRA, Congress would still be fighting for dominion status in 1947.

Book - The Case for India by Will Durant

William James Durant, more popularly known as Will Durant, holds a unique distinction for a singular reason: he is perhaps the only Western scholar-historian-commentator who spoke with blunt candour against the naked evil of European, specifically, the British colonialism of Bharatavarsha. And gave a blow-by-blow account of almost every excruciating detail of the most evil Empire the world has ever seen.

In 1930, he published "The Case for India" while he was on a visit to India as part of collecting data for "The Story of Civilization." The author Will Durant presents before us an unflinching, unwavering and powerful account of the atrocities committed by British rule on the Indian economy, politics and culture.

The Western world still hasn't forgiven Will Durant for this trespass. But it is one thing for Indians to write about the horrors of British colonialism because they are the actual sufferers and victims.

A Raid on the Chittagong Armory, 1930

On April 18, 1930, an attempt was made to raid the police and auxiliary forces' armoury in Chittagong, Bengal. The plan was to seize Chittagong's two main armouries and then destroy the telegraph and telephone offices. It was to be followed by the murder of Europeans. This conspiracy was carried out by 65 people under the guise of the Indian Republican Army. After that, all of the revolutionaries gathered outside the police armoury, where leader Surya Sen took a military salute, hoisted the national flag, and declared a Provisional Revolutionary Government. They then fled to the hills. The police were involved in the investigation. Many of the members were apprehended, tried, and sentenced to life in prison. Surya Sen, the leader, was apprehended in 1933 after a tip. He was probably the last of the militant nationalists to be executed when he was hanged in 1934.

Delhi was announced as India's capital

When King George V arrived in India with the intention of being crowned Emperor of India at the Delhi Darbar, he shocked the world with an announcement. Calcutta was to be replaced as India's capital by Delhi.

New Delhi, India's modern capital with the Raisina Hill complex as its architectural focal point, took more than 20 years to build and was inaugurated on this day in 1931 by Viceroy Lord Irwin. One of the reasons for designating Delhi as the capital was that it served as the financial and political hub for many empires that had previously ruled India.

The city, designed by Sir Edwin Lutyens and Sir Herbert Baker, was christened "New Delhi" on December 31, 1926.

According to the book "Glittering Decades: New Delhi in Love and War," Lord Irwin unveiled four iconic Dominion Columns, each made of red sandstone and topped by a replica of a ship, on the day of the inauguration amid a fanfare of trumpets followed by the playing of the (British) national anthem.

The book says, quoting the Viceroy's speech at the unveiling, "The four columns that are the immediate purpose of our meeting today are tokens of something greater than anything that the past cities of Delhi represent." The columns, which were gifts from Australia, New Zealand, South Africa, and Canada, symbolized friendship and unity within the British Empire.

The British believed they could rule India indefinitely. So, the capital was moved from Calcutta to Delhi. They had only been in power for a decade when WWII broke out.

The establishment of Patit Pavan Mandir was open to all Hindus in February 1931

The Patit Pavan Mandir would be the only remaining symbol of Savarkar's Hindu social reforms. Bhagoji Keer, a "pariah" merchant, opened this mandir on February 22, 1931, with active support from Savarkar. This temple was unique in that it allowed Hindus of all castes to worship freely and without barriers; a pariah boy was given the charge of singing devotional songs; and the chief priest was chosen by Bhagoji Keer himself. In the same month, the sixth annual conference of the Bombay Province Association for the Removal of Untouchability was held in Ratnagiri, where the envoys praised Savarkar's vast social reforms.

Savarkar took it a step further by establishing a Pan-Hindu canteen where inter-caste dining was mandatory. In April of that year, a group of 710 *Somvanshi Mahars* (a former untouchable caste) met in Patit Pavan Mandir in the presence of Savarkar. Two years later, this group held another conference in Ratnagiri, where the participants resolved to remain Hindus and not significantly alter their religious doctrine.

Session of the Karachi Congress - 1931

A "Resolution on Fundamental Rights And Economic Changes" was adopted a year later, in March 1931, at the Karachi session of the Congress. According to constitutional historian Granville Austin, it was "both a declaration of rights and a humanitarian socialist manifesto."

In the Karachi resolution, the "right to keep and bear arms in accordance with regulations and reservations made on that behalf" is listed under the first section on fundamental rights[10] of the people.

This demand was a demand plus a promise, which meant that Gandhi and other Congressmen promised the people of India that if and when Congress came to power, they would make the right to be armed a fundamental right.

They only made this promise because Bhagat Singh expressed such opinions. And because these views had become so popular among

---

10 https://www.constitutionofindia.net/historical-constitution/karachi-resolution-1931/

commoners and activists, Gandhi felt compelled to include them in their books to maintain their market share among activists.

Savarkar, Bose, Bhagat Singh, and many other revolutionaries studied revolutions that had already occurred in Western countries.

They were all well aware that the revolution could not have occurred without the use of arms and ammunition.

When commons are weaponized, the world's most powerful armies decide not to attack that country.

The 1940 Nazi invasion plan, Operation Tannenbaum, was not executed, and SS Oberst Hermann Bohme's 1943 memorandum warned that an invasion of Switzerland would be too costly because every man was armed and trained to shoot.

Armed citizens were responsible for the 1650 revolution in Britain, which resulted in the end of the monarchy and the rise of elected MPs.

The Russian Revolution of 1917 occurred because the Czars began arming citizens in the 1700s. Military service was made almost compulsory in the 1800s, and by the 1910s, as many as 15% to 20% of Russians were armed.

The Chinese Revolution occurred because a sizable portion of the Chinese population was armed.

Azad died on February 27, 1931, in Allahabad's Alfred Park (now known as Azad Park)

Chandrashekhar Azad

Chandrashekhar Azad was assassinated in Alfred Park, Allahabad, on February 27 1931, after an associate betrayed him. For quite some time, with a small pistol and a few cartridges, he held off the well-armed cops who had surrounded him.

However, with only one bullet remaining, he shot himself in the head and fulfilled his vow that he would never be arrested and dragged to the gallows to be hanged.

Gandhi-Irwin Pact, March 5 1931

The Gandhi-Irwin Pact was a political agreement signed on March 5, 1931, by Gandhi and the then-Viceroy of India, Lord Irwin, before the Second Round Table Conference in London.

The proposed conditions were as follows:

- The Indian National Congress has put an end to the civil disobedience movement.
- The Indian National Congress will take part in the Second Round Table Conference.
- Withdrawal of all laws imposed by the British government on the activities of the Indian National Congress.
- Prisoners arrested during the civil disobedience movement are released.
- Allow people living near the seashore to collect or produce salt gratis.

The day Bhagat Singh, Sukhdev, and Rajguru laid down their lives for freedom was March 23, 1931

In the Assembly Bomb Case, Bhagat Singh and B.K. Dutt were tried. Later, in a series of conspiracy cases, Bhagat Singh, Sukhdev, Rajguru, and tens of other revolutionaries were tried. Every day, they entered the courtroom shouting slogans such as *"Inquilab Zindabad,"* "Down, Down with Imperialism," "Long Live the Proletariat," and *"Sarfaroshi ki*

tamanna ab hamare dil mein hain" (our hearts are filled with the desire for martyrdom) and "*Mera rang de basanti chola*" (dye my clothes in saffron colour, the colour of courage and sacrifice). Predictably, this earned them the support and sympathy of people all over the country, even those who believed wholeheartedly in non-violent resistance.

Bhagat Singh became a household name in the country, and many people across the country wept and refused to eat food, attend school, or go about their daily lives when they learned of his execution in March 1931. The country was also shaken by the revolutionary undertrials' prolonged hunger strike in protest of the deplorable conditions in jails. They demanded that they be treated as political prisoners rather than criminals. The entire country supported the hunger strikers. Jatin Das, a frail young man with an iron will, died on September 13th, the 64th day of the epic fast. Thousands of people came to pay their respects at each station visited by the train carrying his body from Lahore to Calcutta. A two-mile-long procession of more than six lakh people carried his coffin to the cremation ground in Calcutta. In the Lahore conspiracy case and other similar cases, a large number of revolutionaries were found guilty and sentenced to long terms of imprisonment; many of them were sent to the Andamans, where Sukhdev and Rajguru were sentenced to death by hanging. On March 23, 1931, the sentence was carried out.

In United Provinces and Punjab, the Viceroy had issued a series of ordinances that effectively imposed "Civil Martial Law."

Congress decided to restart the Civil Disobedience Movement after Gandhi returned from London. Nevertheless, Gandhi was detained within the week. Over the next four months, approximately 80 thousand people were hailed. Protests erupted across India. Picketing liquor stores, burning foreign clothes, and processions were among the main protest activities.

The government dealt with the movement harshly. The congress, as well as other political parties, were declared illegal. The parties' offices and funds were seized. The police had taken over all of Gandhi's ashrams. The movement was crushed in a matter of months. It was suspended in

May 1933 and removed in May 1934. During this phase of CDM, there was an uprising in Alwar, Rajasthan, where Mevs rose up against the local raja, which became known as the Mev Uprising, in protest of his revenue-increasing measures. For many years, Raja was deported to Europe, and his administration was taken over by the central government. Similar uprisings occurred in other areas as well.

Kashmir Martyrs' Day - July 13, 1931

Kashmir Martyrs' Day or Kashmir Day, was a former official state holiday observed in Kashmir in remembrance of 21 Muslim protesters killed on July 13 1931, by Dogra forces of the princely state of Jammu and Kashmir

A guy, while pointing towards the palace of Maharaja Hari Singh in Srinagar, had openly incited a public gathering to wage war against the Maharaja and to raze him to the ground. A case of sedition was filed against him to be tried before a trial court. Can we not appreciate the magnanimity of the Maharaja that he referred to it for judicial scrutiny? In an oligarchy or autocracy, just an allegation of the utterance of such words would have simply catalysed immediate death but despite having numerous precedents warranting the same, the monarch defied them all and made a latitudinarian choice.

That guy namely Abdul Qadeer Khan was charged under sections of sedition and wantonly giving provocation with intent to cause riots under the Ranbir Penal Code. The trial began and on the first four hearings, the courtroom and compound were mobbed. Consequently, it was considered appropriate by the administration to conduct the trial within the jail premises. When the trial commenced from jail on July 13 1931, a mob of around 4000-5000 people thronged its walls, while some even intruded on the jail premises. The mob started sloganeering and intimidating the judge by raising slogans in support of the accused. People became unruly with slogans like Allah-o-Akbar, Islam Zindabad, etc., and tried to barge into the jail premises. Consequently, the police took charge, which resulted in some casualties.

Those unruly lynch mobsters became martyrs for Sheikh Abdullah and his gang. Sheikh Abdullah subsequently conducted a public meeting at the graveyard of the killed mobsters and announced 13th July to be Martyr's day and compared the police action with the Jallianwala Bagh massacre. Immediately after the monarch was forced to leave and Sheikh Abdullah was anointed as his democratic substitute, he declared the Black day for Dogras as martyrs' day for the whole state; the people of Jammu and Dogras were forced to be part of this fiasco as it was declared as a government holiday.

Pingali Venkayya designed the tricolour with a 'charkha' (spinning wheel) in the centre in 1931

From 1919 to 1921, Venkayya continuously kept pushing for the idea of having a national flag of India during the Congress sessions.

"Pingali Venkaiah who is working in Andhra National College, Machilipatnam, has published a book, describing the flags of the countries and has designed many models for our own National Flag. I appreciate his hard struggle during the sessions of the Indian National Congress for the approval of the Indian National Flag," M.K. Gandhi had written in Young India.

The initial flag, called the Swaraj flag, consisted of two red and green bands; the two bands represented the two major religious communities – the Hindus and the Muslims. The flag also had a charkha, which represented Swaraj.

On the advice of M.K. Gandhi, Venkayya added a white band. The white represented peace. Although the first tri-colour was not officially accepted by the All India Congress Committee (AICC), it began to be hoisted on all Congress occasions.

The flag kept being used, but it was in 1931 that concerns were raised about the religious aspect of the flag. Keeping that in mind, a Flag Committee was set up and they came up with a new idea, called Purna Swaraj. They replaced the red with saffron and changed the order of the colours, with saffron on top followed by white and then, green. The charkha was placed on the white band in the middle.

The colours stood for qualities and not communities; the saffron for courage and sacrifice, white for truth and peace, and green for faith and strength. The charkha stood for the welfare of the masses.

Post-Independence, a national flag committee under President Rajendra Prasad replaced the charkha with the Ashok Chakra.

On January 26 2002, the Indian flag code was modified, and after several years of independence, the citizens of India were finally allowed to hoist the Indian flag over their homes, offices and factories on any day and not just on National days, as was the case earlier. Under the revised flag code, now Indians can proudly display the national flag in their homes 24 hours a day including at night, as long as the provisions of the Flag Code are strictly followed to avoid any disrespect to the tri-colour.

From 13th August to 15th August 2022 as part of the celebration of '*Azadi Ka Amrit Mahotsav,*' the 75th anniversary of the country's Independence, on the appeal of PM Narendra Modi 154 crores (1.54 billion) Indians hoisted the *Tiranga* at their homes. A record-breaking flag hoisting movement in the entire world showering respect, love, and affection for our national flag, the tri-colour, a symbol of freedom.

A mass nationalist movement never ever seen before in the last 75 years and a matter of immense pride for all Indians. Our Nation was coloured in Tiranga and a new history was made.

Venkayya was a multi-lingual, with a doctorate in Geology. He had also established an institute in Machilipatnam. Even after his precious contribution to the freedom movement of India and despite being an educationist, Venkayya, passed away in acute poverty inside a hut in Vijayawada on July 4, 1963.

It was only in 2009 that he was dug out of history and a postage stamp was released in his honour. In 2015, the then Urban Development Minister, M Venkaiah Naidu renamed All India Radio, Vijaywada after Venkayya and unveiled his statue on its premises.

Naidu once said that Venkayya was the unsung hero of our freedom struggle who made an immense contribution. He devoted his entire life to the nation and worked relentlessly to make India a free country.

The Second Round Table Conference

Gandhi and the Indian National Congress attended the Second Round Table Conference, which took place in London from September 7 to December 1, 1931.

The session began on September 7, 1931. The main difference between the first and second conferences was that the INC attended the second. One of the outcomes of the Gandhi-Irwin Pact was this. Another difference was that, unlike the previous time, British Prime Minister Macdonald was leading a National government rather than a Labor government. In Britain, the Labor Party had been deposed two weeks before. The British decided to bestow a communal award for representing minorities in India by establishing separate electorates for minority communities. Gandhi was opposed to this.

Gandhi and Ambedkar disagreed at this conference on the issue of separate electorates for untouchables. Gandhi was opposed to segregating untouchables from the Hindu community. The Poona Pact of 1932 resolved this issue. Because of the numerous disagreements among the attendees, the second round-table conference was deemed a failure. While the INC claimed to speak for the entire country, other attendees and party leaders disputed this assertion.

Formation of All Jammu and Kashmir Muslim Conference in 1932

Sheikh Abdullah's rise to power in Kashmir bears an uncanny resemblance to the story of Shah Mir of the 14th century. He was the co-founder of the Muslim Conference in 1932, after successfully orchestrating the first riot in the Valley in 1931, and was an inveterate power seeker. When he sensed the discomfort of Congress with Mahārāja Hari Singh in the late 1930s, he promptly morphed into a nationalist and renamed

"Muslim Conference" as "National Conference." It was in this man that India's leadership placed its utmost trust, to the extent that he managed to prevail on the country's leadership to do something that was not done with the other 560-plus Princely States.

On July 19 1947, a convention of the All Jammu & Kashmir Muslim Conference adopted the "Accession to Pakistan resolution" and demanded the accession of Kashmir to Pakistan. Muslim Conference was renamed as National Conference (probably on the persuasion of Jawahar Lal Nehru) but only the name was changed while the intent and objectives stood conserved. The name was changed just to ensure secular optics, a social engineering technique of Nehru. But their hate for Hindus and Dogra rule can be easily deciphered when Sheikh Abdullah initiated the "Quit Kashmir" movement against the Dogra oligarch.

Poona Pact and Communal Award, 1932

On August 16, 1932, when CDM was in full swing, British Prime Minister Ramsay MacDonald announced the Communal Award, also known as the MacDonald Award, proposing minority representation in legislatures.

According to these awards, (1) provincial legislature seats were to be doubled, (2) separate electorates for communities were to be retained, (3) Muslims were to be given weightage wherever they were in the minority, and (4) 3% of seats were to be reserved in all provinces except NWFP. (5) Minorities were to include the poor, dalits, and untouchables. (6) Amounts were to be allocated to labour, landlords, traders, and industrialists.

In practice, the communal award granted separate electorates to Muslims, Europeans, Sikhs (in Punjab), Indian Christians, Anglo-Indians, the economically backward classes, and even Marathas. (Marathas were given some seats in Bombay.)

The Communal Award's implicit goal was to undermine nationalism and instil parochial loyalty to communities and various spheres of interest. The most painful aspect of the communal Accord for Gandhi was the provision of a separate electorate for the oppressed classes, because this would divide Hindus, and untouchables were an integral part of the Hindu community. Separate electorates for untouchables were primarily the result of Dr B.R. Ambedkar's active efforts in putting such demands in round table conferences. It should be noted that Dr Ambedkar attended all three Round Table Conferences.

From Yarawada Jail, Gandhi wrote to the Prime Minister that if this award, which is related to the poor, is not changed, he will fast until death in the jail itself. Gandhi went on a death fast on September 20, 1932. Dr Ambedkar was approached by Hindu leaders to mediate the situation.

Gandhi and Ambedkar made a pact known as the Poona Pact on September 25, 1932. Ambedkar agreed to joint electorates through this pact, while Gandhi agreed to reserve seats for depressed classes in provincial legislatures that are double the number that exists in provincial legislatures, as well as an adequate representation of Dalits in civil services.

Conclusively, the British were successful in diverting attention away from the Civil Disobedience Movement and creating discord among Hindus through communal awards. For a while, larger issues faded into the background, leaving the common man befuddled about the Poona alliance.

Conference at the Third Round Table

The third Round Table Conference was held between November 17 and December 24, 1932.

This conference also yielded few results. The conference's recommendations were published in a white paper in 1933 and later, debated in the British Parliament. The recommendations were examined, and the Government of India Act of 1935 was enacted as a result.

CHAPTER - XIV

BIPIN CHANDRA PAL PASSED AWAY ON MAY 20, 1932

Bipin Chandra Pal, dubbed the "Burke of India" for his magnificent eloquence and referred to by Sri Aurobindo as one of the "Mightiest Prophets of Nationalism," died in poverty.

Gandhi was chastised for his "priestly, pontificating tendencies." Pal left Congress, but not before launching a devastating attack on Gandhi during the 1921 session.

Between 1905 and 1920, India was rife with the cries of Purna Swaraj, Swadeshi, boycotts, and educational reforms. With eloquence, vision, and initiative, the triumvirate of Lala Lajpat Rai, Bal Gangadhar Tilak, and Bipin Chandra Pal shook the masses' conscience.

Pal, who avoided public life between 1921 and 1932, died in poverty.

Choudhary Rahmat Ali wrote and publicly published the "Pakistan Declaration" on January 28, 1933

In 1933, Mr Choudhary Rahmat Ali, M.A., LL.B., founded the Pakistan Movement.

He partitioned India into two parts: Pakistan and Hindustan. His map of Pakistan included the Punjab, the Northwest Frontier Province, Kashmir, Sindh, and Baluchistan. The rest was Hindustan to him. He planned to create an "independent and separate Pakistan" comprised of five Muslim provinces in the north as a standalone state.

Choudhary Rahmat Ali coined the term Pakistan and moved from England to live in the country he'd named in 1948. His assets were seized due to disagreements with then-Prime Minister Liaquat Ali Khan, and he returned to Cambridge, where he died in 1951, "downtrodden, forlorn, and solitary." Emmanuel College, Cambridge, paid for his funeral, and it took two years of follow-up with the Pakistani High Commissioner for them to be reimbursed.

The signing of the Reichskonkordat on July 20, 1933 in Rome

The *Reichskonkordat* ("Concordat between the Holy See and the German Reich") is a treaty negotiated between the Vatican and the emergent Nazi Germany. It was signed on July 20, 1933, by Cardinal Secretary of State Eugenio Pacelli, who later became Pope Pius XII, on behalf of Pope Pius XI and Vice-Chancellor Franz von Papen on behalf of President Paul von Hindenburg and the German government. It was ratified on 10 September 1933 and it has been in force from that date onward. The treaty guarantees the rights of the Catholic Church in Germany.

In January 1933, Hitler became Chancellor. The passing of the Enabling Act on 23 March, in part, removed the Reichstag as an obstacle to concluding a concordat with the Vatican. The support of the Vatican for anti-Semitism specifically becomes more obvious in the treaty it signed with Nazi Germany on July 20, 1933 called the *Reichskonkordat*.

Hitler gave a speech on March 23, 1933, asking for the adoption of the Enabling Act, where he declared that the Nazis were fighting for Christianity. Thus, when Hitler seized power through the Enabling Act of 1933 and suspended democratic rule "until further notice", Zentrum, the Catholic Center party sided with him. Zentrum leader, Monsignor Ludwig Kaas, who was known to be an advisor to Eugenio Pacelli, (or Pope Pius XII), was one of the leaders who endorsed the Enabling Act.

This led to the implementation of *Gleichschaltung* which was the forcible coordination and assimilation of the Nazi party and the German state. Soon, the Nazi Party dissolved local elections. Reich leaders were then appointed in order to create a Nazi mechanism parallel to that of the state.

Thirty years later, Indian Prime Minister Indira Gandhi had her own Hitlerian moment when President Fakhruddin Ali Ahmed signed the equally-fatal proclamation of Emergency on June 25 1975. Her dictatorship was extremely short-lived in comparison.

But then, Prime Minister Indira Gandhi had her Hitlerian moment. The actual Indian Hitler descended upon the country in the form of her son, Sanjay Gandhi. Both were alike in their pathological lack of and total disregard for basic humanity. Both, quite obviously, surrounded themselves with sycophants, flatterers, mouthpieces, pamphleteers, and...oh well, willing slaves.

1934 - The Night of the Long Knives

The Night of the Long Knives, or the Röhm purge, also called Operation Hummingbird, was a purge that took place in Nazi Germany from June 30 to July 2, 1934.

The SA which was the Nazi Party's paramilitary wing was levelling tacit threats to Hitler. Hitler couldn't take it. On June 30 1934, Hitler ordered the SS to eliminate the SA leadership in what was called the 'Night of Long Knives.' All SA leaders and some other enemies of the Nazi party and conservative figures were slaughtered.

In August 1934, German president Paul Von Hindenburg died. Hitler grabbed this chance to unite the positions of Chancellor and President, thus making his status as the Fuhrer an officially national one. Soon, the German army known as the *Wehrmacht* wore a personal oath of loyalty to the Fuehrer. To Hitler, mind you, not to Germany or its people.

All trade unions were abolished. In replacement, the German Labour Front or the Nazi Organisation was established. All other political parties were dismantled as well leaving just the Nazi Party as the legal one.

Leftist movements were outlawed. Student organizations were dealt with in the same way, leaving only the National Socialist German Student League in existence. The same thing was done to teachers' unions.

On March 31, 1933, the Mufti of Jerusalem visited the German Counsel and assured him that the Muslims "welcome the new German regime & anticipate the spread of Fascism and anti-democratic state leadership to other countries." Arab press had become a tool of Nazi propaganda. Hitler was considered second to Muhammad in the Muslim world for his hatred of Jews. The Grand Mufti of Jerusalem was a great friend of Hitler and it was because of Mufti that the whole Muslim world largely had the support of the Nazis. Hitler was called the 12th Imam in the Arab World. Although "Mein Kampf" included passages against Muslims too, it was specifically translated into Arabic, removing those passages after an agreement with Hitler. In the Arab world, Hitler's image as campaigned against Jews was publicized strongly.

The Royal Indian Marines became the Royal Indian Navy on October 2, 1934

Until 1863, the government of India had its own combatant navy, the Indian Navy, based in Bombay (before 1830, it was called the Bombay Marine). The Indian Navy assisted the Royal Navy in policing Asian waters and conducted regular marine polls. It was abolished in 1863, and it was replaced by two non-combatant marine services based in Bombay and Bengal respectively. In 1877, it was decided to merge the Bombay and Bengal Marines into a new combatant service called HM Indian Marine, with Western (Bombay) and Eastern (Calcutta) Divisions. HM Indian Marine was retitled the Royal Indian Marine in 1892 and the Royal Indian Navy in 1934, and was awarded the King's Color in 1935 for its services.

The Royal Indian Navy had eight warships at the start of the Second World War. By the end of the war, it had grown to 117 combat vessels and 30,000 personnel who had served in various theatres of operations.

Bombay Devadasis Protection Act, 1934

In 1934, the Bombay Presidency brought about a bill to protect women from the devadasi custom by means of an order from the Bombay High Court. It made it an offence to dedicate women to the custom.

The prevailing narrative is that the Devadasi system was nurtured by the Brahminical order and sustained by dominant castes for the purpose of sexual slavery of poor and marginalized women. This narrative fails to take into account the historical status of devadasi women, the participation of multiple castes in the system or the gradation in caste within the devadasi community itself.

Over time, especially with the withering away of the temple economy, the function of courtesan and temple artiste converged. Narratives influenced by Victorian Christian mores further gave a fillip to the worsening social status of these women.

On seeing these breathtakingly beautiful girls sing and dance in temples, these Europeans called them "nautch-girls." It was the first time that a term was used, and understandably so, for the European mind back then, a dancing girl who showed off her body could be nothing more than an entertainer performing for the pleasures of the rich and the famous. Back then, the king, of course, and not the Lord! The whole idea of art as an offering to God was alien to them. This is despite the fact that the Devadasis custom was some 6000 years old and prevalent in ancient Rome, Egypt, Sri Lanka and Indonesia too!

Devdasis enjoyed the same power as the head priest or some of the senior courtiers. They could influence the king, and ask for mercy for the hardened criminals if they thought it was suitable. The peace emissary of any kingdom, they were perhaps the most well-travelled members of the royal court.

In fact, it was customary in those days to invite Devdasis to every festivity in well-to-do families for singing devotional songs and for dancing.

Establishment of the Congressional Socialist Party in the year 1934

The Congress Socialist Party (CSP) was a left-wing faction within Congress. In 1934, it was founded by Acharya Narendra Deva as President and Jay Prakash Narayan as General Secretary.

The emergence of this party was a result of the Indian National Congress's increasing leftist impact. By 1935, one-third of Congress members were socialists. These leaders were opposed to Gandhi's ideas (which they saw as anti-rational). Although they remained active in the workers' and peasant movements, they rejected the Communist Party of India's sectarianism.

Their influence was Marxist-Leninism. The members ranged from those who advocated for armed struggle to those who advocated for peaceful demonstrations.

The Reserve Bank of India was established on April 1, 1935, by the passage of the Reserve Bank of India Act, of 1934

The legislation to establish the Reserve Bank of India was first introduced in January 1927, but it was not until seven years later, in March 1934, that the enactment became a reality. The Reserve Bank's central office was initially located in Calcutta but was permanently relocated to Mumbai in 1937.

Although originally privately owned, the Reserve Bank has been wholly owned by the Government of India since its nationalization in 1949.

The India Government Act of 1935

In response to the Indian National Congress's demand for the establishment of a representative body elected through universal adult suffrage to draft a new constitution, the British Parliament enacted the Government of India Act, of 1935. (It came into effect in 1937) The Congress labelled it a "slave constitution that attempted to strengthen and perpetuate India's economic bondage."

It was based on a report by the Joint Select Committee, led by Lord Linlithgow, which established the two houses of the British parliament. The Act was instrumental in the establishment of the Indian Constitution of 1950.

The Act was founded on:

- Report of the Simon Commission
- The Round Table Conferences' recommendations
- The British government's 1933 White Paper (based on the Third Round Table Conference)
- The Report of the Joint Select Committees

The birth of Pakistan arose from Mohammad Ali Jinnah's frustrations during the 1936–37 Provincial Elections, which were held under the constitutional scheme outlined in the Government of India Act, of 1935.

The Marquess of Linlithgow was appointed as Viceroy of India on April 18, 1936

On April 18, 1936, Victor Alexander John Hope, 2nd Marquess of Linlithgow, was appointed Viceroy of India. Linlithgow carried out the plans for local self-government epitomised in the Government of India Act 1935, which resulted in provincial governments led by the Congress Party in five of British India's eleven provinces, but the princes' obstinacy prevented the establishment of elected governments in the majority of the princely states.

With the onset of World War II, Linlithgow's rejection of the Congress's request for a proclamation that India would be allowed to ascertain its own future after the war resulted in the dismissal of several Congress ministries. On August 8, 1940, Lord Linlithgow expressed an opinion on behalf of the British government. It was known as the August Offer, and it granted the Indian people greater rights in India's governance. Most Indian politicians, including the Congress Party and the Muslim League, declined the offer. He is partially responsible for the Bengal famine of 1943, which killed 3 million people.

Bharat Mata Mandir (Mother India Temple) was inaugurated by Gandhi in the year 1936

Early freedom fighters saw Bharat Mata as a form of Durga. In the Vande Mataram song, she is explicitly identified with Durga.

In her earliest iconography, she was clearly depicted either as a Hindu Goddess or as the Divine cow.

The earliest known anthropomorphic representations of Bharat Mata date back to 1905 when Bengal was partitioned. In the resulting Vande Mātaram movement, Bharat Mata was first painted by Abanindranath Tagore.

Here, she is depicted as a form of Gayatri. She has four arms. She is a saffron-clad woman dressed like a Sadhvi. She holds the Vedas, sheaves of paddy, a piece of white cloth, and a *rudraksha* in her four hands.

Another example of an early representation of Bharat Mata comes from the Bharat Mata temple of Daulatabad Fort. Although it was installed inside the defunct Jama Masjid of the fort in 1947, the specimen dates back to 1906 and is thus one of the earliest known iconographic representations of Bharat Mata.

In this representation, she is identical to Durga. She has 8 arms (*Ashtabhuja*) and holds a trident, sword, chakra, pasha, snake, and fire.

Until 1920, such overtly Hindu representations of Bharat Mata were ubiquitous. Gandhi believed this would offend his Muslim friends. In fact, he approved and sponsored a Bharat Mata temple in Varanasi where she is just depicted in the form of a cartographic map of India.

The Bharat Mata Temple is located at the Mohandas Gandhi Kashi Vidyapith campus, Varanasi and is dedicated to the Bharat Mata (Mother India). It was constructed by Babu Shiv Prasad Gupt and inaugurated by M.K. Gandhi in the year 1936.

Bhikaiji Rustum Cama died on August 13, 1936

Madam Cama spent much of her life in seclusion in foreign nations. She travelled throughout Europe and America to acquire resources and support for her countrymen fighting for their home nation. It should be noted that she was quite successful in her quest. It is not incorrect to say that she was India's first non-governmental ambassador. The American press dubbed her the "Indian Zone of Arch." Madam Cama was old and poor when she returned to India after 33 years. She died on August 16, 1936, after spending nearly eight months in the hospital. Cama remained in seclusion in Europe until 1935, when she petitioned the British government for permission to return home, despite being extremely sick and incapacitated by a stroke earlier that year. She was granted permission to return to India after 33 years, despite the fact that she was unable to participate in the freedom movement.

She had left the majority of her personal belongings to the Avabai Petit Orphanage for Girls. The country had suffered the loss of a glorious leader.

The Indian Posts and Telegraphs Department issued a commemorative stamp in her honour on January 26, 1962, India's 11th Republic Day. The Indian Coast Guard also commissioned the ICGS Bhikaji Cama, a Priyadarshini-class fast patrol vessel in 1997.

Burma was separated from India in 1937

Burma was cut off from the rest of the Indian Empire in 1937, only ten years before India gained independence in 1947.

The British government in India established a penal colony in the Andaman Islands for convicts from the Indian subcontinent in the early nineteenth century, and the Coco Islands served as a source of nutrition for it. According to reports, the British government leased the islands to the Jadwet family of Burma.

The leasing of control over the Coco Islands resulted in poor governance of the islands, prompting the British government in India to hand over control to the government of Lower Burma in Rangoon. The islands were officially incorporated into British Burma in 1882. Even after Burma was separated from British India in 1937, the islands became a self-governing royal colony.

In February 1937, there was an Indian Provincial Election

Provincial elections took place in British India during the winter of 1936–37, as required by the Government of India Act of 1935. Madras,

Central Provinces, Bihar, Orissa, United Provinces, Bombay Presidency, Assam, NWFP, Bengal, Punjab, and Sindh were the eleven provinces where elections were held.

The Bombay Presidency included the following modern-day areas: Konkan extending till Kasargod, Western Maharashtra, North Karnataka, all of Gujarat east of Ahmadabad, parts of Rajasthan, all of Sindh province of Pakistan, and some parts of Yemen and Oman

The electoral results were announced in February 1937. The Indian National Congress gained control of eight of the provinces, with the exclusion of Punjab and Sindh. The All-India Muslim League was unable to form a government in any of the provinces.

In October and November 1939, the Congress ministries resigned in protest of Viceroy Lord Linlithgow's decision to declare India a belligerent in World War II without consulting the Indian people.

Until recently, the only religious separation in colonial India was between Hindus and Muslims. However, the provincial Assembly Elections of 1937 resulted in a political and cultural schism between Hindus and Muslims.

In 1937, Gandhi squandered a hard-won election victory by stepping down from provincial governments as part of his ill-advised Quit India movement. This move had the reverse effect of what was planned. The British were adamant that nothing should get in the way of the war effort. Instead of feeling pressed, they simply reduced their reliance on Congress and, as a result, its clout. Furthermore, the vacuum that was created provided Jinnah with a divinely inspired opportunity. A jubilant Jinnah dubbed the Congress move a "Himalayan blunder."

V. P. Menon, a distinguished civil servant, observed that "by resigning, the Congress Party demonstrated regrettable political wisdom."

On March 24, 1941, Jinnah declared Muslims to be an independent country. This favoured the British strategy. Liaquat Ali Khan was the one who persuaded Jinnah to run in the 1937 elections. Giving up the gains of a massive electoral victory over an ill-timed Quit India movement in 1937 made the British deeply suspicious, opening the door for Jinnah.

1937 May- Savarkar's unconditional release from Ratnagiri internment

Vinayak Damodar Savarkar was expelled from India in May 1937. It had been twenty-seven years since he had been illegally detained by British police on French soil in March 1910. These years in the cold included a decade of agony in the brutal Cellular Jail in the Andaman Islands. Savarkar was then transferred to Ratnagiri on the condition that he refrains from engaging in any political campaigning. His final release was well-received. His next move piqued everyone's attention. Savarkar was elected president of the Hindu Mahasabha later that year.

Savarkar was elected President of the Akhil Bharat Hindu Mahasabha at its 19ᵗʰ session in Karnavat (Ahmedabad)

Following his release from Ratnagiri on August 1, 1937, Mr Savarkar attended a programme commemorating Tilak's death anniversary. Savarkar's decision to join the Democratic Swarajya Party came at an appropriate moment. The political malleability of the time allowed for a plethora of such political outfits to thrive within the confines of Congress. Tilak founded the first Democratic Swarajya Party as an informal platform within Congress. However, Savarkar was powerless to help Hindus in that party. He became a member of the Hindu Mahasabha.

Mr Savarkar attempted to revitalize the Hindu Mahasabha during his tenure as President. On the other hand, Mr Savarkar resigned from the party and chose a solitary life for himself.

Following his election as president of the Mahasabha, Savarkar travelled throughout the country, rallying the Hindu community to oppose the Muslim League's inequitable desires for partition while also shaping his visions of a unified and renewed Hindu society.

On July 10, 1943, in response to the Congress's disinformation campaign about a probable alliance between the Hindu Mahasabha and the Muslim League for elections in the Sindh province of undivided India, Savarkar stated that one day, Congress leaders would be forced to propagate Hindu principles by wearing a *janeu* not only on their bodies but also on their coats.

Subhash Chandra Bose was elected as the Congressional President in 1938

Bose was elected as president of INC in 1938. The situation became more serious when he got re-elected as president after defeating Gandhi's candidate in 1939.

Abandoning all pretence of neutrality, Gandhi declared that Sitaramaiyya's defeat was also my defeat. The old guard and Gandhi supporters immediately went to work, obstructing the newly-appointed President at every turn. Bose may have decided to take over because he was dissatisfied with Nehru's leadership. Gandhi's and Nehru's initial zeal for independence and socialism had waned since he was handed over the Congress Presidency in 1929, and then again in 1936-37. Sitaramaiyya mentions that throughout these years, Netaji largely kept to himself and maintained a bipartisan position on the majority of issues. He cites that it wasn't until the end of September 1938 that it was discovered that Subhas Babu wanted to be President of Congress in Tripuri. In his absence, Gandhi preferred Maulana Abul Kalam Azad as the next president, and Sitaramaiyya was his second choice. However, Maulana later withdrew, leaving Sitaramaiyya and Subhas to compete.

Bose had been a vocal opponent of the British government's federal scheme, as outlined in the Government of India Act of 1935. Unlike other elements within the party who were in favour of accepting the new concessions from the British, he had proposed a mass movement for "Purna Swaraj." The old guard, including Mohandas Gandhi, however, refused to listen to his words. As a result, he contested for re-election to the presidency of the next annual Congress session, which was to be held in Tripuri.

Formation of Razakars

The Razakars were intended to be the armed wing of the MIM (which is a present-day political party that goes by the name "AIMIM") and upheld the Islamic domination of Hyderabad. By 1948, the Nizam didn't want the growing public opinion of Hindus that Hyderabad should accede to India grow roots in the state, and ordered the Razakars to brutally suppress the Hindu population. Qasim Razvi was made the chief of the Jihadi forces.

The Razakars raised 2 lakh Jihadis in their force and raided Hindu-majority villages in Telangana. Over 150 villages in rural Telangana were pushed to Islamic brutality, and over 40,000 civilians fled to the Central Provinces of India from Telangana for refuge. These refugees then proceeded to retaliate against the murderous Razakars through frequent raids to reclaim their land in the bordering areas of Central Provinces and Telangana.

The Razakar militia wanted to preserve Nizam's rule and was inclined towards eventually acceding to Pakistan. They played a brutal role in repressing the majority Hindu population of the Hyderabad princely state because the latter wanted to join India. The group was defeated after India launched Operation Polo to integrate the state with the rest of the country.

The Razakars rampaged in villages, molested women, killed men, and destroyed everything in sight. This army, endorsed by the Nizam, wanted to wreak as much havoc as possible and fill Nizam's coffers as it became clear that the Nizam was losing his hold on his state. One of the tallest leaders of the state and India's ex-prime minister, P V Narasimha Rao, had described the events of Rangapuram and Laxmipuram villages as South India's Jallianwala Bagh. In these villages, Razakars came down heavily on the common people who had celebrated India's freedom from the British in August 1947. Former Prime Minister P.V. Narasimha Rao's Guru and mentor, Swami Ramanand Tirtha's name stands foremost among those who led the resistance from the front.

The Razakars continued their barbaric campaign till the Indian army routed their forces with Operation Polo in 1948, leading to the liberation of Hyderabad from Nizam's control and accession to the Indian Union. These incidents highlight the sacrifices made by Telangana villagers to ensure the survival of Hinduism in present-day Telangana.

The Distress of Hindus under Nizam's Regime

Sir Muhammad Akbar Nazar Ali Hydari (Akbar Hydari is Aditi Rao Hydari's great-grandfather) deserves special mention. He was Hyderabad's Finance Minister for a long time before being appointed as Prime Minister from March 18th, 1937, to September 1941. One of the first things he did was to fire a large number of Hindu employees in the Public Works and Accounts Departments. He eventually broadened his witch hunt to include other departments. Following that, he turned his vulture-like gaze to the private sector. He unilaterally announced the nationalization of several key industries in the state, with the obvious blessings of the Nizam.

As a result, the government acquired a 51 per cent stake in massive industrial conglomerates meticulously constructed by the Hindus. The massive profits from all of these ventures were used to fund the terrorist activities of the Ittehad and, later, the fanatical Razakkars.

In 1939, Osmania University forbade Hindu students from wearing dhotis and kurtas, instead requiring them to wear the dress permitted for Muslim students. On that year's Sri Krishna Janmashtami, Hindus sang "Vande Mataram" in the Hindu prayer hall. The ramifications were immediate. The prayer hall was locked from the outside, and the university administration issued a warning – you will not be able to sing Vande Mataram on the university campus again.

Those who had sung it were required to submit a written apology or face rustication. Following this, the Education Department issued a circular prohibiting the singing of Vande Mataram in all schools and universities. As a result, approximately 1,200 students were expelled from colleges and schools.

The upper echelons actively encouraged the lower rungs to continue the pressure and harassment of Hindus. Physical violence against Hindus can be threatened and enforced at any time, often under fabricated pretexts.

Hindus were barred from constructing or repairing temples in any area where Muslims lived. Temples were frequently desecrated without cause, and perpetrators were "rarely traced, and if traced, never reprimanded." Muslim Ulema and, later, Ittehad members went on a rampage, converting Hindus to Islam.

Hindus' spirits had truly plummeted under his regime. This reality fueled Nizam's fantasy of becoming the leader of the entire Muslim world. The Nizam, on the other hand, was heartbroken when the Western powers permanently crushed the Ottoman Empire.

This heinous state excludes subsequent terrorist acts against Hindus committed by people like Mahmud Nawaz Khan, founder of the Majilis-i-Ittehad-ul-Mussulmeen (the pre-independence incarnation of Asaduddin Owaisi's AIMIM). He was succeeded by the ultra-fanatical Bahadur Khan (Jung), who "insisted on declaring Hyderabad a Muslim state." This "demand" received a boost when Jinnah stepped in and declared that the State of Hyderabad's 87 per cent Hindu majority should be reduced to a statutory minority. The passage of the dreaded Right to Education Act in "independent" India was one of the most frightening methods of reducing Hindus to a statutory minority.

Subhas Chandra Bose resigned as President of the Indian National Congress in March 1939

Gandhi meticulously planned his counter-moves against Bose. There were many Gandhi supporters on the Congress' working committee. So, despite the fact that Bose was now President, he had very little power to exercise because he was not allowed to rule the party.

The final blow to Bose came in March 1939, when the annual party meeting was scheduled. Bose became ill and was unable to attend the meeting. He sent a telegram to Patel, requesting that the meeting be rescheduled for the following annual session. At the same time, Bose sent Gandhi a telegram requesting that the working committee be appointed according to his wishes. Gandhi, on the other hand, did not act or nominate anyone.

Congressmen were outraged by Bose's dictatorial leadership style.

They assumed that Bose did not want the working committee to function at all while he was away. Patel and 11 other working committee members resigned in response to Bose's refusal to apologize. However, Bose refused.

When Subhash was brought to the dais on a stretcher during this session, one of the congressmen remarked, "Why don't you check whether he has any onions under his armpits?" (When onions are kept under the armpits, they raise the body's temperature.) Such was the tragic schism between Subhash and Gandhi and his followers. Subhash resigned from Congress the following month, and he was now on a wholly distinct path.

Subhash Chandra Bose was kicked out of the Congress Party since he possessed the strength of character and competence to win an election against Mohandas Gandhi's desires. His distinct personality shone through when he alone, among all the leading figures in the Congress inner circle, remained unaffected by Mohandas Gandhi's magical charm.

Bose was a staunch opponent of Gandhi's ideologies. Gandhi devised a meticulous plan, not a hasty decision. He did not depose Bose from his throne (as president). It would have been an obvious choice at the time.

According to a declassified CIA record, Bose was later removed from the presidency of Congress by "British influences."

The Second World War began on September 3, 1939. According to the Viceroy, India is also at war

World War II began in September 1939, when Hitler and Stalin invaded Poland and divided it among themselves. According to Hitler and Stalin's friendship treaty, the Nazis would receive half of Poland, while the Communists would receive the entire rest, as well as the Baltic states (Latvia, Lithuania, Estonia), and Finland. In other words, all of the big Communist boasts about resisting Hitler were simply the result of a very loving relationship going sour in 1941. Have you ever noticed how history textbooks conveniently ignore the wonderful friendship that existed between Communists and Nazis? You can infer the political inclinations of those who wrote those textbooks from this.

One of the lesser-known facts about World War II is that India's involvement of men and material bailed out the West.

Over 2.6 million Indian troops played a critical role in the greatest conflict of the twentieth century, assisting Britain in staying in the fight. Indian forces were sent to major war zones around the world. They terrorized German tank divisions in Africa, fought the Japanese in Burma, participated in the invasion of Italy, and were heavily involved in battles in the Middle East.

Indian material assistance was also critical.

Weapons, ammunition, timber, steel, and, most importantly, food, were transported – or, one could argue, siphoned off – in massive quantities to Europe.

Field Marshal Claude Auchinleck, Commander-in-Chief of the British Indian Army from 1942 to 1945, stated that the British "couldn't have survived both wars if they hadn't had the Indian Army."

Even the bigoted and bloodthirsty British Prime Minister Winston Churchill, who had a pathological hatred of Indians ("They are a beastly race with a beastly religion," he once said), acknowledged the "unrivalled bravery of Indian soldiers and officers" during World War II.

Gandhi prioritized the congregation of nonviolent resistance above all else, even India's independence. During the Second World War, he became concerned about the possibility of the British granting India independence, as this would imply India's participation in violent warfare.

During the Second World War, the Hindu Mahasabha and Savarkar's militarization strategy aimed at creating the ultimate push towards freedom by infiltrating the British Indian Army, sowing discontent, and forming a revolt similar to that of 1857. Simultaneously, there appears to have been planning for a post-British scenario in which Hindus would be in direct conflict with Muslims, who had already begun to raise the prospect of a separate land for their faith.

In such a circumstance, where Muslim army strength exceeds Hindu army strength, especially in sensitive territories such as the NWFP and Punjab, not arming oneself militarily would mean surrendering to a powerful and theocratic opponent. This was driven by a belief that Hindus needed to prepare for a power struggle between Muslims and Hindus when the British left India.

The Indian Army had just over 200,000 troops at the start of the war in 1939, enough to keep India in chains and the British safe from Indian revolutionaries. The army's size was increased to 1,000,000 in 1940. In total, India supplied 2,581,726 army, navy, and air force guerillas.

In addition, 14 million Indian labourers worked nonstop to keep the war farms and factories operating.

But what drew so many Indians to fight for the British? Was the British Indian Army, as some historians claim, the largest volunteer force in modern history?

The truth is that Britain had reduced India to such abject poverty over a 200-year period that Indians were willing to seize any opportunity to make a living—even if it was at the expense of life. As soldiers, they could at least send money home instead of living on subsistence wages.

Furthermore, if World War I selection ploys are any indication, not everyone willingly signed up. According to reports, in Haryana, for example, the British cut off irrigation water supplies to those who refused to join the army. Brutal methods such as "stripping people naked and forcing them to stand in front of their womenfolk" were also employed. People were pushed into thorny bushes and forced to stand there for hours until they said, "Yes, I'm ready for enlistment."

The toll on India was high. During the fighting, 24,338 Indian soldiers were killed. In addition, 64,354 people were injured, and 11,754 people went missing.

It is likely that if Indian troops had not been present, at least as many British Commonwealth troops would have died. As a result, hundreds of thousands of British-born people living in the United Kingdom, Australia, New Zealand, and Canada owe their existence to the supreme sacrifice of Indians.

Nonetheless, the sacrifices of these incredibly brave Indians, who received numerous gallantry awards, were not in vain. The returning soldiers had seen firsthand that the British were not eight feet tall, but rather men of small stature and small hearts. Inspired by Netaji Bose's feats, which had struck fear into British hearts, these Indian soldiers were not in the mood to be governed by foreigners, especially racists.

The Hindu Mahasabha's Working Committee

Under Savarkar's leadership, the working committee of the Hindu Mahasabha met in Bombay on September 10, 1939, and passed resolutions stating that the Indian Army is not the British Army, but the army of Indians, and that the government should make every effort to instil this sentiment. That would be the only way they could conscript the troops' support in any global conflict. It urged the British government to increase the size of the Indian Territorial Forces and the University Training Corps, as well as to "establish such military organizations in provinces where they do not currently exist."

It implored the British to Indianize the army by scrapping the dichotomy between "warrior" and "non-warrior" castes; that Indians be inducted into all branches of the Indian defence forces; and that they are granted the same rights and privileges as British soldiers. The meeting also encouraged Hindus to form a "Hindu National Militia" (Hindu Saini Karan Mandals) in their respective provinces for Hindu youth between the ages of eighteen and forty. According to the resolution, the government should encourage the manufacture of arms and ammunition in India.

Rashbehari established the Hindu Mahasabha's Japan Branch

The Hindu Mahasabha's stance drew praise from a variety of sources, including across the border in distant Japan. On September 22, Rash Behari Bose, who had been keeping a close eye on Savarkar and his ideology, wrote him a letter expressing his complete support for the idea of militarization. The revolutionary dream of building on the 1857 war model of instilling disdain in the minds of natives serving in the British Indian Army against their colonial master, resulting in a nationwide uprising in the army and heralding the end of the empire, remained as efficacious as ever. Rash Behari Bose also expressed his deep scepticism about whether this will actually happen, provided that Gandhi – the British Empire's most ardent supporter in India – was strongly opposed to such a move.

Rash Behari Bose volunteered in the summer of 1938 to establish a Japanese branch of the Hindu Mahasabha. On November 14, 1938, Savarkar agreed to this idea with the caveat that the organization be subordinate to the Indian Office. Rash Behari Bose published a detailed article on Savarkar in the Japanese journal *Dai Ajia Shugi* (Greater Asianism). Providing a comprehensive biographical sketch of Savarkar, who was described as a "rising leader of New India," the article lauded him for his "heroism, chivalry, adventure, and epitome of patriotism..." Praise for him is praise for the spirit of sacrifice.

The resilience of the Royal Indian Navy's officers and sailors was expanded after the declaration of war

When World War II began in 1939, the Royal Indian Navy was a meagre force of about 114 officers and 1,732 sailors, with only 16 officers manning the Naval Headquarters, which was situated inside the Naval Dockyard at Bombay. Since New Delhi served as the focal point of command and control during the war, a Naval Liaison officer was stationed there in October 1939 to shorten the time it took to process important documents.

However, because this was also inadequate, the Naval Headquarters was relocated from Bombay to New Delhi in March 1941.

By the end of the war, its resilience had nearly fifteen folded. It had 2,438 officers, 214 warrant officers, and 21,193 ratings in December 1945. Several uprisings occurred in the service during this time period.

The Royal Indian Navy was the heir to the great seafaring traditions of South India's coastal kingdoms. During World War II, it played a minor but critical role in the fight against the Axis powers. Although initially limited to protecting Indian ports and the sea lanes leading to them, its responsibilities grew to include local naval defence.

It also performed combat duties and served admirably in the Middle East and the Bay of Bengal. Its ships also operated in European waters, including the Mediterranean and the Atlantic. The Red Sea was, perhaps, the most important and early combatant assignment, with Indian ships actively participating in the capture of Massawa from the Italians and fighting the Italian navy off the coast of Somaliland. They were also successful in the Persian Gulf, where their duties primarily involved patrolling the coast and escorting supply ships. Following Japan's entry into the war, Burmese waters became the Royal Indian Navy's primary field of operation.

It participated in patrolling and worked well together in combined operations. Movements through treacherous changes and along the highly indented Arakan coastline were perilous, but the Indian Navy did not falter and delivered a magnificent display of valour and skill, laying the groundwork for subsequent generations to emulate and implement.

CHAPTER - XV

THE FORWARD BLOC

In 1939, at the first intra-congress, Bose concocted his own independent party, The Forward Bloc.

Bose stepped down from Congress in 1939 and founded the All India Forward Bloc as a rebellion within the Indian Congress, which was attacked and nearly destroyed by Communists in the 1950s, who formed the "All India Forward Bloc" out of it. His goal was to free India from colonial yokes.

When Netaji founded the Forward Bloc after resigning from Congress, the insecure Nehru stated, "Bose formed the Forward Bloc to target the Congress in response to a question from an American journalist."

In Bombay, Bose met with Savarkar to discuss the possibility of collaboration between the Hindu Mahasabha and the Forward Bloc. Savarkar advised Subhash Babu to seek axis support and raise an army from prisoners of war. When the Times of India bragged about their meeting, it became rage news. This prompted British officials to keep a close eye on Subhash Babu. He was under surveillance for days before finally fleeing to Germany via Afghanistan.

Michael O'Dwyer, The Colonial Official, was shot by Udham Singh

Udham Singh, born on December 26, 1899, held Michael D'wyer, the Lieutenant Governor of Punjab at the time of the Jallianwala Bagh massacre, responsible for the massacre.

Bhagat Singh and his revolutionary group influenced him a lot. In 1924, Udham Singh joined the Ghadar Party, a multi-ethnic party that challenged the British Empire's ownership of India and is also credited with laying the groundwork for future Indian revolutionary movements for the Indian independence movement. On the orders of Bhagat Singh, Udham Singh returned to India in 1927, bringing with him 25 associates as well as revolvers and ammunition. He was arrested, however, for having unlicensed firearms and was sentenced to five years.

He was released in 1931, but his movements were constantly monitored. In 1934, he moved to London and worked as an engineer while secretly plotting the assassination of Michael D'wyer. In Singh's diaries from 1939 and 1940, he misspells O'Dwyer's surname as "O'Dyer," raising the possibility that he mistook O'Dwyer for General Dyer, who actually led the troops.

When Michael D'wyer was scheduled to speak at a joint meeting of the East India Association and the Central Asian Society at Caxton Hall in London on March 13, 1940, Udham Singh entered the hall with a handgun to execute his plan. At the end of the meeting, Singh shot O'Dwyer twice as he approached the podium, one bullet passing through his heart and right lung and killing him instantly.

Udham Singh was apprehended for the murder. The charges were formally levied for the murder of Michael D'wyer on April 1, 1940, and while awaiting his trial, he went on a 42-day hunger strike during which he had to be force-fed. Singh was declared guilty and sentenced to death. Four months later, on July 31, 1940, he was hanged at Pentonville Prison. Udham Singh's remnants are still on display at Amritsar's Jallianwala Bagh.

Subhas Chandra Bose's flee to Germany

Bose openly challenged British rule. On March 19, 1940, he presided over an All India Anti-Compromise Conference in Ramgarh, Bihar, organised by Swami Sahajan and Saraswati, in which he expressed his displeasure with the Congress's compromising nature. "As soon as the war began, Mohandas Gandhi proceeded to Shimla without caring to seek advice from the Congress Working Committee and without notifying the

Viceroy that he was in favour of rendering unconditional help to Great Britain in the prosecution of the war."

He organized a mass demonstration against the British's false narrative, which claimed that Nawab Sirajuddaula pushed around 160 British into a small room, resulting in mass deaths. This was based on General Holwell's accounts. Netaji was arrested on July 2, 1940. In captivity, he went on a hunger strike and was eventually released in November 1940. All the while, he urged Congress to initiate civil disobedience. On May 20, 1940, Nehru stated that launching a civil disobedience campaign at a time when Britain was engaged in a life-or-death struggle would be a betrayal of India's honour. Gandhi also refused to participate, claiming that he did not want to gain independence from Britain's ruins. After facing sustained opposition from pro-Gandhi factions within the Congress and severe restrictions from the British Raj, culminating in his house arrest in Kolkata, Netaji took a flight of imagination and vision and escaped in a most idiosyncratic manner to mobilize Indians abroad towards an armed struggle against the Britishers to free India from their clutches.

In January 1941, Netaji's audacious attempt to flee from India was to later emerge as the Commander-in-Chief of Azad Hind Fauz and liberate India through military means.

Netaji utilized every tactic. He worked with the British to promote Indian independence. He attempted it in the manner of Gandhi and Nehru, as well as their Indian National Congress. When that failed, he travelled from Calcutta to Peshawar to Kabul before fleeing to the Soviet Union to seize the opportunity raised due to World War II. From there, it's on to Germany.

RSS leadership

In 1939, at a Gurudakshina festival, Hedgewar announced that Golwalkar would be the next general secretary (*sarkaryavah*, the second-most-important position in the RSS). A day before his death on 21 June 1940, he gave Golwalkar a sheet of paper asking him to be the RSS leader. On 3 July, five state-level *sanghchalak* (directors) in Nagpur announced Hedgewar's decision.

Golwalkar was different from Dr Hedgewar in his approach to politics. Unlike Dr Hedgewar, who came from the background of the Calcutta-based revolutionary group Anuseelan Samiti, Golwalkar had taken spiritual initiation from Swami Akandananda, a direct disciple of Sri Ramakrishna. Swami Akandananda was known for his humanitarian services.

In the 1940s, there were several reports by the British Home Department which held RSS and Golwalkar suspicion of their anti-British activity.

To cite reports-

"Golwalkar condemned those who were selfishly helping the British Government. He declared that his organisation has resolved to do its duty even if the whole world turns against them, and they are ready to sacrifice their lives for the cause of country even after the partition." - No. 28, Section F, Home Dept (27/04/1942)

British anxiety had good reasons. A report warned, "Cadres had infiltrated the Army, Navy, Post & Telegraphs, railway and administrative services, so that there may be no difficulty in capturing administrative department when the time comes." It further stated. "the organisation is intensely anti-British and its tone is increasingly becoming militant." – 13/10/1943, Home Department (G.A Ahmed)

Jinnah Proposes a Two-Nation Theory

On March 24, 1941, Jinnah declared the Muslims to be a separate nation. This gave fire to the British strategy. The British were making Gandhi utterly worthless by bolstering Jinnah. Amid a difficult war, his loud proclamations of nonviolence did not sit well with the British.

"If they (the Germans) take possession of your beautiful island if Hitler chooses to occupy your homes, vacate them." Gandhi told Viceroy Linlithgow in 1940, "If he does not give you free passage out, allow yourself, every man, woman, and child, to be slaughtered."

Besides the NWFP and Balochistan, Jinnah's plan for Pakistan included all of Punjab, all of Delhi, all of Sindh, as well as Assam and Hyderabad as well as a corridor connecting East and West Pakistan.

Veer Savarkar towards the youth in May 1941

Veer Savarkar urged Hindu youths to enlist in large numbers in the Indian army. Even before Britain's direct involvement in WW2, Savarkar emphasized militarization.

The following is the memorial that Savarkar presented to the Provincial and Central Indian Governments and Legislatures in 1938, a year before the invasion of Poland (which drew the UK into WW2): We, the undersigned citizens of India, demand that the Provincial and Central Governments institute forthwith compulsory military training in high schools and colleges, and establish at least one modern military college in each Presidency to recruit officers and soldiers.

Furthermore, on April 23, 1939, Savarkar sent a cablegram to US President Roosevelt advocating India's independence from British imperialist rule.

Savarkar's critics must explain why a supposed "British stooge" would ask the US President to persuade the UK to withdraw its armed occupation of Hindustan.

It is now necessary to investigate the reasons cited by Savarkar for this militarization drive. On the eve of his 59th birthday, May 25, 1941, Savarkar sent a letter stating, "Unforeseen facilities are being made available to you. Unexpected opportunities have arisen in front of you. If you use these facilities and opportunities to militarize Hinduism, you help no one more than yourself! If you don't get this done, nothing else will work."

On April 8, 1942, Savarkar stated, "If Hindus are thus trained, armed, and prepared in their millions, then and only then will they be able to defend their hearths and homes from the ravages of war and to suppress any internal anti-Hindu anarchy." To accomplish this, one must join the government's military force for the motherland.

It is worth noting that, as a result of WW2, Britain was ready to arm the Indians that it had previously disarmed. Savarkar saw this as a perfect opportunity to militarise the Hindus, which he believed would result in

India's freedom, as evidenced by the phrase "to further the cause of the political emancipation of our motherland," as well as to curb "anti-Hindu" developments, which must refer to the growth of the Muslim League.

The British were willing to train and militarize long-disarmed Indians. Savarkar saw it as an opportunity to rekindle the Hindus' martial spirit. As Bose himself acknowledged, Savarkar's militarization drive aided the INA's efforts. According to Goreges Ohsawa, a Japanese writer, in his study of Subhas Bose and Rash Behari Bose's activities: "The chief of the Indian National Army proceeded alone to the front line and talked to Indian officers and soldiers in the British Army in strong heart-stirring words not to be false to their love of India and the Independence of India." The impossible was accomplished. The shooting has been halted. During World War II, Savarkar's militarization policy began to take shape.

In addition, there is an important aspect to note that the naval recruitment that Savarkar emphasized, as previously described, was instrumental in achieving independence. Clement Atlee, the British Prime Minister during India's independence, later admitted to retired Calcutta High Court Chief Justice Phani Bhushan Chakraborty that it was the Naval Mutiny that forced the British to leave.

On September 3, 1939, Viceroy Linlithgow declared, "Britain had automatically turned India into a belligerent in the allied cause." In response, Congress issued a demand for immediate independence. As a result, Linlithgow attempted to sway Muslims in his favour. He promised Muslims that their opinions and interests would be taken into account.

In March 1940, Jinnah declared the Muslim League's goal to be the establishment of a separate Muslim state, and he also actively supported the British in their subsequent war efforts.

In retrospect, it is clear that Savarkar was correct on this point. During partition, the Muslim regiments of the army were assigned to Pakistan, while the rest of the army was divided along religious lines in response to the Muslim League's demand. In fact, "any Muslim domiciled in Pakistan would not be able to serve in India, and any non-Muslim domiciled in India would not be able to join Pakistan's armed forces." Pakistan received 140,000 of the 410,000 army men, 40% of the navy, and 30% of the air force.

The Japanese leadership approved a "Plan for Acceleration of the End of the War with America and Britain" just before the attack on Pearl Harbor

Several recommendations were made in the plan, such as the separation of Australia from Britain and the encouragement of Indian independence movements.

Japanese Prime Minister Hideki Tojo urged Indians to use World War II to rise up against British power and establish an India for Indians in a series of speeches to the Japanese parliament, the Diet.

Following the surrender of British forces in the Battle of Singapore in February 1942, Tojo stated, "The true prosperity of Greater East Asia cannot be achieved without the liberation of India." "We have decided to strike a decisive blow against British power and military establishment in India," he stated on April 4, 1942.

Japan's problem was that Mohandas Gandhi's Indian National Congress was hostile to it. Indian leaders were concerned that Tokyo would turn India into a vassal state. They had made a mistake. In The Indian National Army and Japan (June 2008), Joyce C. Lebra, an American historian of Japan and India, writes: "Contrary to the suspicions of many Indians in the independence movement, Japan at no time planned a major invasion of India or actual incorporation of India into the Greater East Asia Co-Prosperity Sphere."

The attack on Pearl Harbor changed the course of World War II

The attack on Pearl Harbour on December 7, 1941, was one of the most poignant moments of the war, as it signalled the official entry of the United States into the tension, which eventually led to the dropping of nuclear bombs on the Japanese cities of Hiroshima and Nagasaki in 1945.

Relations between the United States and Japan were already deteriorating before Japan attacked Pearl Harbor in 1941.

Japan annexed Korea in 1910 and invaded China in 1937, raising concerns in the United States and other Western powers about Japan's open expansionism.

Between December 1937 and January 1938, the "Nanking Massacre" or "Rape of Nanking" occurred, in which Japanese soldiers killed and raped Chinese civilians and combatants.

The United States opposed Japan's belligerence in China and imposed economic sanctions and trade embargoes following its invasion. Japan was heavily reliant on imports of oil and other natural resources, which was one of the reasons it invaded China, and later French Indo-China (present-day Vietnam, Laos, and Cambodia). The plan was to seize control of major Chinese ports to gain access to resources such as iron, rubber, tin, and, most importantly, oil.

On December 7, 1941, at nearly 7.55 in the morning, approximately 180 Imperial Japanese Navy aircraft attacked the US Naval base at Pearl Harbor on the Hawaiian island of Oahu.

Over 2,300 Americans were slain in the bombing, which also destroyed the battleships USS Arizona and USS Oklahoma. Approximately, 160 aircraft were destroyed, and another 150 were damaged.

"AIR RAID ON PEARL HARBOR X THIS IS NOT A DRILL," the naval officer at Pearl Harbor commanded in a frantic dispatch to the fleet units and major Navy commands that morning.

The Emergence of the Rani of Jhansi Regiment (RJR) of the Indian National Army (INA)

When the world was talking about women's empowerment, The Rani of Jhansi regiment, founded by leader Subhash Chandra Bose, was the first of its kind in Asia and was only for women.

Captain Lakshmi Swaminathan (also known as Lakshmi Sahgal), a doctor by profession, was the commander of the women's regiment in Netaji Subhash Chandra Bose's Azad Hind Fauj.

She was ranked as a colonel, but she was always referred to as a captain.

Lakshmi Sahgal assisted wounded prisoners of war during the British armies' surrender to Japanese forces in Singapore, which was then Burma, in 1942. For the Azad Hind Fauz, she recorded the army song, *Chalo Dilli* (On to Delhi). On March 4, 1946, she was apprehended and brought to India to receive a heroic embrace. She was awarded the Padma Vibhushan in 1998.

This unit was the first in recorded military history to be made up entirely of women. Although the Soviet Union's Red Air Force had a few squadrons of female pilots during WWII, the support staff was mostly male. In any case, these squadrons were not officially known as "women's regiments." The RJR's position as the world's only all-female ground forces fighting force is considered one of the best.

Eventually, Lakshmi Swaminathan's selection was a key figure in the formation of the RJR. She had it all, and she emerged from the battles and struggles with a larger-than-life image.

The book contains many interesting vignettes about the formation of the Rani of Jhansi regiment, its impact on the resident Indian populations of Singapore, Malaya, and Burma, and the difficulties faced by Netaji and his senior officers in forming the unit. There were many sceptics, but they were eventually won over. It's unclear whether the Ranis (as the regent's members were dubbed) would be sent to the battlefield. Subhas was unequivocal in his belief that the presence of combat female soldiers in Indian territory would cause men in the British Indian Army to desert to the Indian National Army.

The Bombay session of the AICC passed the Quit India resolution on August 8, 1942

It was a watershed moment when Mohandas Gandhi launched a civil disobedience movement during World War II at the Bombay session (now Mumbai) of the All India Congress Committee (AICC) on August 8, 1942, demanding the end of British rule in India. The *Bharat Chhodo Andolan*, also known as the August *Kranti*, was the final act of British rule in India in the history of the Independence struggle.

As the INA prepared to fight the British Indian Army on the battlefield, Gandhi launched the Quit India movement in 1942, which was similar to what Bose had demanded in 1939. The movement was launched with the proper zeal. But sadly, it was crushed within three weeks, and it was all over in a matter of months.

It is true that Gandhi did wonders for India. But to say that the Quit India movement resulted in independence would be misrepresenting the facts or having partial views. Savarkar had recognised early on that the "Quit India" movement could devolve into "Split India."

On August 16 1942, at Chimur in Maharashtra, many RSS workers participated directly in a Quit India agitation which resulted in brutal suppression by the British. Dada Naik, who was also the head of the Chimur RSS branch, was sentenced to death by the British. The Hindu Mahasabha leader, Dr N.B Khare, took up his case with the authorities. Ramdas Rampure, another RSS cadre, was shot dead by the British.

Confidential reports blamed two persons for these uprisings. One was Dada Naik who, the report said, was 'largely behind the recent disturbances' and the other was Sant Tukdoji Maharaj, who was closely associated with the RSS, and was suspected to have been involved in disturbances at Chimur.

Formation of the Indian People's Theatre Association

Indian People's Theatre Association (IPTA) is the oldest association of theatre artists in India, formed on May 25 1943. Needless, the goal of IPTA was to spread the Communist venom in the wider Indian society by capturing theatre, and to an extent, folk and performing arts.

The launch timing of IPTA was near-perfect – in Bombay in May 1943, when the CPI was holding the First Congress. And it met with spectacular success. The IPTA called itself an autonomous and independent cultural body not affiliated with any political party, but in reality, it was entirely controlled by the Communist Party Of India (CPI). Like most Communist activities, IPTA was a subterfuge for naked propaganda, hidden skilfully in plain sight.

Subhash Chandra Bose was elected President of both the Indian National Army and the Indian Independence League in 1943

Bose saw the Second World War as an opportunity to depose the British and liberate India. As a result, he approached Germany and Japan to gain support for India's catalyst. The formation and activities of the Azad Hind Fauj, also known as the Indian National Army (INA), were significant developments in the struggle for freedom during World War II. Rash Behari Bose, an Indian revolutionary who had fled India and had been living in Japan for many years, founded the Indian Independence League with the support of Indians living in Southeast Asian countries.

Former British India army officer, General Mohan Singh, was pivotal in organizing this army.

On June 13 1943, Bose arrived in Singapore in a German submarine to lead the Indian Independence League on the invitation of Ras Bihari Bose. Netaji Bose was appointed as the head of the Indian Independence League and was also designated as the leader of the INA or 'Azad Hind Fauj.' Bose gave his famous battle cry *'Chalo Dilli'* and promised independence to Indians saying, *"Tum mujhe khoon do, main tumhe Azadi dunga'* (You give me blood, I will give you freedom.)

Subhash Babu sided with the Axis powers. The Azad Hind Fauj consisted of approximately 45,000 soldiers, including Indian prisoners of war and Indians who had settled in various Southeast Asian countries. On October 21, 1943, he established the Azad Hind Government in Singapore with Japanese support, with jurisdiction primarily over the Andaman and Nicobar Islands, even as it later struggled to make inroads into India's North-East. The provisional government commanded a large army made up of Indian POWs (Prisoners of War) captured by the Japanese during the Malayan campaign in Singapore, and it maintained diplomatic relations with several countries, including Germany, Italy, Croatia, Thailand, Japan, Burma, the Second Philippine Republic, and Manchukuo. If a government's legitimacy is measured by the extent and population of its jurisdiction, as well as international recognition, Netaji was the first Prime Minister of free (and, dare I say, undivided) India. Nine countries, including Germany, Italy, Japan, and Myanmar, recognised this government.

Soon after its formation, the Azad Hind government declared authority over Indian civilian and military personnel in Southeast Asian British colonial territory, as well as prospective authority over Indian territory that would fall to Japanese forces and the Indian National Army during WWII.

The provisional government not only allowed Bose to negotiate on an equal footing with the Japanese but also allowed him to mobilize Indians living in East Asia to join and support the Indian National Army, which played a critical role in the national movement, providing much-needed impetus to India's struggle for independence.

Under Bose's leadership, the Azad Hind government established its own bank, currency, civil code, and stamps. In that era, Bose even formed the INA's first women's regiment, the Rani Jhansi Regiment, laying the groundwork for equal opportunity for women in the armed forces.

Azad Hind declared war on the British and allied forces on the Indo-Burma Front immediately after the formation of the government-in-exile. As part of the Imperial Japanese Army, the Azad Hind Fauj fought against the British Indian Army and allied forces in the Imphal-Kohima sector. The existence of the Azad Hind Government provided greater legitimacy to India's independence struggle against the British. Subash Chandra Bose's valiant actions and the decision to establish the country's first government triggered a chain of events that eventually forced the British government to leave India in August 1947.

In 2018, Prime Minister, Narendra Modi, hoisted the National Flag at Red Fort, to commemorate the 75th Anniversary of the formation of Azad Hind Government, formed by Netaji Subhas Chandra Bose.

The 1943 Bengal Famine

Under Winston Churchill's leadership, the United Kingdom engineered a famine in 1943 that killed nearly 3 million people in Bengal alone. Three million Indians literally starved to death, and Bengal's streets were littered with the dying and dead bodies of men, women, children, and infants.

The episode is the first in a series that explains how England methodically and systematically destroyed not only Indian food production but also Indian culture, attitude, manners, customs, and conception of food, passed down since time immemorial by our *Rishis* and ancestors.

Famine broke out in the state of Bengal in 1943, during the Second World War. The situation quickly deteriorated, and within a short period of time, death by starvation became common. Friends witnessed their friends' pain in front of them. Women witnessed their partners' deaths before succumbing to their own. Children then witnessed their mothers' deaths before succumbing to the heinous realities of Bengal. As the days and months passed, more and more families were seen dying on the streets, their carcasses devoured by wild dogs. This was replicated by the millions throughout the state of Bengal.

The most heinous and infamous of Winston Churchill's actions were those that directly contributed to the Bengal Famine in the 1940s. His actions, which included exporting rice out of India while Bengal was suffering from famine, were directly responsible for the deaths of an estimated 3 million people.

The United Kingdom also implemented a "denial policy" in India, confiscating large quantities of rice and thousands of boats to deny the Japanese adequate resources should they invade India in the future. He was explicitly told that continuing to export rice out of India could lead to food shortages in the country. However, Britain continued to export rice out of India to other parts of the world to sustain its war efforts.

Winston Churchill blamed the famine on Indians when the Indian Viceroy requested 1 million tonnes of emergency wheat supply in 1942-43 due to the famine. "I despise Indians," he declared. "They are beastly people who worship beastly gods. It was their own fault for breeding like rabbits that caused the famine."

As a result of Winston Churchill's actions, millions of people died due to the Bengal famine and the subsequent spread of diseases such as malaria and cholera in India. There was significant social upheaval, which completely altered Bengal's landscape.

Given all of this and his statements, it is an undeniable fact that Winston Churchill was a racist, and claiming otherwise is sheer denial.

It was one of the darkest periods in Bengal's history. And this dark period was fueled by Winston Churchill's evil policies, which stemmed from his hatred for Indians. To claim that he was not a racist simply because he opposed Adolf Hitler is to deny the obvious. Opposition to Nazi Germany is not a sufficient criterion for naming someone a hero.

Stalin killed millions as well, and no rational person can deny that he was a genocidal maniac.

To put it simply, Churchill's policy in Bengal was one of mass murder. Although not carried out in the same manner as the Nazi extermination camps, the scale and outcome of the Bengal Holocaust were comparable to what happened to Jews in Germany. Both atrocities were motivated and exacerbated by the racism of the "leaders," Winston Churchill and Adolf Hitler. This is not to diminish the horrors of the Jewish Holocaust; rather, it emphasises how horrific and vile this man-made tragedy, the Bengal Holocaust, truly was.

Churchill's defenders claim that the famine was caused primarily by natural disasters that could not have been controlled. Crop failure is cited as the leading cause; they also blame a cyclone that devastated large swaths of coastal Bengal and a crop disease for the crippling shortage of foodgrains and, consequently, the famine. However, Churchill's defenders overlook the fact that, at first, the extortionate British administration was solely responsible for the crop failure that was caused.

The British, as foreign rulers whose sole goal was to plunder India and fatten their coffers, did nothing to boost agricultural productivity. In addition, the British were responsible for the famines of 1770, 1783, 1866, 1873, 1892, and 1897, which killed over 14 million people in all. Sharply declining agricultural yields and drastically reduced crop area (due to farmers' being forced to cultivate indigo and opium) combined to create a disaster waiting to happen. Bengal went from being a net exporter of rice (until the last days of Mughal rule) to a net importer of rice under British rule. Many other British actions, such as the construction of a vast network of railway lines built on embankments that cut off natural drainage and thus laid waste to large tracts of fertile farmland, contributed to the famine.

During the Bengal famine, the relief camps were opened and operated by Shyama Prasad Mokherjee, all the services were provided by Mokherjee, where many Subhash Bose supporters also worked.

Viscount Wavell was appointed Viceroy of India on October 1, 1943

Field Marshal Archibald Wavell, viceroy from 1943 to 1946, was the first to recognise India's strategic importance to the survival of the British empire. He recognised that British power was dwindling and that it was only a matter of time before Britain was forced to withdraw. According to him, the Congress party that would rule India would not cooperate with British interests. He reasoned that if the Muslim League was successful in separating the Northwest from the rest of India, this gap would have to be filled.

In his diary, Wavell noted that Churchill, too, had imagined the division of India. Churchill's idea was to divide the country into three parts: Pakistan, Hindustan, and Princestan. Wavell, on the other hand, had envisaged India's division at the time. This plan was known as the Wavell plan for Pakistan within the British leadership.

By early 1947, the British military and leadership had reached a unanimous decision to maintain strategic control over Northwest India. Following that, they played a complex game to deceive a befuddled Congress Party, use Jinnah to achieve their strategic goal and deceive Americans who had different ideas.

Even though Wavell was initially popular among Indian politicians, concerns about the likely structure and timeframe of an independent India grew. With the Wavell Plan and the Simla Conference, he attempted to move the debate forward but received little support from either Churchill (who was opposed to Indian independence) or Clement Attlee, Churchill's successor as Prime Minister. He was also hampered by disagreements among Indian political factions. Rising Indian expectations remained unfulfilled at the end of the war, and inter-communal violence increased. Attlee eventually lost faith in Wavell and replaced him with Lord Mountbatten of Burma in 1947.

Bose hoisted the first independent Indian flag in Andaman and Nicobar in December 1943

On December 30 1943, Netaji Subhash Chandra Bose hoisted the National Flag for the first time at Port Blair's Gymkhana Ground (now Netaji Stadium). He also announced the islands as the first Indian territory to be liberated from British control.

Japan, which captured the island during World War II, liberated it from British rule at the time.

Netaji landed at Port Blair aerodrome in the Andamans on December 29, 1943, accompanied by Sarvashri Anand Mohan Sahay, Captain Rawat-ADC, and Col. D.S Raju, Netaji's personal physician. At Port Blair, he was greeted by the Japanese admiral. The enthusiastic Indians and Burmese also greeted him warmly.

On this day in 1943, Netaji Subhash Chandra Bose hoisted India's first independent flag. Bose renamed Andaman Island Shaheed and Nicobar Island Swaraj, respectively, and appointed INA General, A.D Loganathan, as governor. The Azad Hind government was no longer just a government in exile; it had its own land, currency, civil code, and stamps.

By hoisting the Azad Hind flag, Bose, the Provisional Government of Azad Hind, fulfilled his promise that the INA would be on Indian soil by the end of 1943.

CHAPTER - XVI

GANDHI AND MEMBERS OF THE CONGRESS WORKING COMMITTEE WERE ARRESTED ON AUGUST 9, 1942

In any case, Gandhi's Quit India Movement was exactly what the British wanted, as they brutally suppressed it by baton-charging thousands, shooting hundreds dead, imprisoning thousands, and bombing freedom fighters from the sky using armed forces. All in a day's work for Churchill, who had wished to use chemical weapons on Indians several years before.

Gandhi, Nehru, and the entire Congress leadership team were detained. In reality, Gandhi was housed in the comfortable and opulent surroundings of the Aga Khan palace in Pune, while Nehru was imprisoned in the minimum-security Ahmadnagar prison, where his daily routine included regular morning exercises, reading, writing, and gardening, all done with ease. On the contrary, the legit freedom fighters, such as Veer Savarkar and the revolutionaries, were sent to the horrors of Kala Pani in the Andaman and Nicobar Islands, where third-degree torture was predominant, resulting in numerous sleepless nights in dark dungeons.

Savarkar resigned as President of the Mahasabha in July 1943 due to health concerns

With Savarkar's health rapidly deteriorating, the working president, Syama Prasad Mookerjee, became Mahasabha's de facto president. He was asked to officiate on behalf of Savarkar.

Mookerjee, along with Vinayak Damodar Savarkar, is recognised as the godfather of modern Hindutva. He saw Hindutva as a tool for reawakening a sense of nationalism. It was a gateway to India's rich civilization and sacred culture, which carried the message of universal brotherhood for him. Mookerjee was the first to apply Hindutva in Indian politics, founding the Bharatiya Jan Sangh (BJS) in 1951, which later became the Bharatiya Janata Party (BJP).

If the Hindu Mahasabha and their fight for a Hindu Rashtra had not existed, West Bengal would have been a part of East Pakistan after the partition. The Bengali Hindu Homeland Movement, as well as the resistance of Mookherjee and others, was the driving force behind West Bengal's admission to the Indian Union.

The Japanese launched operation "U Go," provocative against the British in March 1944, leading to the Battles of Imphal and Kohima

The Japanese army advanced towards India to prevent a planned British invasion of Burma and to make inroads into India. They planned to seize the British supply bases on the Imphal Plain and cut the road connecting Dimapur (Nagaland) and Imphal at Kohima (the state capital). The Japanese hoped that by seizing Imphal, they would be able to cut off air supplies to China, gain control of the city, and establish a base from which to launch further attacks against the British in India.

To achieve these objectives, the Japanese launched an attack on Kohima on April 5, with 15,000 troops. The British Indian army in Kohima numbered only 1,500 men, and the Japanese were able to effectively alienate the city.

The fierce fight put up by the Gurkha, Punjabi, and Scottish regiments prevented them from taking over Indian and British food supplies and other munitions to keep their siege going. Despite being vastly outnumbered, the British Indian army was able to inflict massive casualties and prevent the Japanese from advancing beyond Kohima with the help of air-dropped firearms and grenades. After receiving reinforcements in the form of additional battalions of Punjabis and Gurkhas, the Japanese were pushed back from Kohima, having suffered massive casualties.

The Japanese also besieged and surrounded Imphal. The British Indian army won the siege of Imphal, which began in March 1944 and lasted until July.

The Japanese were given orders to retreat from Imphal into Burma on July 8, 1944. The fight by Indians and other allies was so fierce that the Japanese lost 53,000 men (dead or missing) in total. The two battles helped the Allies turn the tide in the CBI theatre, and the Japanese were eventually driven out of Burma as well.

The defeats at Imphal and Kohima were the Japanese's most significant in World War II up to that point.

Imphal Peace Museum just outside Imphal was inaugurated on June 22 2019 as part of the 75th Anniversary commemoration of the Imphal battle. This is a joint project of the Nippon Foundation and the Sasakawa Peace Foundation, in collaboration with the Government of Manipur, the Manipur Tourism Forum and the 2nd World War Imphal Campaign Foundation. It showcases both the war era and the post-war period in Manipur.

Gandhi was freed in 1944, just in time to see his deceased wife

Gandhi was arrested in the early hours of the morning under Defense of India Rules following the 'Quit India' resolution and lodged in Aga Khan Palace Jail. On May 6, 1944, at 8 a.m., he was unconditionally released.

In the case of his wife, Gandhi demonstrated his aversion to modern medicine selectively. When Gandhi's wife became ill with pneumonia in 1944, British doctors advised Gandhi that a penicillin injection could cure her. However, Gandhi refused to have modern medicine injected into her body, and she died as a result. However, Gandhi had an emergency appendectomy, a modern surgery, 20 years earlier to remove his inflamed appendix.

Gandhi's blatant hypocrisy was defended by the British and Western media, as well as the Indian National Congress. Jinnah referred to M K Gandhi as "wily Gandhi" for a reason.

Azad Hind radio broadcast on June 25, 1944

In the Azad Hind's radio broadcast of June 25 1944, Subhas Bose criticised the Congress for discouraging Indians from enlisting in the Army while applauding Veer Savarkar's militarisation efforts.

When, due to misguided political whims and lack of vision, almost all the leaders of the Congress party are decrying all the soldiers in the Indian Army as mercenaries, it is truly inspiring to know Veer Savarkar's fearlessness with Indian youth. He quoted, "These enlisted young people provide us with trained men from whom we recruit soldiers for our Indian National Army."

Congress made a strategic blunder

The Muslim League, a party with no popular base, was now propped up and allowed to consolidate. Given how easily Muslims are swayed by threats to their religion, rallying support for the League was not difficult. Without the Congress leaders to explain what was going on in the country, the Muslims defected to the League.

By 1944, Wavell was determined to strengthen Jinnah's Muslim League while withdrawing British forces to the strategic northwest, where they would seek to maintain their bases. Pakistan, he envisioned, would become a Commonwealth dominion, while the rest of India would be left to its own devices. Prime Minister Churchill had long opposed any form of Indian independence, but by March 1945, Wavell noted that Churchill's position had shifted – he "seems to favour partition of India into Pakistan, Hindustan, and Princestan" – Hindustan referring to the Hindu regions of India, and Princestan referring to the numerous princely states that Britain had long cultivated to ensure colonial control. The mention of Princestan demonstrates that the British intended to balkanize India.

Archibald Wavell, India's arch-racist Viceroy from 1943 to 1947, believed that Congress leaders would refuse to cooperate with Britain on military and foreign policy matters, whereas the Muslim League, which had been demanding a homeland for Indian Muslims since 1940, would agree. The inability of the British to defend the Middle East and the Indian Ocean could be filled if the Muslim League had been successful in separating India's strategic northwest from the rest of the country, a conceivable goal given the close ties that Victor Linlithgow (Wavell's predecessor and Churchill's alter ego in his hatred for Indians) built up with Muslim League leader Mohammad Ali Jinnah during World War II.

Rash Bihari Bose's death

Rash Behari Bose died on January 21, 1945, in Tokyo. He was 58 years old. The Order of the Rising Sun was bestowed upon him by the Japanese administration.

He saw Japan as a chance to free Asian nations from colonialism. At the same time, he was uneasy about Japan's imperialist plans. Although he would go silent during the Second World War and concentrate solely on the liberation of India, he had warned Japan as early as 1934 not to antagonize the United States (US) and (then non-Communist) China, as well as the Soviet Union. He expressed concern that "an American-Japanese War will destabilize these two great powers, who are grave rivals of the United Kingdom." Patriotic Americans and Japanese should work hard to promote American-Japanese friendship.

Marxism and communism

When the Communist Party of the Soviet Union (CPSU) and Stalin were at peace with Hitler, they saw the war as an imperial one waged by capitalist-imperialist forces, and thus they opposed the British and the war. When the Nazis attacked the Soviet Union, the war was annotated as the "People's War." They began to denigrate national leaders and India's freedom movement.

The CPI launched a vulgar campaign against Netaji Bose through People's War magazine, dubbing him "the running dog of Japanese Fascism." They did not hold back when it came to character assassination. They wrote authoritatively that Bose was living a luxurious life in a

Rangoon villa with the Axis powers' corrupt money. They even claimed to know the name of the bank that provided funds for Bose's lavish lifestyle – the South Regions Development Bank. The magazine declared in its January 10, 1943 issue that if "Bose's mercenary army of liberation, of rapine and plunder... dares to set foot on Indian soil to commit acts of pillage and robbery," it would "feel the wrath and indignation of our people."

During the Bengal Famine, the Marxists not only supported the British but also started a communal campaign against Hindus in Bengal. In the attacks, Comrade P.C Joshi singled out Mookerjee, saying, "Dr Shyamaprosad gives the lead, the Hindu hoarders pay the cash and call the tune, and the Fifth Column provides the cadres." It's an odd mix of the factionalist, the profiteer, and the traitor. And who were the members of the Fifth Column? The front line and Anuseelan Samithi. "People's War," on the other hand, would publish a cartoon depicting Bose killing the famine-starved Indian children. However, Bose's Marxist betrayal and backstabbing went beyond propaganda.

There was a communist Indian who pretended to be a nationalist collaborator with Bose while concealing his true ideological affiliation. Bose's plans were severely harmed as a result of his treason.

Thus, by sabotaging Bose's plans and engaging in a defamation campaign against him, Marxists actively supported British genocidal policies.

Surprisingly, yet evidently, India is the only country where the mutually hostile troika of Islamism, Christian Evangelism, and Marxism are friends due to their similar vision – to break India.

Babarao Savarkar passed away on March 16, 1945

Babarao had become frail by 1944. His body had already been battered by the perilous confinement and strain of his work. On July 31, 1944, Dr Syama Prasad Mukherjee, President of the Akhil Bharat Hindu Mahasabha, paid a visit to Babarao.

Babarao Savarkar passed away on March 16, 1945. The events of Indian history that followed would prove Ganesh Savarkar correct. He would not live to see the day when India would gain independence. On the other hand, the Congress party and its ecosystem persisted in vilifying and attacking his brother, Veer Savarkar.

The Wavell Plan was implemented on July 19, 1945

The Wavell Plan was first presented in 1945 at the Simla Conference. It was named after Lord Wavell, Viceroy of India. The Shimla Conference was held to agree on the Wavell Plan for Indian Self-Government, which called for separate representations as well as communal lines.

In his diary, Wavell noted that Churchill, too, had imagined the division of India. Churchill's idea was to divide the country into three parts: Pakistan, Hindustan, and Princestan. Wavell, on the other hand, had imagined a division of India at the time. This plan was known as the Wavell Plan of Pakistan within the British leadership.

By early 1947, the British military and leadership had reached a unanimous decision to maintain strategic control over Northwest India. Following that, they played a complex game to deceive a befuddled Congress Party, using Jinnah to achieve their strategic goal and fooling Americans who had different ideas.

In 1946, the new Viceroy, Wavell, thought of a new strategy, which Wali Khan explains in his book, "The disputed areas between the Congress and the Muslim League were located on the border." Pakistan's concept was divided into two sections: northwest and northeast. These were areas with a Muslim majority. Wavell suggested that the areas with a Congress majority should be handed over to them and be given complete autonomy. The British military, civil servants, and families should relocate to Muslim-majority areas.

Since Wavell was a professional soldier, he knew that if the North East and North West were separated from India and left under British control, what effect would it have upon the Indian defence policy? The territories were specified; in the East, Bengal and Assam; in the West, the Frontier Province; Punjab and Sindh. "Delhi would be under direct British control and the rest would go to the Congress."

Wavell's strategy was consistent with Churchill's advice to the viceroy on his way to India: "Keep a little bit of India." Essentially, the British were anticipating the Balkanization of India.

The Muslim League accepted Wavell's proposal. The League leader, Liaquat Ali Khan, who would later become Pakistan's first Prime Minister and be assassinated in fast succession, told the British, "If your excellency was willing to give the Muslim League only the Sindh desert, I would still accept it."

Referring to the "Wavell Plan" in Madras, Dr Shyama Prosad Mukherjee explained the Hindu Mahasabha's position on the proposals and stated that the country should reject the plan because it would result in the destruction of the Hindu majority's rights and the continuation of foreign rule in the country.

Although the Wavell Plan was formed to break the political deadlock in India, he abandoned the proposals due to disagreements between Muslim League and Congress leaders, which eventually resulted in their dissolving at the Shimla Conference.

August 18, 1945 - the plane crash

Netaji was said to have died in a plane crash on his way to Taiwan, but this was extremely controversial and never proven. Many people believe and claim that "Netaji" did not perish in the plane crash. He made it safely to Russia, where he lived for years before returning to India. Many people believe that the hermit "Gumnami Baba," who lived in disguise in Uttar Pradesh, was none other than "Subhash Chandra Bose."

The real mystery is who invented the story of Netaji's death in a plane crash that never happened and then tried to hide the actual fact for 70 years.

First, we can examine the well-established key facts. Netaji was not killed in a plane crash in Taiwan in 1945 because there was no plane crash. And this was known to all governments, including the Indian government led by Pandit Nehru at that time. The question is who benefited the most from this cover-up? The Japanese may have wished for Bose to speak on their behalf with the Soviets, who had just declared war on Japan.

Nehru was concerned that Bose's return would jeopardize his position. From 1945 to 1950, there is evidence that Bose was a Soviet guest-cum-prisoner. That was just before the Korean War when Mao's China and the Soviet Union were on a collision course.

The Soviets and Nehru may have agreed that in exchange for Nehru obeying a pro-Chinese policy, the Soviets would hold Netaji in custody. Nehru did follow a strongly pro-Chinese policy, initially declining a permanent seat on the UN Security Council and then surrendering Tibet against the advice of Sardar Patel and others. The documents could shed some light on it.

If true, this would explain why Nehru and subsequent Congress governments felt the need to censor these documents.

This is just a guess. While plausible, only the release of all Netaji-related records can put an end to it.

World War II comes to an end

World War II in Europe ended on May 8, 1945. As word of Germany's surrender spread around the world, joyful crowds gathered in the streets to celebrate, clutching newspapers proclaiming Victory in Europe (V-E Day). Later that year, US President Harry S. Truman declared the surrender of Japan and the end of World War II. The news quickly spread, and festivities suddenly appeared across the country. The official Victory over Japan Day was established on September 2, 1945, when formal surrender documents were signed aboard the USS Missouri (V-J Day).

The British Field Marshal Claude Auchinleck, Commander-in-Chief of the British Indian Army from 1942 to 1945, stated that the British "couldn't have come through both wars without the Indian Army."

Even the racist and bloodthirsty British Prime Minister Winston Churchill, who had a pathological hatred for Indians ("They are a beastly race with a beastly religion," he famously stated in the past), praised the "unrivalled bravery of Indian soldiers and officers."

However, India was a volatile place after WWII. The INA trials in Delhi were closely watched by serving Indian military officers and men. More than two million soldiers returned from Europe after WWII, having witnessed firsthand poor British soldiering. The majority of these battle-hardened Indian soldiers were primed for revolutionary action. All INA soldiers were quietly released by the British.

What the Japanese accomplished with the INA was exactly what they had intended. The INA was the biggest secret weapon that fueled Indian revolutionary activity while instilling fear in British hearts. For over two centuries, Indian soldiers have ensured the British's security in India. The military's loyalty was the ultimate sanction for British rule in India. With that assurance gone, the British realized their time had come to an end.

Cambridge University historians Tim Harper and Christopher Bayly write in their accounts of the end of the British Empire, Forgotten Armies and Forgotten Wars, that "it was Indian soldiers, civilian labourers, and businessmen who made the 1945 victory possible." Their cost was India's quick independence.

At the end of World War II, the total number of Royal Indian Navy officers was 2,438 and sailors (Ratings) 21,193 in December 1945, compared to 1,615 before the war, both officers and men.

As the world celebrated the end of World War II in Europe in May 1945, one evil figure plotted the annihilation of the world's oldest continuing civilization. British Prime Minister Winston Churchill directed his generals to prepare a policy report "to safeguard the strategic interests of the British Empire in India and the Indian Ocean" with an enormous hatred for Indians and apprehension about the arrival of Russia as a superpower.

On May 19, the War Cabinet's Post-Hostilities Planning Staff tabled a top-secret document outlining four reasons why India was useful to Britain:

- British forces based in India could be deployed throughout the Indian Ocean, the Middle East, and the Far East.
- India served as an air and sea communications hub.
- It had a large reserve of combat-ready personnel.
- Northwest India was ideal for air power deployment against Russia.

Crime and its Ramifications

While Britain has apologised to other countries, such as Kenya for the Mau Mau massacre, those facing similar genocides in India continue to be ignored. Other nationalities have served as role models for us. Israel, for example, cannot forget the Holocaust, but more importantly, it will not allow others, least of all the Germans, to forget. Germany continues to provide Israel with cash and weapons worth hundreds of millions of dollars.

Armenia will never forget the Great Crime – the systematic slaughter of 1.8 million Armenians by Turks during World War I. During the final weeks of World War II, thousands of Polish Army officers were massacred in the Katyn Forest by Joseph Stalin.

Then, there's the odd case of the Ukrainians, who like to refer to the mass starvation caused by Stalin's economic policies as genocide, which it clearly wasn't. There's even a term for it – Holodomor.

And yet, India is the only country that refuses to seek punitive damages, let alone an apology. Could it be because the British were the last of many invaders, so why bother with a post-imperial England? Is it because the English-speaking elites in India feel beholden to the British? Or are we simply destined to repeat our historical mistakes? Perhaps, we are too quick to forgive and let go.

But forgiveness is not the same as forgetting, which Indians are known for. Airbrushing the Bengal Famine – and other great colonial crimes – is an insult to the millions of Indians whose lives were cut short as a result of Britain's greed and racial practices.

British attitudes toward Indians must be viewed in light of India's contribution to the Allied war campaign. By 1943, over 2.5 million Indian soldiers had joined the Allies in Europe, Africa, and Southeast Asia. Vast quantities of arms, ammunition, and raw materials were shipped to Europe – mostly at no cost to the United Kingdom.

Indian rulers and business families had contributed hundreds of millions of pounds to build RAF fighter squadrons and pay British Army troops' salaries.

Britain's debt to India is too large for either country to ignore. Cambridge University historians Tim Harper and Christopher Bayly say "It was Indian soldiers, civilian labourers, and businessmen who made the 1945 victory possible." Their cost was India's quick independence.

There is insufficient wealth in Europe to compensate India for 250 years of colonial plunder. Forget the money, do the British have the decency to apologize? Or, like Churchill, will they continue to believe that English rule was India's *"Golden Age"*?

The blatant Red Fort trials

After the Second World War, officers of the INA captured by the British Raj were subjected to the heinous Red Fort trials. During the war, the British downplayed the INA's role, claiming it was a collection of Japanese-inspired forces.

The trials, on the other hand, brought to light the magnitude of Netaji's and his troops' efforts. This electrified people all over the country. After all, here was a leader and an army that had been poorly supplied and ill-equipped but had not flinched even once in their willingness to lay down their lives for India's independence.

Massive demonstrations and a hartal (strike) were held in Lahore, Rawalpindi, and Lyallpur during the first two days of the trial, while "INA days" were held in Vellore, Salem, Karachi, Madras, and other Indian cities and towns. Posters began to appear in Calcutta and Delhi, threatening to kill 20 Britishers in exchange for the execution of every INA hero.

The governor of the Central Provinces even expressed doubts about the willingness of Indian troops to reign in the mobs, comparing the situation to the Sepoy mutiny in 1857.

Ironically, the Muslim League, even after having a rivalry and significant hostility with Bose, supported the INA heroes. Netaji's dharmic cosmopolitanism in welcoming Muslims, even at the highest levels of his army and government, made it impossible for the League to remain neutral. Even Nehru, who had retired from the bar a quarter-century earlier, joined the INA officers' legal defence team. This was also ironic because Nehru had publicly condemned the INA while they were fighting pitched battles in India's North-East, while Netaji was gracious enough to name an entire brigade of the INA after Nehru.

Due to protests and riots, the General of the British Indian Army, Claude Auchinleck, was forced to release all three defendants in the trials. Within three months, 11,000 INA soldiers were released after being cashiered and having their pay and allowances forfeited. The British were so paranoid that, on Lord Mountbatten's recommendation and with Nehru's agreement, no INA soldier was to be allowed to join the armed forces of independent India as a condition for independence! Following the commutation of the officers' sentences, there was a massive celebratory rally in Delhi attended by approximately 100,000 people. Similar crowds were seen in Punjab in support of the heroes.

The magnitude of how loved and respected these officers was is reflected in a communication by Sir Bertrand Glancy on November 17, 1945, in which he stated that executing these war heroes would result in a situation worse than in 1919 (before the Jallianwala Bagh massacre) or in 1942, making a peaceful, constitutional settlement extremely difficult. Given that Punjab was an important recruitment centre for the British Indian army, the ripple effect of the trials and the subsequent electrifying effect of the officers' release could seriously jeopardize the army's ability to stand its ground in the near future.

The British Raj in India was based on the strength of the British Indian army, as their approach to acquiring clout and power had been mercantile and then militaristic. While Netaji did not achieve his ultimate goal with the Azad Hind Fauj, his efforts did incite a nationalistic fervour that threatened to bring the Raj down in India. Indian soldiers began to speak of their loyalty to the Congress and the Indian forces rather than their British overlords. In January 1946, 5,200 pilots and officers abruptly went on strike, effectively crippling the Royal Indian Air Force (RIAF).

General election in India in 1945

In December 1945, general elections were held in British India to elect members of the Central Legislative Assembly and the Council of State.

In this election, the Congress campaigned for a united India, while the Muslim League campaigned for the establishment of Pakistan. There were 30 Muslim constituencies in this election and the Muslim League won all of them.

That clearly demonstrates what Muslims desired at the time! They desired Pakistan, which India could not resist.

Furthermore, even among the very few Muslims who opposed Pakistan, many, such as Mufti Kifayatullah, did so not to give the Muslims a piece of land, but to have Islam rule over all of India.

Dr Ambedkar's book "Pakistan or the Partition of India"

In 1940, shortly after the Muslim League passed the "Pakistan Resolution" in its Lahore session (on March 22nd), Ambedkar published Thoughts on Pakistan. In 1945, it was republished as Pakistan or the Partition of India.

"Pakistan or Partition of India," Ambedkar's book, is brilliant and eye-opening. Reading this book explains why the left-wing academy would have wanted this book to be removed from public view.

This book deconstructs many carefully and deftly crafted Communist fake narratives, which are widely used to mislead the youth. Many people blindly follow their narrative, believing that it is ordained by Dr Ambedkar himself to follow the left.

How could the left, say, educate today's Ambedkarites that the Indian partition was caused by Savarkar's ideology? How could they still have been duped into believing anti-Hindu propaganda that Hindus wanted partition?

He talks about how Hindu politicians for a long time believed that India was one nation, and how Hindus felt betrayed when Muslims insisted that they were another nation. "This assertion cuts the entire ground from under the feet of Hindu politicians," Ambedkar writes. It's natural for them to be annoyed and call it a "stab in the back."

Ambedkar attempts to analyse the mind of an Indian Muslim, writing that the Muslim mind is constantly aware that the Hindus around him are encroaching on him and de-Mussalmanising him. There are numerous other things, unbelievably factual and deeply analytical, that Ambedkar cited in the book, such as the difficulties of Hindus and Muslims living in a unified nation, as well as the financial and security benefits of partition.

CHAPTER - XVII

Clement Atlee Was Elected as the Prime Minister

Churchill lost the election in 1945, and Clement Atlee became Prime Minister. Unlike Churchill, Atlee preferred working from behind the scenes. His goal was to partition India while making it appear that the Congress wanted it. His second goal was to persuade Jinnah to accept a truncated Pakistan. As we have seen, there was a Wavell plan for Pakistan, which was essentially how Pakistan was created.

The Royal Navy Ratings Mutiny

It was dubbed "Navy Mutiny" rather than "Navy Revolt" by hired textbook writers and historians. In 1946, one of the defining movements that are thought to have accelerated the British exit from India and convinced them that there was no future for them here transpired in Mumbai. The Great Indian Naval Mutiny swept through Westminster like wildfire from the naval base in Mumbai. For the first time since 1857, a significant portion of the Indian armed forces revolted, turning their guns on the British. Between the 18th and 23rd of February 1946, naval ships along Mumbai's docks carried banners challenging the British to 'Quit India.' Over 60 ships and shore establishments, as well as 10,000 sailors, joined the battle. Despite condemnation from both the Congress and the Muslim League, Mumbai residents overwhelmingly supported the rebellion.

The 1946 Royal Naval Ratings Mutiny, like the 1857 Mutiny, began in a rather mundane manner. However, resentment was already building among the naval ratings and other Indian members of the army. The INA mutiny was the most serious of all, shaking British confidence. The Royal Air Force Mutiny, which occurred in 1946 over working conditions for Indians in the Air Force, and the demobilisation of British troops after the war, are less well known.

Navy Day was held at HMIS Talwar

Navy Day was a celebration of British traditions that glorified the Royal Navy and its naval saga. On Navy Day, all ships and naval establishments are adorned, known as "Dress Ships," and are open to the general public.

Due to the preoccupation with victory celebrations at the end of World War II, the Royal Indian Navy decided to celebrate Navy Day on December 1, 1945. The officers and ship's company of HMIS Talwar had worked tirelessly to prepare their establishment for Navy Day celebrations. It was a well-known incident that this naval establishment was horribly congested with sailors awaiting discharge. The majority of them were dissatisfied with worsening operational conditions and the prospect of an uncertain future staring them in the face. They may not have been completely enthralled by these celebrations, but they did set up shop for Navy Day.

During the middle watch (0000-0400 hours), when the ship's company had gone to sleep and others had closed up for duty, a group of disgruntled ratings, previously unknown to naval authorities, hoisted brooms and buckets on the signal masthead. They secretly and silently painted subversive slogans on the parade ground and walls. Some of these slogans had political overtones, such as "Inqilab Zindabad" and "Quit India," while others were anti-British, such as "Kill the white dogs."

Lieutenant Commander Coles, the Commanding Officer of Takwar, took the action of erasing the painted slogans and other symbols of smacking insolence in his establishment while also reporting the incident to higher naval authorities in Bombay. With the Navy Day publicity, word of mouth would have spread like wildfire about slogan writing at Talwar.

The first signs of mutiny appeared on the night of December 1, 1945. If the 1857 mutiny was known as *"The First War of Independence,"* the sailors' mutiny deserves to be known as *"The Last War of Independence of India."*

During the period 1942–1945, the Royal Indian Navy experienced nine recorded mutinies. These acts of disobedience or abstinence from food were not on the same scale as the men's uprising during the 1946 Naval Mutiny by junior sailors.

The Naval Ratings Mutiny's Emergence

The Naval Ratings Mutiny made its debut on January 16, 1946, when a contingent of naval ratings arrived at the Castle Barracks on Mint Road in Mumbai's Fort Area. The contingent came from the training ship HMIS Akbar, which was docked in Thane and arrived at around four o'clock in the evening. When the contingent arrived, the galley cook took out 20 loaves of bread, casually added some water to the mutton curry and dal (preserved from the previous day), and served it. The food was so bland and unappealing that only 17 of the ratings ate it, while the rest went ashore.

This was not a one-time phenomenon. Such neglect was common, and worse, repeated complaints to senior officers about the appalling working conditions heard nothing back. As the number of complaints grew, the ratings became increasingly dissatisfied, both with the conditions and with the chiefs' indifference. The trial of the INA leaders only added fuel to the fire. The ratings began to be fed stories about Netaji Subash Chandra Bose's fight for freedom and the exploits of the INA during the Siege of Imphal. It inspired them and gave them hope that the might of the British Empire was not invincible.

Commander King is the new commanding officer

To control the deteriorating situation, immediate administrative action was required. So, the Commanding Officer was replaced. On January

21, 1946, Commander King was appointed as the Commanding Officer of HMIS Talwar, succeeding Lieutenant Commander Cole. Miscreants staged another subversive incident in HMIS Talwar on February 1, 1946, before Commander King could adjust to his new surroundings.

At midnight, a prominent telegraphist, B.C Dutt, was discovered moving around suspiciously and was arrested. However, Dutt's arrest did not put an end to slogan writing in Talwar. Their happiness was short-lived.

The problem caused by bad messing began at supper time on February 17, 1946

CO King referred to the insurgents as "you sons of bitches" and "sons of bloody junglees."

When the ratings pressured them for more good food, British officers referred to them as "beggars." The problem began with bad behaviour at supper time.

Mutiny in the Royal Indian Navy on February 18

The HMIS Talwar, a shore establishment in Bombay, becomes the focal point of the mutiny.

In HMIS Talwar, the Navy's Wireless Communication Establishment in Bombay (in naval parlance, even shore establishments are referred to as "ships"), and then spread to various naval ships and establishments all over the country and even beyond Indian shores. HMIS Talwar was the British Empire's second-largest training facility.

Rating in the Navy on HMIS Talwar, MS Khan led a revolt, and a "strike committee" was formed. MS Khan and fellow Naval Rating Madan Singh had taken control of the mutiny by this point, and it was spreading. On February 18 1946, Naval Rating MS Khan led a revolt on HMIS Talwar, resulting in the formation of a strike committee. Ratings on the HMIS Hindustan, which was anchored off the coast of Manora Island in Karachi, began to revolt. MS Khan and fellow Naval Rating Madan Singh had taken control of the mutiny by this point, and it was spreading. Ratings from Castle and Fort Barracks had joined the revolt by the 19th of February 1946. Ratings left their jobs and drove around Bombay in trucks, carrying photos of Netaji Subash Chandra Bose, who had become their excellent role model by this point.

It quickly spread to Kochi, Vizag, and Kolkata. The officers who opposed the strike were thrown off ships, and the mutineers communicated using radio sets. HMIS Talwar became the epicentre of the mutiny as strikers used radio sets to communicate with one another. It was a well-coordinated revolt that was now retaliating. Other Navy personnel from sloops, minesweepers, and offshore establishments in Mumbai soon joined, along Hornby Road (near Chhatrapati Shivaji Terminus), now Dadabhai Naoroji Road. The British White Ensign was lowered from all ships, and British officers were targeted for attack by mutineers armed with hockey sticks, crowbars, and whatever else they could get their hands on.

Flora Fountain soon echoed with "jai hind" cries and liberation slogans. Protesters forced British officers and their wives to yell "jai hind." Throughout the day, guns were trained at the Taj Mahal Hotel and the Yacht Club. The Royal Indian Air Force joined the strikers in solidarity, and 1,000 men from the Andheri and Marine Drive camps arrived. The Gurkhas of Karachi, one of the British Army's sword arms, refused to fire on the mutineers. The mutiny spread like wildfire, with slogans like "Strike for Bombay," "Release 11,000 INA prisoners," and "jai hind" echoing through Kolkata, Vizag, Chennai, and Karachi.

The tri-colour was now swinging on all ships, and by the 20th of February, British destroyers were stationed near the Gateway of India. The British government, now led by Clement Attlee, was alarmed and directed the Royal Navy to put down the rebellion. The Royal Indian Navy's Flag Officer in Command, Admiral JH Godfrey, issued an ultimatum to the mutineers – submit or perish. On the other hand, a patriotic wave swept in favour of the mutineers. The mutineers had taken control of all the ships and were planning a last-ditch attack. Every Indian, from the clerks to the cleaners, cooks, and wireless operators, was prepared for combat.

On the third day, the Royal Air Force flew a squadron of bombers near Mumbai Harbor while Admiral Arthur Rullion issued an ultimatum to the mutineers, requesting unconditional surrender. Meanwhile, the 2nd Battalion of the Black Watch quietly secured the island of Manora near Karachi.

Soon after, the decision was made to confront HMIS Hindustan, which was now under the control of the mutineers. The Royal Artillery on Manora Island issued an ultimatum to either surrender or prepare for war. The guns opened fire on HMIS Hindustan at 10:33 a.m., and the naval ratings fired back. HMIS Bahadur and HMIS Himalaya were soon subdued, and the revolt in Karachi was put down.

With the bombardment intensifying and little hope of winning a long war, the mutineers began to surrender, and on day 4, negotiations took place in which most of the strikers' demands were conceded in principle. Immediate steps were taken to improve the quality of food and living conditions, and the petition for the release of INA prisoners was given favourable consideration. Seven Royal Indian Navy sailors and one officer were killed, 34 were injured, and 476 were discharged from service.

The news of the naval strike in Bombay broadcasted on All India Radio and in newspapers on February 19

The news of the naval strike in Bombay was widely disseminated via All India Radio and newspapers.

Castle and Fort Barracks ratings had joined the revolt. Ratings left their jobs and drove around Bombay in trucks, carrying photos of Netaji Subash Chandra Bose, who had become their inspiration by this point.

Platoons of Marathas in Bombay on February 20

A platoon of Maratha Light Infantry was deployed. No food was prepared on the ship. Armed with rifles, the rating began sniping at the military guards. HMIS Khyber, Patna, and Kalavati also joined the Bombay mutiny. Sailors in Calcutta and Jamnagar went on strike. Protests erupted across the Indian naval services.

At the rally, Hindu Mahasabha leaders Veer Savarkar, N.C Chatterjee, Dr N.B Khare, and others rallied in support of the Indian National Army and Indian National Navy.

It is quite possible that if the abusive language used toward sailors had not been used, these ratings could have been pacified and would not have resorted to mutiny.

Thousands of civilians brought milk, fruits, bread, vegetables, and cooked food at the Gateway of India for the starving people. Motorboats were used by the ratings to collect the offerings. The Hindu, Muslim, and Iranian restaurants opened their doors and asked the public to do whatever they could to help the suffering people. They were not stopped by the Indian soldiers on duty.

The sailors' mutiny ended in unconditional surrender on February 23

The Army retaliated by firing indiscriminately. In just two days, 229 civilians and three police officers were killed. Over 1,000 people were injured, including 91 police officers and soldiers.

The sailors' mutiny ended in unconditional surrender.

The ratings were tried in court. More than 500 ratings were kept in deplorable conditions in Mulund (Bombay) and Maliar (Karachi). They were suspended and then sent home.

The Tragedy

Unfortunately, the Indian National Congress offered no support to the mutineers. Far from it, they were sentenced for their actions. Mohandas Gandhi issued a statement in which he chastised the mutineers for revolting without the support of a political party. Aruna Asaf Ali, a lone voice in the Congress who supported the mutineers, stated that she would rather unite Hindus and Muslims on the barricades. The Muslim League, too, condemned the mutineers, arguing that street unrest was not the best way to address grievances and that protest should be limited to constitutional means only.

One reason for these negative reactions could be that spontaneous uprisings like these pose a threat to the centralised political authority of both the Congress and the Muslim League, affecting their interactions with the British government. Another reason was that neither the Congress nor the Muslim League were truly mass-based organisations. Both remained the preserve of the upper class and upper caste elite, and such mass uprisings made them uneasy.

The Communist Party of India was the only political party that supported the mutineers, while the others simply ignored them. Both Sardar Patel and Muhammad Ali Jinnah condemned the mutineers' actions, and Aruna Asaf Ali was the only Congress member who supported them. On surrender, the mutineers faced a court martial and imprisonment. Worse, even after independence, neither the Indian nor Pakistani governments supported the mutineers.

The Royal Naval Ratings Mutiny lasted only four days and was quickly put down. However, the impact was far-reaching. The British were now completely convinced that they could no longer rely on the armed forces to help them maintain control of India. So far, the British have been able to maintain control of India solely through armed forces, but when the soldiers began to revolt, the British realized that their time was up. The INA revolts were followed by the Naval Ratings Mutiny. Add to this, the revolts in the Air Force and the fact that World War II effectively bankrupted Britain. All of these factors influenced the British decision to leave India far more than the 1942 movement.

With Mohandas Gandhi's repeated failures, whether in 1920, 1939, or 1942 and Attlee's derision of the pacifist approach, it is safe to say that the Azad Hind Fauj delivered the proverbial death blow to the British Raj, albeit not in the way they may have wished. To conclude, I'd like to highlight and celebrate a rarely-seen aspect of Netaji – his Dharmic moorings and spirituality, which defined and guided his actions in service to the nation while also emphasizing the critical role he and his Azad Hind Fauj played in securing India's independence.

British fright

For the British, the post-World War II period was terrifying. The German armed forces, the Wehrmacht, had routed the British Army in several battles around the world. Adolf Hitler's V2 rockets had reduced London to rubble, and the city's inhabitants had been hiding in subterranean shelters for more than five years. Japan had soundly defeated Britain in the Asian theatre, exposing British weakness in the face of subject Asian nations.

The British were humiliated and demoralized, and they desperately wanted to keep India. For 200 years, India was a never-ending money pit into which Britain could dip whenever it needed to. Indian science and technology, combined with the unparalleled wealth looted from the colony, sparked the British Industrial Revolution. It was terrifying to think about losing it. In this context, a mutiny in India sent shivers down the spines of the British.

Lord Wavell, then Viceroy of India, wrote to King George VI on March 22, 1946, saying, "The last three months have been anxious and depressing." They have been marked by continuous and unbridled abuse of the government, of the British, of officials and police, in political speeches, virtually the entire press, and in the Assembly; by serious rioting in Bombay; by a mutiny in the RIN; much indiscipline in the RIAF; and some unrest in the Indian Army; by unprecedented drought and famine conditions in many parts of India; and by threatened strikes on railways, post, and telegraph. *"It's a sad story of misfortune and folly..."*

"The most troubling aspect is that unrest is beginning to appear in some units of the Indian Army, almost entirely in the technical arms so far. Auchinleck (commander of the Indian Army) believes that the majority of the Indian Army is still intact, and I agree. If the Congress and Muslim League decided to use all of the propaganda power at their disposal, it may not take long to shake their resolve."

The continuation of British rule in India was impossible without the support of the Indian military. "It is my opinion that the naval mutiny, which came as the culmination of a number of similar incidents in the Indian defence services, was largely integral in persuading the British that holding India was no longer feasible without the use of large-scale British force and was, inter alia, responsible for ushering in freedom," says Lieutenant Kohli.

The British Indian Army had 2.5 million Indian soldiers under the command of 40,000 British overlords. If more of the former had become mutineers, the Empire would have faced a massive disaster. A public outpouring of rage quickly erupted in Bombay, Karachi, Madras, and Calcutta. The British were eager to redeem the situation and extricate themselves from the wreckage. Coincidentally, a Cabinet mission was dispatched to India in March 1946 to discuss the details of a power transfer.

Due to inadequate or contradicting source materials, the relationship between the INA and Savarkar has remained a mystery.

Recognition and dismissal

All navy personnel involved in the mutiny were fired and many faced court martial. Despite shaking the foundations of the British Empire, these brave young men, who were barely in their twenties, became unpersons, to borrow a phrase from George Orwell's 1984. That is, they did not exist for India's political leadership.

Former Prime Minister Morarji Desai, a staunch Gandhian who took over as Home Minister of Bombay a few months after the mutiny, best exemplifies the cavalier attitude toward freedom fighters.

However, Desai was adamant that the ratings had no right to revolt, regardless of whether they were serving under a foreign power or not because they were volunteers, not regular soldiers. Regarding freedom fighters' pensions for ratings who participated in the rebellion, he was emphatic that they were not entitled to any such pension. He stated that he was opposed to the ratings being reintroduced into the service after they had mutinied.

Desai disagreed with the ratings' claim that their actions hastened the country's freedom. In his opinion, the INA was not the harbinger of independence, and it was Gandhi who brought the country independence.

However, 476 RIN sailors who were discharged, dismissed, or "released" from service as a result of the mutiny were granted a freedom fighters' pension in 1972. This decision was made with the understanding that these categories of RIN ex-sailors lost their jobs as a result of their involvement in the mutiny.

The INA revolts were followed by the Naval Ratings Mutiny. Add to this, the revolts in the Air Force and the fact that World War II effectively bankrupted Britain. All of these factors influenced the British decision to leave India far more than the 1942 movement. This post was originally published on the blog 'History Under Your Feet.'

The Indian government recognised a few as freedom fighters in 1973. The majority of pension claims went unanswered. In the 1990s, there were two navy tugboats named B.C Dutt and Madan Singh.

Such is the story of India's political leaders' betrayal of the Royal Naval Mutiny of 1946. Nobody spoke up for the hundreds of ratings who were suffering in the Mulund camp.

After independence, the ruling Congress party was so afraid of the truth being exposed that a Bengali actor named Utpal Dutt was arrested in 1965 for writing a passionate play about the Royal Navy Uprising. Utpal Dutt also appeared in the Bollywood blockbuster "*Golmal.*" On December 27, 1965, he was arrested under the Preventive Detention Act.

The Bengal government and India feared he was "subversive." Why? Because he based his play "Kallol" (Sound of Waves) on this sunk chapter of the Indian freedom struggle. This would take the lustre off our popular heroes and gods like Gandhi and Nehru, right? He was imprisoned for several months during the run of his show at Calcutta's *Minerva* Theatre.

The uprising was commemorated with a statue in Colaba in 2001 – a recognition that came more than half a century later!

A memorial to a sailor holding the wheel can now be found in Cooperage, Colaba, Mumbai. The first thing they did after the mutiny began was to storm the naval prison and free B.C. Dutt, the man who sent a strong message to England.

Endgame

To comprehend the significance of the INA and the naval mutiny in driving the British out of India, one must first comprehend the British attitude toward India.

According to Valentine Chirol, head of The Times' foreign department, it is "impossible that we would ever concede to India the rights of self-government that we have willingly conceded to the great English communities of our own race. We must continue to govern India as the greatest of the British Crown's dependencies."

The concept of a free India, according to Robert Crewe, secretary of state for India from 1910 to 1914, was "a world as remote as any as Atlantis or Erewhon (an anagram of nowhere) that ever was thought of by the ingenious brain of an imaginative writer."

Finally, how did Winston Churchill, the ultra-racist, react to Gandhi's nonviolent approach? "Gandhi ought to be bound hand and foot at the gates of Delhi, and then trampled on by an enormous elephant with the new viceroy seated on its back," said the British Prime Minister.

Last but not least, India gained independence only because of guns, not because of the Charkha run by Gandhi and the Congress. Because of WW2, the British had to train over 40 lakh Indian soldiers and military engineers. In 1945, Indian engineers were capable of producing guns and bullets, so unlike in 1857, Indian soldiers would not have run out of bullets in 1946. Since 1857, there has been apprehension about Indian soldiers revolting. However, until 1930, the British were able to suppress them because Indian citizens did not know how to make bullets and gins. However, the British realised in 1946 that if Indian soldiers revolted, they could not be suppressed.

The Navy Revolt (also known as the Navy Mutiny by shameless Indian-paid historians) was the final nail in the coffin. Fear had become the truth of the matter.

Do you need any more proof that the British withdrew from India only after a bloody struggle?

The ban on Savarkar's book "Indian War of Independence 1857" was finally lifted on May 1946

Most historians, both British and Indian, have described and dismissed the 1857 uprising as a "Sepoy Mutiny" or, at best, "The Indian Mutiny." On the other hand, the Indian revolution has been characterised by nationalist leaders and thinkers as a planned and organised political and military uprising aimed at destroying British power in India. Mr Savarkar's is an attempt to examine the events of 1857 from an Indian perspective.

Veer Savarkar himself, was attracted and inspired by the burning zeal, heroism, bravery, suffering and tragic fate of the leaders of 1857, and he decided to re-interpret the story and to relate it in full with the help of all the material available to him at the time. He spent days and months at the India Office Library studying the period

Savarkar's book, "The Indian War of Independence (1857)," was published in 1909. The entire story of its publication and eventual demise is told in detail elsewhere in this volume. We will only mention here that the government prohibited its entry into India even before it was published. The Congress government of Bombay finally lifted the ban in May 1946, and this is the first authorised edition of the book to be published in India.

Conclusion

1857 First War of Independence - Sepoy Mutiny	1946 Mutiny in the Indian Navy - The Last War of Independence
Dissatisfaction in Sepoy Rank with British Officers'	Dissatisfaction among junior sailors under British officers
Pig/Cow greased cartridges. Overtones of Religion	Officers' unacceptable behaviour
Sepoy Mangal Panday was hanged on April 8, 1857, sparking a mutiny.	Subpar food; sailors went on strike on February 18, 1946.

The mutiny spread throughout the country and lasted until the end of 1859.	Violent mutiny in all major naval bases across India
Proclamation of British Sovereignty over India on August 2, 1858	India gains independence on August 15, 1947.

On June 3, 1947, Louis Mountbatten made the historical announcement on behalf of the British government – England was quitting India. Mohandas Gandhi's botched Quit India Movement five years ago was now a success. Of course, the Congress Party was quick to pocket the full credit for this success. In reality, it was not success but surrender.

There are stories, and there are untold stories, whose number is often more numerous, which is perhaps why they remain buried

Objectively speaking, Indian freedom was achieved by an infinite combination of several forces. In the end, the British didn't actually "give" us freedom. They were just happy to dump India to its own devices and decamped as soon as they could. But some of the most decisive forces that propelled their exit was the Naval mutiny at Bombay and Subash Bose's INA. And Veer Savarkar, who by the 1940s, had transformed into a renewed headache for them.

THE WHITE INVADERS LEFT INDIA BECAUSE THE INDIAN NAVY BEGAN A REVOLT, WHICH WAS IMMEDIATELY JOINED BY THE AIRFORCE AND THE ARMY.

NOT NON-VIOLENT SATYAGRAHA, INDIA WON INDEPENDENCE BY VIOLENT INTENT AND STRIKING FEAR INTO BRITISH HEARTS.

As a patriotic person, many deep insights pass through my mind. "*Saare jahan se acha hindustan hamara, hum bulbule hain iske, yeh gulistan hamara,*" we sing. This Gulsitan has strong impressions of true warriors that have been fine-tuned before being presented. Many people are destroying our history for their own amusement. Our history has been pawned and destroyed. We are not educated on the truth. As an Indian first and a writer second, I believe that every Indian should be aware of this. Jai Hind!

REFERENCES

Savarkar: Echoes from a Forgotten Past, 1883-1924 by Vikram Sampath

Savarkar: A Contested Legacy, 1924-1966 by Vikram Sampath

www.opindia.com

www.swarajyamag.com

www.dharmadispatch.in

www.amritmahotsav.nic.in

www.organiser.org

www.timesofindia.indiatimes.com

www.indiafacts.org.in

www.mea.gov.in

Untold Story 1946 Naval Mutiny: Last War of Independence by G. D. Sharma

The Indian War of Independence by Vinayak D. Savarkar

www.ingramcontent.com/pod-product-compliance
Lightning Source LLC
Chambersburg PA
CBHW051134130726
47988CB00005B/1831